What's On Your Mind?

WAYNE SPURRIER

Copyright © 2016 Wayne Spurrier

All rights reserved

ISBN-13: 978-1539454199
ISBN-10: 1539454193

Printed by CreateSpace, An Amazon.com Company
Available on Kindle and other devices

Cover image courtesy of www.myfreetextures.com

DEDICATIONS

To Simon – for giving me the inspiration!

To Chris, for putting up with me during the writing of this book and your constant support throughout the process.

To Hazel and Jayne. Two amazing people and the most treasured friends a person could wish for.

And finally…

To mom and Paul, without whom I simply could not have survived the events detailed in this book. Your unfailing support will never be forgotten.

INTRODUCTION

16 January 2016

It wasn't that I wanted to die!

Far from it; I simply couldn't bear the thought of living with the future I'd convinced myself lay before me. I hadn't reached this point overnight. It had been a long time coming but, the time had arrived. Everything was in place and in less than one hour I would be dead. It would all be over. I'd made peace with the decision to take my own life and I was ready.

The brightly-lit screen of my mobile phone displayed 4.35am as I turned it off for what I intended to be the final time. I felt nothing; I had been released from sadness, fear and pain the moment I made the decision and all that remained was emptiness. A hollow void consumed the space that had once harboured love and happiness and I had made my choice. No more torment; an end to the worthlessness and hopelessness I was feeling and, most importantly, peace.

The morning air was crisp outside. A light-frost dusted the cars, sparkling in the moonlight from the clear, wintry sky. The air was still. The dawn chorus was yet to burst into life and the soft rustling of trees was the only sound.

I'd arrived home an hour earlier from work and remained outside for at least ten minutes, in freezing temperatures, gazing into the sky at the swathe of brightly-lit stars which adorned the blackness, wondering if there really was something waiting for me on the other side?

The decision had been made just one day before.

I'd researched a number of methods and made my choice. The most important factor was to die in my own bed, holding a photograph of the two most important people in my life; my beautiful children. It was also important to me that, since it was likely to be a family member who discovered my lifeless body, I should look as peaceful as possible. Jumping from a bridge, whilst effective, would not be pretty for whoever had to identify my remains. I knew this would devastate a number of people, but I had reached the point where I had no choice other than to put myself first and take action, however drastic that was.

Before leaving for work the previous night I had made sure all the practicalities were dealt with. The apartment was spotlessly clean, the dishes were washed from dinner and I had carefully laid out my final words; letters written to my mother, two very close friends and of course, my children. I knew what I was about to do would hurt them all in different ways, but I needed them to know how much they meant to me, how grateful I was for all that they had tried to do and, most critically, that there was nothing more they could have done to save me.

From my girls I begged forgiveness. I tried to explain my actions and urged them to pursue whatever made them happy in life. These were the hardest letters to write, but ones which would likely be read over and over again throughout their lives and therefore, they had to be right.

One additional letter had been written; a set of instructions which included my funeral wishes, financial information and the lock-pattern to access my mobile phone, where numbers for my friends could be found. No stone was left unturned and I wanted to make the process as easy as possible for my mom, who would inevitably be the one to ensure my wishes were met. It might seem crazy to anybody who has never felt so desperate, that one could be so clear in thought about the practicalities for others while caring so little for your own life, but that's how it was.

I lay on the bed, placed the baseball-cap on my head and pulled the thick plastic-bag over it. Hands shaking, I lifted the cable-tie to my throat and fumbled to make the two ends meet, the intention was to prevent oxygen from entering through the gap, allowing me to slowly lose consciousness and drift away. The baseball-cap was there to create a ridge and stop the bag from being sucked against my mouth when drawing breath, thus alleviating the panic of suffocation. Death would ultimately come from carbon-dioxide poisoning.

I lay there motionless, staring at the ceiling, clutching a treasured photograph of my girls to my chest – a truly happy memory from just a few months earlier – a snapshot of our time together during a walk in the Lickey Hills.

There were no tears and, surprisingly, no fear about what I was doing. Nobody would be likely to question the lack of response to any phone calls or messages until at least mid-afternoon, as they knew I'd been out working all night and would therefore assume I was merely catching up on lost sleep. Therefore, there was no question in my mind I would be discovered before the lack of oxygen had done its job, leaving no chance of revival.

Time stood still.

I have no idea whether I lay there for two minutes or ten. The bag had begun to perform its grim obligation and, with each new breath, my chest became tighter and more painful, my quickening heart-rate forcing me to breathe faster, as if mocking my intentions. In the blackness of the room I could see nothing, and yet tiny specks of light began to dance sporadically into my vision, their mesmerising, sinister pirouettes calling to hold my gaze.

In spite of my body's valiant struggle to battle the effects of the diminishing oxygen and the burning sensation beginning to form within my lungs, calmness remained. For a while, a peaceful, floating sensation washed over me as I drifted but, without warning or conscious thought, my mind quickly became flooded with questions.

What was I doing? How could I be so selfish? What long-term effect would my actions have on my children?

Visions of my funeral flashed in my mind, a sinister show-reel of despair and mourning before my very eyes; the faces of my own flesh and blood, etched with sadness and pain. A tsunami of guilt washed over me, each thought crashing down upon the other with greater force than the last, and I realised suddenly how much they would hate me for doing this.

I couldn't bear it!

One final thought broke through the chaos of my mind with alarming clarity; I remembered what it felt like to hold them. Not just a memory; I could literally feel the warmth of their arms wrapped around me and the soft weight of their heads resting on my shoulder, as it had done so often before in happier times. It was as if they were there in the room, reaching out and comforting me in what was undoubtedly my darkest hour.

Instinctively I tore at the bag, gasped as the oxygen surged through my body, and began to sob uncontrollably.

ONE

They say fact is often stranger than fiction.

The greatest writers of our time would be pained to conceive the crazy twists and turns real-life can sometimes take, or the intriguing, complex-characters who join us along our journey. I'm nobody special, just an average guy plodding through life and trying to make the best job of it I can.

As you'll discover I've had some pretty exciting, daunting and life-changing moments along the way, yet I wouldn't consider my story any more extraordinary than most. I've not suffered any life-threatening illness, lost any limbs or been taken hostage in a bank-robbery, but the events which have formed the last few years of my life have been game-changing and – at 41 years old – I believe I have finally found the secret to true happiness.

For many of my adult years I harboured the secret dream of becoming a writer. I'm one of those types who always thought they had a book in them – no wonder it was uncomfortable sitting down – but never quite knew where to start in writing the damn thing.

Over the years I've spent many hours contemplating plots, characters and scenarios; basically looking for a tiny seed from which the branches of a truly great story could unfurl. Something worthwhile that would be of interest to the rest of the world in some way. Needless to say, the majority of what I came up with was average; uninspiring at best and at worst, downright lame.

You'll find out later in the book about my interest in ghost hunting and the paranormal, a pastime which led me to consider creating a masterpiece of fiction based around something spooky. I pondered how I could send the reader on the journey of a terrifying ghost hunt; a crazy night of exploration in a haunted house, in search of spirits and ghosts.

The action would follow me, the protagonist, as I immersed myself in this unique and frightening experience. The story would unfold to disclose a horrific encounter with a number of seemingly malevolent entities, before the denouement revealed it was actually I who was the ghost. However, I realised that ship had already sailed with the supernatural thriller *The Sixth Sense*, and trust me when I say that Bruce Willis was a far better leading-man than I could ever be. For starters, I don't look good in a white vest!

Next up, I wondered if I could spin the story of the infamous Pendle Witch Trials into a romp through England, shifting between the trials of 1612 and the plight of a modern-day historian, hell-bent on revealing THE TRUTH. This would develop into a fight for survival and a battle against the might of the most powerful institution in the country – the monarchy – equally as hell-bent on protecting the memory of their ancestor, James I, who led the persecution of witchcraft in the name of his faith. Cut back to reality; I'm basically trying to write what would surely result in a poor-man's version of *The Da Vinci Code* and once again, I realised I'm no Dan Brown. Cue sad emoticon.

Amidst all of this I had a life (honestly). I had a wife, two children, a good job and......a Facebook page. All of these demanded my time and as a result, my foray into the realms of literary-genius failed to materialise. There was always something more pressing making demands on my time and despite several false-starts, nothing came to pass.

Over the course of a few years my life took some dramatic twists and turns. I took a massive chance on a career which didn't go to plan, my earnings plummeted, my 'better half' (we'll come back to that) divorced me and then moved a hundred miles away with our children. I switched jobs several times, plunged into depression, had my first gay relationship, ended my first gay relationship (we will definitely come back to that one) and eventually found my dream man, with whom to begin my 'happily ever after'. In the space of four years my whole world changed and most of the big changes happened in just 18 months.

Anyway, I have strayed from the point (brace yourself because that will happen a lot). Having spent many years trying hard to find the perfect story to tell, one with some dramatic twists and turns and of course the obligatory journey through misery to happiness, I suddenly had an epiphany.

My story was probably just as interesting as anything I could create from fiction. After all, four job changes, a divorce, losing my children, coming out, discovering you were in an 'open relationship', coming very close to suicide and then finding a happy ending; all this in just 18 months. Surely that's more than average right?

Ah, but here's the kicker. Did I really want to spend goodness knows how long writing about myself, with the potential that nobody would actually want to read my book? After all, a celebrity-biography is one thing for the Christmas list, but who is going to be interested in reading the story of a regular guy – a complete unknown? It would need to offer something different, or at least have an 'idea' to support it.

Then fate took an interesting turn. An ex-colleague

sent me a message via Facebook, telling me he'd love to read *my* story. He'd witnessed all of the ups and downs on my timeline and seen newfound happiness unfold in the form of photographs, memes, videos and the occasional Dub Smash.

That's when it hit me!

All those Facebook posts meant something to me personally. My life was already documented in short headlines and comments. Among them were literally hundreds of sarcastic, thought-provoking and sometimes witty observations about current affairs and celebrities. I realised I'd got all the material I could possibly need already written, or at the very least the signposts to follow in order to narrate the journey.

So, with an excited skip in my step, I began trawling back through my life on Facebook, and in the next few-hundred pages I'll share with you the good, the bad and the downright ugly moments that shaped who I am today.

So sit back, grab yourself a cuppa and hold on tight. Prepare yourself for the Facebook ramblings of Wayne Spurrier, aged 41 ¾ (at the time of writing).

Let's pick up where my Facebook journey begins.

...... *You Joined Facebook* – Feb 2009

Seven years down the line I honestly have no idea what unstoppable force drove me to make the leap into the world of Facebook.

After all, I had managed to live a perfectly happy and successful life without it. Did I really need to know what my work colleagues were having for dinner that night? Would my life be enriched somehow by knowing how well my friends' children were doing in their school open evenings? Could I go to sleep at night without having discovered the *'Ten Things You Never Knew You Could Do With Tin-Foil'*? I felt I could!

However, what it seems I couldn't cope with was the

overriding feeling the rest of the world – circa 360m people at the time – knew something I didn't, or that they were part of something I wasn't. Basically, the inner-voice inside kept telling me I just had to be a part of this growing phenomena, and who was I to ignore the voices in my head?

So without a second thought for my privacy, which I have always valued, and with complete disregard for the impact it may have on my ability to hold a conversation – without checking my mobile or computer every five minutes – I leapt feet first into the unknown.

Within a matter of hours I had reconnected with 'friends' I had schooled with many years before, stumbled across work-colleagues from my past who I'd forgotten even existed, and trawled through the pages of 'people you might know' in some desperate attempt to bolster my friends list right from the off.

I would look at the ridiculous number of connections some people had and think to myself, how can that be possible? How can one person know over 500 people? Leap forward seven years and my friends list stands at 665 (at the time of writing), but I can honestly say that every single one is either a relative, colleague, genuine friend or at the very least, somebody I have met and had a meaningful conversation with along the way.

What's more, some of the people I have met through social functions and work have gone on to become great friends. Without the existence of Facebook I feel sure our paths may never have crossed again and several of these people became fundamental in helping me survive some very dark times which, at the time, I was blissfully unaware were coming my way.

I'm just as aware as everybody else that social-media can be as much a curse as it is a blessing. I have witnessed many vile exchanges and conversations between people I wish I'd never been privy to. Thankfully, I am very conscious of how easy it can be to become embroiled in somebody else's argument and, to date, have managed to avoid being dragged into those murky waters.

It never ceases to make me smile when somebody breaks-up with a partner and posts something scathing about them, to then witness their 'friends' go on the attack, with comments such as 'I always thought he was a dickhead' or 'you're better off without him'. I would love to be a fly on the wall at the next 'social' night when the couple are back together and all these people are in the same room. Two HUGE slices of humble pie served with lashings of awkwardness please waiter.

Like most of us I've also borne witness to some vile displays of violence, racism, homophobia and hatred via my timeline.

I'm not an avid follower of the news and I choose very carefully the things I expose myself to in this world, but being a part of the Facebook 'community' does remove an element of choice, with videos of beheadings, beatings, racial and homophobic abuse and horrific accidents appearing unexpectedly on my wall. None of these are things I would ever go in search of, but they have made their way into my world as a result of social-media.

When I created my profile my intentions were simply to connect with people, share my thoughts about anything on which I had a strong opinion and generally have some fun. I also saw Facebook as an opportunity to create a scrapbook of my life; a kind of virtual photo album on which I could look back in years to come, and reminisce about the memories I have made.

As I look back over literally hundreds of posts to write this book I think, in the most part, I have done just that. Some are deep and meaningful, some are funny and some are completely nonsensical, such as the following post I shared when I first joined Facebook.

......says next week's lotto numbers are.......05, 14, 17, 29, 47 & 49. Now you know you're going to! – 15 Feb 2009

I have absolutely no idea whether anybody rushed out to buy a ticket using these numbers on the Lotto, but I know for a fact that I did and I won......absolutely nothing!

So before we go any further I'd like to take this opportunity to apologise to anyone who wasted £1 at the time. You may have lost your money, but I'm sure you felt good about the fact you supported some great Lotto-funded causes as a result of your blind faith in my ability to predict six random numbers.

As you will see further down the line (if I haven't bored you yet), I don't have a great track-record with making predictions or good decisions! After all, I'm the guy who purchased shares in oil off the Falkland Islands one day before they crashed, and which are now running at -87.49% profit.

TWO

......found a grey chest-hair. Is this the beginning of the end? – 5 May 2009

We've all been there!

You're happily going about your daily business when you are suddenly stopped in your tracks by something completely unexpected. For me it happened on 5 May 2009 with the discovery of a grey chest-hair, and my head was sent spiralling out of control.

In the grand scheme of things this may not seem like a major event. It would have no bearing whatsoever on the economy, people were still starving in third-world countries and war would continue to rage in the middle-east. For me though it was a moment that had a profound impact and would go on to ignite a whole host of insecurities about my achievements in life, as well as a reminder that the clock is always ticking.

It prompted me to reflect on the dreams and aspirations I had when I was younger, how I compared to those school friends I had been checking up on now that we had connected on Facebook and, most importantly, where I was heading from here. I wasn't about to have a breakdown (just yet) but I've always felt a certain level of inferiority and would often compare myself unfavourably to others.

I quickly realised that while Facebook is an amazing tool with which to keep in touch with distant acquaintances, it can also be a dangerous place if you aren't feeling great about yourself or the way your life is going. You must always remember that what people portray to the outside world may not be the reality they are living; the saying 'one smile can hide a thousand tears' is never more true than where social media is concerned, and this would be something I would come to prove myself many years later.

Whilst I have never been driven by material things such as designer-brands, expensive cars and luxury holidays, the reality that my peers *appeared* to be more successful than me in achieving their dreams really did begin to play on my mind. In addition, I would look at photographs and feel a pang of jealousy because my shoulders weren't as broad, my waist as slim or my stubble as perfectly-formed as theirs. I'd often look at other guys and wish I looked like them.

Sadly though I was born to be one of the masses. Average looking and a physique with nothing to shout about other than an A-cup, a wobbly belly and oversized ears. As a child of the '70s I had worn brown NHS glasses from the age of five and had always been a skinny kid. I often look back and wonder how I wasn't bullied to within an inch of my life as a result of the way I looked, but can only put it down to my quick-witted charm (still present today I'm told) that I managed to survive into adulthood pretty much unscathed.

Of course it didn't help that I was the younger brother of two, so I also had the pleasure of wearing hand-me-downs for many of my formative years. I'm no psychologist, but feel sure this must have some lasting effect on a person's psyche.

As a child I don't recall any strong desire for a particular career when I grew up. The typical train-driver or fireman aspirations seemed to evade me, and to this day I've never really found my niche. I know that one should never carry regrets as they achieve nothing, but if I were to pinpoint one thing I wish were different, it would be that I never really knew exactly what I wanted from a career and therefore had no specific goal to aim for. This would go on to be a constant into adulthood and have a massive impact upon my life as I swerved uncontrollably into my 40s.

One thing I never doubted about myself was my work-ethic, which I believe I gained from my parents.

Born in the back-bedroom of a council house in 1974, I had grown up in Redditch, Worcestershire, and throughout my formative years both parents had worked incredibly hard to make ends meet. Mom managed to raise two boys whilst working a daytime job as a dinner lady at the local primary school and evenings at the local newspaper, as a typist and cleaner.

In my younger years dad worked in a factory for a company called Alcad, before becoming a driver for a local coach company. I don't ever recall being truly poor, but I do know that, like many families back then, we didn't have a lot of money.

Money aside, growing up in the '70s was great. When I went on to have children of my own, the difference in the restrictions they had to endure was vast compared to what I experienced as a child. In reality the dangers were still there 35 years ago; people still got attacked, children still went missing and the horse-and-cart was long-gone on the roads, so we already needed to be road savvy. However, things were different!

I grew up surrounded by a group of other kids – all within around a five year age gap – and we would disappear in our gang for hours on end, swinging from ropes in the woods, crashing our BMXs and generally creating mischief as kids do. Back in those days all we needed was a football, a few coins, some marbles and an empty can of Coke and we had a full week's gaming sorted. Skinned knees and grazed hands were the hallmark of a great day!

I was an absolute nightmare as a child. I'd managed to knock-down two members of the same family on my BMX, sent my toy tractor bouncing down all thirteen stairs in our home (with me on it) and been swept out into the sea by a freak-wave, causing my brother to run in the opposite direction and almost into the path of an oncoming car.

I was obsessed with women's bodies – boobs in particular – and recall walking into a shop on one occasion before promptly lifting the skirt of a mannequin to investigate what lay beneath. Yes, you guessed it - she was real.

My mom eventually accepted that providing me with steel toe-capped shoes was the only way I would make a pair last longer than a month, and my knees were almost always visible through the holes in my jeans; the result of the constant scrapes I would find myself in. In fact, it's a minor miracle that to this day I have never broken a bone or had a serious injury.

My 'nightmare' status changed dramatically as I reached my teens. With dad driving tour-coaches around Europe for much of the year and my brother having pretty much flown the nest already, I found myself the primary source of support for my mom, who suffered a serious bout of depression in the early '90s.

If you were to speak to my friends I'm sure they would tell you I'm a naturally compassionate and empathic person, but as a young man I found it difficult to show feelings. Between us we got through it, but I would be lying if I said there hadn't been times when school friends had called and I'd made excuses for not going out; I simply couldn't be certain that mom would be safe left alone at the time.

This was a very difficult time, but one which shaped me in ways I didn't realise until much later in life, and inevitably gave us a closer bond than I think we otherwise may have had. I don't know whether I had just worn myself out before hitting my teens or if it was the result of the circumstances, but I calmed down massively and never gave them any further cause for concern – well, until I was about to hit 40.

Back to 2009 where the discovery of this intrusive silver-thread of insecurity suddenly made me begin to reflect upon what I had achieved in my life. In short, I had planted a seed of doubt in my own mind that I would nurture for many years to come; one which would very nearly get the better of me.

I'm not a naturally shy person but, when confronted with a group of people, part of me always felt less capable than everybody else; I'd find myself on the outskirts of conversations because I never really felt I had anything worthwhile to say – especially in groups of guys.

So it was a massive challenge for me when I found myself spending two days in the company of a bunch of men for a camping trip in South Wales.

……is preparing for his first ever camping trip…with a group of blokes I haven't met yet & sole responsibility for my two children. Wish me luck! – 18 Jun 2009

Anyone who knows me would testify that I'm most certainly no Bear Grylls, and if you asked me to spend a month on a deserted island my survival skills would most certainly leave me dead within the first week.

Despite the scrapes I found myself in as a child I have never been one for getting dirty, and camping is so far down the list of my preferred holiday pursuits it barely even features. However, in 2009 I found myself agreeing to join my wife's boss and a group of guys I had never met before on a camping weekend with the children, in sunny south Wales. Every year this group of dads would take their children camping for Father's Day weekend, and now I was about to join them.

I cannot be certain what drove me to agree, but hindsight leads me to think I was feeling guilty about the amount of time I spent with my children. I had become one of those dads who worked far too many hours and didn't appreciate the speed at which my two daughters were growing up. Whatever the reason I had agreed and was about to embark upon a proper guy-weekend; I was feeling pretty nervous.

I have never seen myself as a proper bloke. I would rather boil my own bollocks than watch or play football and as for motorbikes or cars, you'd be better off talking to your grandma about those. I can just about find my way around the oil, water and screen-wash beneath the bonnet – and maybe change a tyre on a good day – so the thought of spending a weekend with a dozen guys I had never met, and who I perceived to be 'real men', filled me with mild terror. However, I sucked it up for the sake of the kids who were really looking forward to the trip, and off we went.

This turned out to be a pivotal moment for me.

Over the preceding weeks I had considered fabricating an excuse on several occasions, but something within me kept telling me that I must go. It would have been so easy to back out; to listen to the inner-voices of my own insecurities which have always prevented me from experiencing some of what life has to offer. As the weekend loomed several of my friends and family applauded my courage in going away with a group of strangers.

'You're so much braver than me', my mom had said.

'I don't think I could spend a weekend with strangers, but then you're really confident aren't you!' one of my work colleagues had added.

The truth was I felt terrified, but I'd made a commitment to my children and was determined not to let them down. I also acknowledged the generosity of the guys who had invited us along and felt duty-bound to go.

It turned out to be a great weekend!

These guys had camping down to a tee; the tents went up in a flash, there was a marquee with a huge gas-fired barbecue and an electric hook-up for the drinks fridge. I finally spent some quality time with the girls (for the first time in ages) and to my surprise I got on really well with everyone. It dawned on me that I had faced up to a fear and conquered it. I realised that I had allowed my insecurities and fear to dictate the decisions I made in the past and genuinely believe this moment was pivotal in changing my outlook.

I hadn't just conquered Everest or spent a month surviving on a desert island, but something had changed. I had challenged myself to do something which was so far out of my comfort zone you'd need 20/20 vision and a pair of binoculars to see it; I had faced a fear and won!

I didn't realise at the time just how empowering this was, but looking back I firmly believe this was the moment I stopped allowing myself to be crippled by what others thought of me. I finally stopped worrying about how people perceived me and found a confidence in myself I had never experienced before.

People often refer to turning 30 as a milestone for a change in their attitude and confidence in life. For me it came in my mid-thirties and this camping trip certainly added to it. There's a fine-line between being confident enough in yourself to do things your way, versus simply not giving a damn about other people. I'd like to think that I fall into the first category, and it makes me cringe to hear people say 'I don't care about anyone else, I just do what I want.'

Although I began to worry less about what people might think of my actions, to this day I still *care*. It may no longer dictate the final decision I make, but I would always consider whether my choices had an impact on others, and it makes my blood boil to see people using the 'I don't care' attitude as an excuse to do whatever they want, regardless of the consequence.

'I speak my mind and say exactly what I think' is another phrase which gets my goat. Honesty and integrity are without question two of the noblest qualities a person can possess, although I've witnessed so many occasions where this is just used as an excuse to be mean, bitchy or controversial.

For as much as I love social-media and believe it to be a great medium for creating honest, open debate about current-affairs, it also provides a faceless opportunity for its users to make statements for which they have no supporting evidence and worse, no accountability.

In my opinion there's a lot to be said for filtering your true thoughts for the sake of others' feelings. Having the confidence to share your opinion is a very different animal to shoving your thoughts so far down the throats of others that their farts begin to smell of your toothpaste. Honesty is not always the best policy, and there's a lot to be said for telling a little white-lie when it spares somebody embarrassment or hurt.

Having said all that, I do feel I owe an apology to Jason Donovan for airing my views in a rant I shared with the world towards the end of 2009.

......will not be held responsible for my actions if I am forced to endure that bloody Iceland Xmas advert with Jason Donovan any more. Please note that if he is ever discovered with his hands and feet bound together with half his body weight in Iceland party food rammed down his gullet - I have an alibi – 29 Nov 2009

I'm a regular shopper at Iceland and have nothing whatsoever against them and to be honest, I have sung along on more than one occasion to some old-school

Jason Donovan, but it seems I just couldn't cope with him swaying around a table of Black Forest Gateau, party sausages and Vol-au-Vents with festive music playing in the background.

If I'm totally honest, I think my issue was more with Christmas than it ever was with Jason or Iceland.

I have incredibly fond memories of childhood Christmases; the excitement and anticipation of Christmas Eve and waking up early on the day itself and sneaking downstairs to find a pile of presents waiting to be torn open. The smell of the turkey in the oven, which had been slow-roasting since the early hours, is another memory I cherish. My brother and I both used to hide a present somewhere so that we could be the last one to open something, and this would often result in a gift being forgotten and found many hours later, unopened.

This was that time of the year when the spare chair would come into use. Every family home has one; that makeshift seating which doesn't see daylight for 364 days of the year, but is always there to help you cater for the family gatherings. With grandparents around for dinner the table would be set and every conceivable seat would be needed; even the piano stool was used and, as I was the smallest, this was always my perch (which I secretly loved).

Christmas Day consisted of opening presents, mom cooking the dinner, dad washing up before falling into a food-coma on the sofa and my brother and I watching Top of the Pops on TV. Nan was somewhat less than tolerant of this.

'Bloody thump, thump, thump,' she would grumble, fingers shoved firmly in her ears.

I recall waking one year to find the most amazing BMX bike waiting for me, concealed with enough wrapping paper to provide shelter for a small African village. It was yellow and blue and a far cry from the Grifter I had been used to. This wasn't just a bike – this was a BMX or, put another way, an opportunity to create havoc and almost kill two separate members of the same family who lived around the corner.

As a child I had a thirst for speed and would tear around the pavements outside our house, slamming on the brakes to skid around the corners. In fact, it took me less than seven days to wear down the rear tyre of my brand-new killing machine and actually pop the damn thing! It was New Year's Eve when it went bang, and I then found myself without a bike for two days, until the shops opened again to purchase a new tyre.

At least this meant the locals were safe for a few days; but not for long!

Over the course of a few weeks sometime throughout the following year, I managed to take-down two of our neighbours by speeding around the corner without warning. No serious injuries were sustained thankfully, although I don't think they were too impressed and I'm sure a few choice words were said to my poor mom.

It was many years before my love for Christmas would be tainted, but the moment came as a result of work. I spent a couple of years working in a men's clothing store and discovered first-hand what Christmas was really all about; money.

It was awful.

While everyone is packing up early on Christmas Eve, retail employees are working twice as hard to cater for all those last-minute shoppers. Then the real kick in the teeth comes. Once the doors are closed, it's time to put out the New Year sales posters and tickets, ready to re-open as soon as the public have recovered from eating their own body weight in turkey and Ferrero Rocher.

Worse still, these poor sales staff have also been subjected to festive music on a constant loop since the beginning of November and, since my stint in retail was way before the advent of MP3s, we only had one or two CDs available. By the time we finally closed the doors on 24th December, we had been subjected to Noddy Holder screaming 'It's Chriiiiiistmaaaaaas' around 300 times.

Seeing the reality of this spoilt Christmas for me and, although I still love the day itself, I'm quite happy to see the back of it when it's over.

So, how I came to find myself in the back-seat of a Ford KA, on a seven-hour road trip to Billingham in 2014 to watch a pantomime – with the worst hangover of my life – I'm not quite certain. But that's exactly what happened.

One of my close friends Craig, a successful drag-artist by the name of Cherry Darling, was making a name for himself as a panto dame. So a couple of friends and I decided it would be fun to make the journey to Billingham, near Stockton-On-Tees, to see him do his stuff. Now for some reason I didn't look at a map when booking the tickets and assumed this was Stockton near Manchester – just a couple of hours away from Redditch.

How wrong was I?

It was actually some 220 miles north, via the M1 motorway, on which there were several sections of roadworks with speed restrictions.

To make matters worse I had spent the previous evening at my mom's house with family, getting somewhat drunk on every conceivable colour of alcoholic beverage known to mankind. Needless to say I was not in a great state by the time I fell onto my bed that night, even managing a whole conversation with my brother on Facebook of which I had no memory, until I found it the next day.

The plan for our road trip had been for Carolyn to drive to mine from Dudley, then for me to drive to Hazel, who lived in Nottingham. Hazel would make the drive to Billingham, thus breaking up the journey for everyone and sharing the time behind the wheel evenly. I had promised Carolyn a delicious bacon sandwich at my apartment, but here's how the conversation went as I opened the door that morning.

'Morning Carolyn, I'm still a little bit drunk from last night,' I said sheepishly; head bowed and eyes looking up, like a puppy who knows he's done wrong.

'You look dreadful,' she replied.

'Not as bad as I feel. I've tried to sober up by drinking coffee but I'm still drunk and there's no way I can drive to Nottingham,' came my response.

I'm not sure if you have ever been so drunk that the room has continued to spin, even after you've woken the next morning, but it was a first for me and needless to say I most certainly didn't relish the idea of eating anything straight away, let alone cooking bacon.

'Well I guess that's my bacon sandwich out of the window,' Carolyn said, helping herself to coffee and toast.

With a plastic bowl in hand we set off to Nottingham in Carolyn's car, where Hazel would then pick up the driving; or so we thought.

'Would you mind driving to Billingham please Wayne?' were Hazel's first words. 'My windscreen wipers have broken and I can't risk driving the car all that way in this weather.'

'Err……I'm still drunk,' came my reply, the guilt now growing for my actions the night before.

Yes, you've guessed it!

Off we went - poor Carolyn beginning her third-leg of driving with Hazel in the passenger seat and me squashed into the back seat of a KA – sick-bowl by my side – with a blanket, a pillow and a lifetime's worth of regrets. When we stopped en route at the services you could almost hear our spines click as we unfolded ourselves and headed for the nearest Costa.

What made it worse is that I don't even like panto. We were making this trek up the M1 and all I could think about was this dreadful hangover, and the fact that I would be spending two hours locked inside a theatre, surrounded by excited, screaming children.

The performance was great and Craig took to the

stage to rapturous applause, alongside actor Jake Canuso who plays Matteo in the TV comedy series *Benidorm*.

After the show Carolyn, Hazel and I headed for the stage-door, where we were due to meet Craig for a drink before making the journey home. We waited and waited but he didn't show up. It turned out he was in the bar waiting for us and as we stood outside in the cold Jake was signing autographs and taking pictures with fans.

It soon became apparent he thought we were waiting for him, as he kept looking across at us as though we were stalkers.

'Are you waiting for a photograph?' he asked.

'Err...no,' came Hazel's rather awkward reply, 'we're waiting for Cherry.'

The look on his face was priceless!

But not quite finished yet, Hazel then interrupted him while having a photograph taken with a young lady to add;

'If you see Cherry, could you send him up to the bar where we will be waiting please?'

One of the many things I love about Hazel is her absolute disregard for celebrity-status and I don't know Jake from the proverbial Adam, but I would imagine that a random stranger asking him to play messenger – to a cast member further down the billing – was not a moment he might remember fondly.

Either way, despite the worst hangover I have ever experienced and the need for chiropractic intervention to straighten my spine, this turned out to be an amazing experience, restoring my faith in the true purpose of Christmas; family, friends and making great memories.

THREE

......spent 15mins alone in the cellar at Station Hotel with a night-vision camera - how Yvette am I??? – 11 Oct 2009

I've never been quite sure where my beliefs about the paranormal lie, but one thing I have always truly felt is that everything in life happens for a reason; that the people we meet along the way are brought into our lives for a specific purpose. I'm not sure whether you'd call it destiny but I've always believed that, in some way, we each have a path already laid out for us.

Little did I know that a chance meeting at a ghost hunting event in October 2009 would massively change my life, and introduce me to someone who would grow to become a huge part of it; both in work and later as a close personal friend.

Earlier in the year I had attended a spooky night at The Station Hotel in Dudley and, after a few unexplained things happened, I really wanted to return. It was almost nine months before it happened but I rebooked to return to the same place, this time with a company called Haunted Happenings.

When I was around five years of age I had an

experience which has remained with me ever since.

It was summertime and possibly due to the humidity (we did have summers in the late '70s) I couldn't get to sleep. I recall standing at the window of my bedroom, gazing out across the lawn-area – over which the house looked – and seeing the dark figure of a person standing against the wall of the house opposite. My dad came into the room and I remember asking him what they were doing.

'There's nobody there,' he insisted, trying hard to see what I referred to.

I felt completely perplexed!

Why couldn't he see this person when they appeared so clear to me? Was I imagining it? Did it actually even happen, or had I dreamed the whole thing?

We never spoke of it again and I would be very surprised if he even remembered it after all these years, but that experience remained lodged somewhere deep inside my brain and left me with a deep-seated fascination for ghosts – for I convinced myself that this must have been what I had witnessed.

It was just a few years after this that the groundbreaking movie *Ghostbusters* hit the cinemas, instantly becoming one of my favourite childhood films.

Years later I remember finding myself completely engrossed in a one-off show called *Ghostwatch*; a British mockumentary broadcast on BBC1 on Halloween night in 1992. I later learned that the show had been recorded weeks before, but on the night it was presented as live television and involved BBC reporters carrying out an investigation of a house in London, at which poltergeist activity was believed to be taking place.

The story told of a malevolent entity nicknamed Mr Pipes; thought to be the spirit of a disturbed man called Raymond Tunstall – a child-killer from the 19th century.

During the course of the programme the activity at the house became increasingly sinister until, at the end, the reporters deduced the programme had acted as a national-séance, serving to provide the entity with even greater power.

Finally, the spirit took control of the BBC studio, possessing host Michael Parkinson in the process. All hell broke loose and without warning the show went off air, leaving viewers in a state of shock and completely unaware the whole thing was just a lavish performance.

Everyone was talking about it two days later at school and it was all over the national press for days. This show went on to achieve cult-status, was banned from being repeated on UK television and left a lasting impression on the UK public; it also left an indelible mark upon me and brought back those memories of my ghostly apparition all those years before.

Jump forward ten years and *Most Haunted* hit the small-screen, with children's TV presenter Yvette Fielding as host and paranormal investigator.

I was instantly hooked!

The team would investigate a new 'haunted' location each week with a resident medium and a parapsychologist in tow, each offering their own perspective on these allegedly haunted places.

The programme seemed to provide a genuine ghost hunting investigation and soon amassed a huge following, with impressive viewing figures for such a niche genre.

On 31st October, precisely 10 years after *Ghostwatch* was aired, the first *Most Haunted Live* was broadcast from Dudley Castle in the West Midlands. Little did I know at the time that this would be a place I would come to spend many nights investigating myself years later, even capturing a ghostly figure on camera during a children's birthday party one Sunday morning.

Back to 2009 and my chance meeting with the owner of Haunted Happenings, Hazel.

Having opted to bravely carry out a lone-vigil in the cellar of the Station Hotel – with only a camcorder for company – I had missed the coffee-break and become separated from the rest of my group. When I returned to the ballroom I began chatting with Hazel, and just a few days later I received a message via Facebook asking if I would like to join the team to help with future events.

'Are you serious?' I replied, typing the words faster than I ever had before. 'I'd absolutely love to!'

Within weeks I found myself wandering the corridors of some amazing locations all across the UK, meeting all sorts of interesting people, exploring places I never imagined I would have the opportunity to see, and loving every moment of it.

As I write this almost seven years later I still consider myself sceptical about the existence of spirits and the paranormal in general, but through my subsequent work with Haunted Happenings I have experienced some crazy things for which I can offer no logical explanation, and would say that my beliefs have most certainly been challenged on many occasions.

I have always been a very rational and balanced person. The need to have everything in my life placed into neat boxes, both literally and figuratively speaking, is key to my sanity, and I've always had a very black & white approach to most things.

My default-setting is to question 'why' or 'how' when told something, and I never take things on face-value unless I feel they make sense to me. This has been my personal approach to all of the ghost hunts I have attended and shall always remain so.

With that in mind I would only need five fingers to count the number of *personal* experiences I have had in seven years of ghost hunting, for which I could find no other explanation and would therefore consider paranormal. That said, those which I have encountered have left me baffled, and the open-mind with which I attended my first ghost hunt has been opened much wider as a result.

WHAT'S ON YOUR MIND?

……I AM TOTALLY PERPLEXED. I threw a coin in the cellar at Station Hotel into an empty part of the room and everyone heard it land. How the hell it then it was found right in front of me just a second later I will never know! What a freaking bizarre experience!!!!!! – 4 Nov 2012

Before I tell the full story, let me just say that I don't expect anyone to believe what I say. After all, I might have embellished the tale. There could be a perfectly rational explanation. It's possible I made the whole thing up. But, I haven't! I have no reason to lie because it doesn't matter to me whether people believe me or not.

One of the things we always remind the guests on these types of events is that nobody has to believe anything anybody tells you. Participants are urged to make their own decisions about what they experience and I can only share with you what happened to me and how I perceived it.

At the beginning of the night I found myself in the large cellars of the hotel with a small group of guests, all of whom had attended ghost hunts before and were therefore thrown straight into the investigation, while the newer ones learned about the equipment we would use later in the night.

The room we were investigating is fairly significant in size (around 30ft x 20ft), and is one in which many people have reported strange occurrences in the past. The five participants were seated around a small table with their hands upon it, conducting a séance, while I stood a few feet away – in complete blackness – calling out for the spirits to make themselves known by making a noise in the room.

After a few moments, with no sign of any activity, I decided to try something different and removed a coin from my pocket.

'I'm going to throw something,' I warned the group, not wanting to frighten them and cause mayhem and panic when they heard the inevitable noise it would make upon landing.

It's important to remember that each of these people were sat in complete darkness (with their hands upon the table) and had absolutely no idea what I was about to throw. Also bear in mind this investigation was taking place in a cold cellar in the middle of November, so everybody was dressed suitably in layered warm-clothing, which would make it almost impossible to move without making a noise.

As I finished speaking I threw the coin overhead, towards the empty part of the room and away from all of us. Some 20ft away the familiar chink of metal upon brick was heard by everyone in the group, so we knew the coin had landed somewhere in the distance.

I had taken-part in hundreds of ghost hunts by this time and, if I'm completely honest, had absolutely no belief whatsoever that anything would happen. Then, just as I drew breath to request for any spirits to move the coin, I heard a noise immediately to my right (the guests were seated to my left). I reached for my torch to investigate the source and was astonished to find a 1p coin on the floor, just a few inches from my right foot.

'Err folks,' I nervously mumbled, 'there's a coin here next to my foot'.

'Is it the one you threw?' asked one of the guests excitedly.

'I can't be sure,' I replied. 'It was dark so I don't know whether I threw a 5p or a 1p coin, but I know from the size that it was one *or* the other.'

I was completely mystified – even considering the possibility one of the group had somehow hoaxed me – but they couldn't possibly have known what I was about to do and surely I would have heard them move?

So without hesitation we set about searching the room for the coin I had thrown, assuming it must just have been a brilliant coincidence. That's right, we couldn't find another coin in the room anywhere!

In fact, we spent around five minutes scouring the area to no avail. We even tried rolling the coin from one end of the room to the other; none of us had heard it roll back and the floor is made up of brickwork – preventing it from travelling even half the required distance – not to mention the small gulley it would have had to traverse to reach its final resting place.

Needless to say this became the talking point of the night, and to this day I can find no explanation for how it happened, despite having tried on several other occasions to recreate it.

A sprawling Gothic-revival mansion, buried deep within a valley in Gloucestershire and surrounded by National Trust woodland, was the setting for another ghostly experience I will never forget.

Woodchester Mansion was built on the site of an earlier house, Spring Park, sometime around the mid-1850s. The mansion is built largely from local limestone and since work was never completed it offers visitors an opportunity to see how a house of this period was constructed.

Fireplaces remain suspended in mid-air, where floors were never installed, and the exceptional craftsmanship of the stonemasons employed to work on the project is astounding to witness. The house has long been a favourite of ghost hunters and paranormal enthusiasts, with many myths and legends surrounding its history.

The mansion acted as a base for Canadian troops between 1939 and 1945, using the adjoining lake as a training site for bridge-building in preparation for the D-Day landings in Normandy – scheduled to take place on 6 June 1944. Legend has it that several soldiers lost their lives in the lake following the collapse of one of the bridges, and another story tells how those working on the construction of the house suddenly downed tools in 1868 and left, never to return.

Regardless of the history you could not ask for a building with a more 'haunted' appearance. Stone gargoyles adorn the exterior of the façade, long passageways and empty rooms perpetuate inherent feelings of unease, and the gothic architecture throughout serves to make Woodchester Mansion one of the most enigmatic and spooky houses in Britain.

On the particular night in question the event was underway and small groups were in different areas of the building, carrying out experiments and vigils in an attempt to illicit paranormal activity and make contact with the spirit world.

I had just walked my group along a passageway leading from the cellar to the kitchens and stopped at the junction where the corridor meets another leading back to the main doorway, offering us an unobstructed view of the entrance.

It was a clear night and the moonlight cascaded through the open door, some 60ft from where we stood.

As I shone my torch toward the entrance, to help the group obtain their bearings for our position in the mansion, a figure walked briskly across the doorway, perfectly silhouetted in the moonlight. With a clear line-of-sight towards the area, both myself and one of the guests witnessed the same thing; a human figure walking at pace, arms swinging and with a real purpose. I immediately returned the glare of my torch to the spot, fully expecting to see one of the team or guests in front of us; there was nobody there!

I, and the lady who also witnessed this, ran straight toward the doorway, in search of whoever it was we had just seen. It was then that we realised if it had been a living person they would have had to either turn left (towards us) or right (out of the doorway). The flooring at the time was made up of small chippings of gravel and stone and impossible to navigate without making a significant noise; we hadn't heard anyone and upon checking, nobody was out of their group roaming the corridors.

The figure had been moving forwards at a brisk purposeful-pace, but in a split-second had seemed to vanish into thin air. A small gate offers access to a spiral-staircase at precisely the spot from which our mysterious visitor had disappeared, although closer inspection revealed this was firmly secured with a padlock and – even if it had been unlocked – the gate opened outwards so would not allow time for somebody to open it and start climbing the stairs before we were already heading toward them.

Despite these experiences I still don't know for sure what my thoughts and beliefs are regarding spirits and the paranormal, but what I do believe is that 'ghosts', or figures from the past, can be witnessed – given that magical combination of timing, location and circumstances – and this is what I truly believe we saw that night. A full apparition; the holy grail for any ghost hunter.

The way I describe it to people is that we all leave an imprint in this world.

Imagine your morning routine; you get out of the same side of the bed each day, into the bathroom, down the stairs to open the back door to let the dog out. Maybe you walk past the kettle and switch it on to boil while you pop back upstairs to jump in the shower.

Whatever your personal routine, could it just be possible that this repetition leaves some form of energy imprint, one which another person may witness at some point in the future?

When they tell friends they saw a figure disappear through a wall, could this once have been the position of a door while you lived at the property, long-since modified and repositioned? Could this explain the disappearance of our ghost at Woodchester?

Nobody knows!

The true joy about ghost hunting and paranormal investigations is that there is no irrefutable evidence to-date which either proves or disproves the existence of ghosts and spirits. As with anything, the thrill of the chase is paramount to the enjoyment of the activity.

Through my participation in these events I have encountered many interesting people from all walks of life, all careers and all ages. I have found that – whatever our differences – one common thread binds us all together; we would love to know whether there really was something waiting for us when we shuffle off this Earth.

One thing is for sure - when I'm dead and gone you won't find me lurking in the basement of a cold, derelict building, knocking twice for yes and once for no in answer to your questions.

Instead, I'll be that ghost who haunts the cosy armchair of a local pub, positioned right next to the open-fireplace and, if it's at all within my power, I'll train the landlord to leave me a vodka each night too.

But every good ghost needs a background story – preferably ridden with angst and torment – so maybe that explains why the next few years of my life delivered so many challenges for me to overcome.

Perhaps my time on Earth has no other purpose than to craft my spectral after-life attributes; the character-development for a much bigger story.

I guess only time will tell!

FOUR

......laughed so much a bit of wee escaped. You'll never forget the night you get acquainted with your Cherry!!! – 19 May 2010

One of the many people I was introduced to through Haunted Happenings was a larger than life character called Craig, a medium and professional drag artist.

It's not a combination you'd normally expect to encounter on a day-to-day basis and they were two very separate identities until 19 May 2010, with the launch of an exciting new venture, aptly titled *Scream with a Queen*.

Ghost hunting was becoming increasingly popular with hen-parties, looking for a night out with a difference. Some groups wanted the standard experience offered by the company, while others wanted a fun night with an element of spookiness thrown in for good measure.

With the average age for women getting married increasing from 24.7 years in 1970 to 33.6 years in 2010, it's understandable that an increasing number of hen-parties were now seeking something more than just a night on the town in a pink Tutu, waving an inflatable penis at the long-suffering doormen of clubs and bars. Picture it; a haunted castle, a six-foot drag-queen and a set of dildo-style dowsing-rods.

The concept for *Scream with a Queen* was born!

I can't remember exactly how my part in this came about, but at some point I agreed to get involved and I believe the conversation between Craig and Hazel went something like this:

'What I really need to make this work is a geek,' Craig had pondered.

'What on Earth for?' Hazel asked, completely puzzled.

'Well, I need someone who is prepared to dress up as a complete nerd, have the piss mercilessly ripped out of them all night, but then also be able to lead the ghost hunting experience for ladies afterwards,' he replied.

'I know the perfect person!' Hazel said with a glint in her eye.

In that moment, Duane was born!

It was just a matter of weeks later that I found myself standing in front of a dozen leery hens, dressed in a check-shirt, tartan bow-tie, trousers which were several inches too short and a pair of geeky glasses. Not my proudest moment and certainly not my best look! What made it worse was that I had been instructed not to speak; I just had to take whatever abuse came my way and laugh nervously.

Trust me when I say I didn't need to fake the nervous laugh that night, but once Cherry's banter kicked in I was able to fade into the background and enjoy listening to her turn her attention to the ladies and tear them apart instead. This was the first time I had seen a proper drag-artist at work and my God, what an experience it was.

Nothing was off limits. Nobody was safe!

If I recall correctly the hen's mother didn't fare well at the hands of Cherry's vicious wit, and one of the more vertically-challenged ladies was rebranded as Gollum from *The Hobbit*. There were jokes about the royal family, one about licking grass and one which involved a prawn; you can make up your own punchlines.

I hadn't laughed so much in years and it was certainly a night I wouldn't forget in a hurry, and yet for me the worst embarrassment was still to come.

With more than an hour to drive in order to reach home the fuel warning-light illuminated my dashboard, just as the castle disappeared in my rear-view mirror. Well of course I'd packed a change of clothing hadn't I?

Err.......NO!

Imagine the scene; it's 3.30am and there's a guy on your forecourt wearing a bow-tie, trousers so short they wouldn't have looked out of place in Michael Jackson's *Billie Jean* video, and a shirt that looks like it belongs in your great-grandad's wardrobe. I'd searched for a 'pay at pump' option in some desperate attempt to avoid having to make any form of communication with the attendant, but alas there were none. I'm not sure to this day who was more relieved that the shop itself was closed and payment had to be made through the security-window, the guy behind the till, or me?

Either way, with a full tank of fuel and my self-respect in tatters I spent the rest of the journey praying the car didn't break-down, otherwise I'd have to call the recovery services to rescue me, and you can imagine how that would have turned out.

Thankfully Duane's part in these nights was short-lived because the format worked perfectly well without his character. However, I did join Cherry's *Scream with a Queen* venture on one more occasion (as myself), but as a result of the night's events I've never been able to look at a shoelace in the same way since.

......has arrived at the Golden Fleece in York to host a hen night for 11 crazy women, with a Butler in the Buff, a male stripper and the infamous Cherry Darling! Wish me luck folks!!! – 9 Apr 2011

The venue was the infamous Golden Fleece pub in York. The occasion was another hen-party, but this time they had also booked a male-stripper who would arrive later.

Needless to say the ladies were full of excitement when they arrived, and following several lashings from Cherry's barbed tongue, a few verses of Gaga's *Born This Way*, and a rousing rendition of Gloria Gaynor's *I Will Survive*, they were ready for some cock.

I'm not quite sure of the best words to describe the stripper. Old would definitely be one but handsome most definitely would not. If I could summarise his look it would be a combination of the Incredible Hulk and Roy Cropper from *Coronation Street*, with a fake-tan that could easily have been sponsored by Cuprinol.

This was to be my first experience of a male-stripper (and thankfully my last), so I wasn't quite sure what to expect or quite how far he would go.

It turns out I didn't have to wait long to find out!

It seems he wasn't a big fan of the traditional tease, opting for the 'get your kit off as quick as possible and wave your willy around' routine instead.

Before the trousers came off I had already spotted the monster bulge. There was clearly something significant going on in there and when the buttons were undone and the culprit revealed I didn't know where to look. Well actually I did; I was mesmerised – but not for the reason you'd expect.

This guy had a raging boner!

I don't just mean swollen; you could break rocks with it. Worse still, it was tied-off so tightly with a shoelace the poor thing was choking to death and had turned a rather alarming shade of purple. Not a soft gentle-hue – this was borderline aubergine. In fact, the skin-tone between the two was so different you could be mistaken for thinking a black man's willy had been surgically attached to a white guy's body. The look of horror on some of the women's faces was one I won't forget in a hurry, as this thing bobbed around in front of them for a good ten minutes.

Moments like these don't happen very often and, although mildly traumatised by what I had seen, I truly appreciated every opportunity life was throwing at me. I still had my day job to bring me back down to Earth from Monday to Friday every week, but pretty much every weekend I was doing something I loved *and* notching up some fantastic stories along the way.

Needless to say though, whenever I tie my shoelace I am instantly transported back to this moment and the emotional scarring is something I believe will stay with me until the day I die.

It was probably a good thing that Duane's part in these outings was retired early, as just a few months later I took a huge leap-of-faith and made the decision to fix something about myself which had been a bug-bear since my youth; my eyesight.

Those huge geeky-glasses on which Duane's character was built would no longer be required, and he just wouldn't have been the same without them.

......is having laser eye surgery in 62hrs 45mins! 31yrs of being a speccy twat are about to end......I'll no longer be speccy! – 22 Nov 2010

I always hated wearing glasses, but from around the age of four I was stuck with them.

As well as being long-sighted in both, my right eye was also esotropic and amblyopic; that's right – not only was I born with big ears, I was also half-blind and cross-eyed with a smidgen of laziness thrown in too. Oh yeah, just to add real insult to injury they discovered a couple of years later that I was also suffering from orchiopexy (undescended testicle), a condition where one or both of the testicles don't move down correctly into the scrotum during development in the womb. In my case it was just the right one but hey, still not a great start right?

Once my parents realised the reason I was bumping into things was less to do with poor spatial awareness and more to do with the fact everything around me was blurry, I was furnished with a pair of standard-issue NHS specs. Unfortunately I also had to suffer the humiliation of an eye-patch for several weeks in an attempt to develop the lazy-eye's capacity to see as well as the preferred one.

God can be so cruel sometimes!

Naturally, once I started school I had to endure the usual torment of being one of the few kids wearing glasses. 'Four-eyes', 'Speccy' and 'Joe 90' were all names to play a large part in my formative years, and I honestly believe the self-confidence issues which haunted me later in life can be traced back – at least in part – to wearing glasses as a child.

In contrast, I would suggest that feeling like an outsider for so many years as a child also had an unexpected, but positive, impact upon me too.

Moving into adulthood I have never been able to tolerate seeing one person ostracised from a group. I absolutely loathe witnessing anybody being deliberately excluded, simply because they are different in some way from the rest, and can't even begin to imagine the effect this must have – for children and adults alike – particularly where disabilities are concerned. As if dealing with the condition itself wasn't enough of a challenge, to find yourself being victimised as a result must be absolutely heart-breaking.

Thankfully this quality and compassion appears to have been picked up by both of my children along the way. Kids can be cruel, particularly girls at school, and I have always tried to impress upon them the importance of being kind to others.

My eldest daughter had her moral compass tested to the fullest during her time at middle-school, and I can honestly say one of my proudest moments was to hear her tell me she had fallen out with some of her friends because she supported a girl who was being pushed out of their group for no good reason. She was incensed at the injustice and, rather than see this girl alone she turned her back on the 'clique' in order to support her, showing both courage and compassion beyond her years.

It staggers me how often this happens even today, both in social groups and also in the workplace. It may not be overt, but if you watch closely there will always be somebody within a group of five or more people who will feed their own insecurities at the expense of others.

Nowhere is this more prevalent than through the social-experiment which crashes at high speed into our lives in the UK each summer; the crazy messed-up world of *Big Brother*.

A dozen or so people enter the house looking for an experience (and fame if they're really honest with themselves), and within weeks an alpha-male or dominant-female will usually begin the process of systematically isolating anyone who dares to challenge their opinion, or presents any kind of perceived threat to their position. The division within the house is clear and will occasionally result in the complete isolation of an individual housemate.

My childhood was nothing like that, but feeling different definitely shaped the person I am today.

Cut back to 2010; I find myself with a spare £3,000 and the burning desire to re-shape my eyeballs so that I can finally dispense with the contact-lenses I had been wearing for the past 10 years.

I don't tend to think of myself as impulsive, but when it comes to some of the bigger decisions in life I probably rush in faster than some.

Following the recommendation of a clinic by a friend, whose partner had already used for the same procedure, I felt confident I'd found a reputable company in which to place my trust (and my eyesight). Of course I did the usual research in terms of testimonials and checked out their certification, but as for reading up on what to expect from the operation itself I did none. Thankfully, during the consultation and examinations they didn't offer up the gory details, and I was definitely of the mind that I would be better off not knowing exactly what the procedure entailed. That way I would have less to worry about on the day.

Well thank God I didn't, because as anybody who has ever had it done will testify, it isn't pleasant at all.

Having doused my eye with a clear fluid and prising it open with a clamp – akin to a scene from *A Clockwork Orange* – the surgeon positioned the machine over my right eye and off we went.

'Now, all I want you to do is look directly at the dot in front of you,' he said, with a reassuring tone. 'Don't worry if your eye moves because the laser is tracking the iris two-hundred times per second, so if you make any movements, it will follow.'

'Don't worry about me moving,' I replied nervously, 'I've paid £3,000 to lie in this chair so I'm not going anywhere.'

I'm unsure whether he appreciated my comment or not but in hindsight, cracking jokes while placing my vision in the hands of another probably wasn't the way forward.

Oddly, it wasn't until this very moment that I first considered just how big a deal this was. After all we take our sight for granted and here I was, putting myself in a position where I could potentially damage it further or worse, lose it altogether.

Questions raced through my mind about my real reason for doing this.

I hated wearing glasses and was struggling now with contact lenses due to dry-eyes, but was my loathing for glasses really to do with the practicalities I kept convincing myself of, or was this actually a deeper issue of vanity? Even more importantly, was I reacting to the comments from more than twenty-five years ago at school? Honestly,

I don't know, but one thing of which I was certain; it was too late to back out.

I have never lay so still in all my life and, after what seemed like a lifetime of staring at that dot, the surgeon removed the machine and I saw his hand move towards my eye with what looked like a pair of tweezers. My brain couldn't comprehend what my eyes were seeing. He had just lifted something from my eye which resembled a contact lens. *You're not wearing any, so what the hell was that?* I don't know if it was standard practice or whether my face alerted him to my confusion, but he went on to explain:

'I've just lifted the flap of skin covering your eye. Now all you need to do is look at the dot again and the laser will do the rest.'

Whaaaaaaat? I had just witnessed a crucial part of my eye lifted from the place it had sat comfortably since the day I was born. This was like a scene from a horror movie, but as if this wasn't bad enough, nothing could prepare me for what came next.

If you have ever been unfortunate enough to burn yourself with an open flame then you'll understand exactly the smell I'm referring to.

As the laser went about its work reshaping the eye, the aroma of burning flesh wafted into my nasal passage and I'm sure if I were hooked up to a heart-monitor it would have registered a significant rise in the number of beats per minute it was kicking out.

This was serious stuff and I couldn't run away. After what was probably as little as two minutes he removed the machine and placed a protective lens onto my beautiful new eyeball.

'All done!' he announced proudly. 'Now, we just need to do the other one.'

What's worse than having your eyeball cut apart and burned? You guessed it – having to sit through the next one, now fully aware of what was coming. At least with the first one I didn't know what to expect.

In less than twenty minutes since entering the room the procedure on both eyes was complete and, after a short wait and a check-up, I was sent home wearing dark sunglasses (on a cloudy day) looking like a celebrity sneaking out of a plastic surgeon's clinic.

One week later the protective lenses were removed and, following an eye test, I skipped out of the building with genuine 20/20 vision for the first time in my life.

This was honestly one of the most hideous yet rewarding things I have ever done. To wake up each morning and be able to see without reaching for a pair of specs or faffing around putting contact lenses into your eyes was an amazing feeling, and to this day it still makes me smile.

A short while later I discovered that, despite all of the brilliant after-care provided, there was one important reminder they missed.

......has discovered a hidden problem they don't warn you about when having laser eye surgery. Today, I had to change my Mii character on the Wii to remove the goggles! – 6 Jan 2011

FIVE

......Apparently when they said 'do not over-fill hole with foam as it will expand to fill the cavity' they meant just that. I did read the instructions, but just didn't agree with them. Oops! – 16 Jan 2011

I like to think when it comes to DIY skills I'm slightly above average, but we're all allowed one mistake aren't we? Well okay, there's been more than one along the way, but this is one of those which makes me smile when I recount the story, predominantly because it could so easily have been avoided had I only taken note of the instructions - and followed them.

I inherited the majority of my DIY skills from my mom. In all my years growing up I can't recall ever seeing dad with a saw, hammer or spanner in his hand, never mind anything more technical. As for decorating, mom was always the one hanging wallpaper, painting walls and creating havoc with a tin of gloss and a two-inch brush. I never really asked how this came to be, but I just accepted that's how it was and never questioned it.

As every kid does I begged and begged for the privilege of slapping paint onto the wall with a roller, and over the years I picked up all the basics of decorating. I discovered the perils of hanging heavily-patterned wallpaper, learned precision cutting-in with a paintbrush and even how to wire a plug; all courtesy of mom. One thing I certainly didn't learn from my mother was how to drill holes or hang shelves; basically, she couldn't do it.

On one occasion, while recuperating at home from a hernia-repair operation, I watched her channel a recess into the wall, from ceiling to floor, to bury a piece of cable. Having done all of this and feeling very proud of herself it suddenly all went wrong.

'Effing hell,' came a colourful outburst from the corner in which she was working (I have censored the real words).

'Errr, excuse me?' I chirped up, trying desperately not to burst my fresh stitches with laughter, or allow my stomach muscles to contract too much:

'I've managed to do all of this but I can't even nail the mesh-protector in place to cover the cable.' Tears of frustration were beginning to form as she continued. 'Why the hell can't I do this? I can do everything else and I can't even hammer the bloody mesh into place without bending the nails!'

'Maybe it's because you're a woman,' I replied, gently prising the hammer from her clenched fist, just in case she didn't appreciate my humour and chose to respond with a swift blow to my tender stomach.

Now of course I was joking, but who knows why such a seemingly simple task would defeat someone who can hang wallpaper with the best of them? I guess there are just some things in life which evade us and some at which we excel. Either way, this outburst resulted in a ridiculous scene with me hammering nails into the wall – wearing pyjama bottoms – whilst holding myself gingerly and hoping the nerve-blocks would hold out long enough to complete the task without causing excruciating pain.

As the years rolled on and I became the proud owner

of my own home my skills developed and, just like my mom, I became a dab-hand at decorating and DIY. I exceeded my own expectations with the addition of coving and new skirting-boards to several rooms, after eventually working out how to cut the angles properly following several botched attempts. I had even laid floor tiles in the bathroom, working out carefully how to cut around the sink-pedestal and toilet-bowl for the perfect finish. I impressed even myself!

On another occasion I almost succumbed to trench-foot, shovelling and wheeling five tonnes of hard-core and an additional three tonnes of pea-gravel into the garden to create a new seating area, in what turned out to be the worst week's rainfall we had seen in years.

……hates the fact that I've got five tonnes of hard-core on my drive that needs to be in my garden and only one shovel – 12 May 2009

Just ten days earlier I had already begun to regret the task in hand after moving unwanted turf and dirt from an area covering around 36ft x 12ft, in preparation for the task ahead.

…… has a new dance craze going on - big skip, little skip, Christ I'm f*cked. Why did we buy a house with a big garden??? – 2 May 2009

Guess what - just like mom, I wasn't destined to drill things!

Despite my best efforts I still wasn't to be trusted with a power-drill and would certainly never risk attempting to mess with gas or electrics; these are pesky little critters and I always enlisted the help of my father-in-law on those occasions, who was a master of all things DIY.

He was the Mr Miyagi to my Daniel; a true Sensei.

This was my perception of him until the day he kindly helped us to remove the pipework from an old back-boiler and cut through what turned out to be a live gas-pipe with a junior hack-saw.

How we didn't blow the house and ourselves to a thousand tiny pieces in that one moment I'll never know?

It was like a scene from *Fawlty Towers*; lots of panicked shouting and a desperate rush to locate the gas-main at the back of the under-stairs cupboard to switch off the supply. Kids' shoes, roller-boots I've owned since I was 18, coats, jackets and boxes – unopened since we moved into the house two years before – all ended up in a heap in the hallway: a desperate attempt to prevent us being gassed, or creating the greatest firework display Redditch has ever seen.

Needless to say we survived, but it just goes to show nobody is infallible. It also shows that DIY is dangerous, which is why I now avoid it at all costs; nothing to do with the fact that I just hate doing it.

Anyway, back to my hole.

When it came time to decorate the master-bedroom, I wanted to block up the original airbrick and plaster over it. Nothing screams 'pre-combi boiler' more than an ugly air-vent and I wanted it gone. So, off to Wickes I went (other DIY stores are available) to purchase a can of expanding foam filler with which to block up the cavity.

Now the fun begins!

I'm not one of those types who completely ignores instructions. When it comes to flat-pack furniture in fact, I'm quite the opposite. Even when something seems obvious I follow them to the letter, having been caught out before when I went with the obvious, only to find there was a damn good reason they wanted me to fix parts D & E together earlier in the process.

However, when it came to the very clear instruction NOT to 'overfill the hole', it seems I came to the regretful conclusion they didn't know what the heck they were talking about. I proceeded to spray the foam and, despite their warning to allow time to expand, kept on spraying. Only once I felt I had filled the hole sufficiently did I remove my trigger-happy finger from the aerosol.

Needless to say the instructions were in fact correct. As I stood back and waited, the foam continued to expand further and further. If you have ever added too much Radox to a Jacuzzi-bath you'll know exactly the look I had achieved.

Rather than a nicely-filled cavity, I was faced with something resembling the Hiroshima mushroom cloud and it continued to grow outwards, into the room!

When the expansion finally subsided, the now hardened foam-cloud stood around seven inches proud of the rest of the wall. Worse still, I had to leave this monstrosity for several hours before I could attempt to reduce its size and try to conceal my folly from the rest of the family.

Once hard, it took several minutes of hacking away with a saw to bring it in line with the rest of the wall, but I won.

The score was man-1, expanding foam-0.

As with everything in life, the mistakes we make are far less important than the lessons we learn from them and needless to say, I have never repeated this mistake. In fact, where gas, electrics, plumbing or expanding foam-filler are concerned, I know my limitations.

Just get a *proper* man in!

As I sat back and contemplated my error of judgement – having ignored the expert advice offered – I was reminded of a small rant I'd posted some months before.

……OMG - Experts reckon we waste a year of our lives looking for parking spaces! Not nearly as much time as these twats waste in useless research. GET A PROPER JOB!!!!! – 25 Oct 2010

Love them or hate them, the world is full of so-called 'experts' and we spend our whole lives being provided with information from them. Whether it be the economic forecast or the weather forecast – both of which have seen spectacularly incorrect predictions just in my lifetime – we are continually force-fed statistics about a whole host of weird and wonderful things.

Remember Michael Fish giving absolute and unequivocal assurances to UK viewers that there was no hurricane on its way in 1987? Here are his exact words:-

'Earlier on today, apparently, a woman rang the BBC and said she heard there was a hurricane on the way... well, if you're watching, don't worry, there isn't! Having said that, actually, the weather will become very windy, but most of the strong winds, incidentally, will be down over Spain and across into France.'

That evening 18 people died in the Great Storm, when winds of up to 122mph battered the UK. Around 15 million trees were uprooted, blocking roads and railway lines, cars were crushed, houses were damaged and thousands of homes were left without power for several days. The bill for damages was estimated (by experts) at around £2bn, and the country was left devastated.

Let's face it, weather is the single-most unpredictable thing to forecast, yet we rely on the experts on a daily basis to tell us what will happen, so that we may plan our Bank Holiday barbecue, or the annual trip to the mud-flats of Weston-Super-Mare.

We believe what we are told because these people are trained meteorologists and experts in their field. Of course, the statement from Michael was in no way intended to mislead us or play down the gravity of the impending winds; it was simply incorrect information, based solely on the facts available to him at the time.

When push comes to shove predictions are basically guess-work; hypothesis based on the limited information we have in the moment, combined with just a smidgen of personal opinion. History has proven time and time again that people get it wrong.

I'm reminded of the following quote from the UK's first female Prime Minister.

'It will be years – not in my time – before a woman becomes Prime Minister' – Margaret Thatcher 26 Oct 1969

When the Government announced plans in 2009 to allocate research funding according to how much impact it has, academics were up in arms. Speculation, driven by curious minds, has led to some of the most important scientific breakthroughs in history – including Penicillin and the theory of evolution – a fact that cannot be denied. Every single one of us reaps the benefit of somebody else's research on a daily basis and without it, our lives would be vastly different.

Genuine research for the growth and development of mankind is one thing, but what really makes my eggs boil is the incessant flow of ridiculous information we are presented with, especially with the advent of social-media.

We are confronted daily with a completely useless tirade of pointless 'facts and figures', often from unknown sources, of which we have no desire to consume.

Give me a cheap petrol-station calculator and a scrap of paper and I can estimate how long the average adult will spend looking for a parking space each year, or how many hours of our lives we spend washing our car. I could even tell you how many hours each year the average adult-male spends on the toilet, reading pointless research or expert-predictions on their mobile phones.

Does this make me an expert?

No, it just shows I have nothing more pressing to do with my time than calculate information which will add no value to my life, or the lives of anyone else.

For example, I don't feel my existence became any

more meaningful with the discovery of the 'fact' that the average human will swallow eight spiders every year while sleeping. For starters this goes completely against both spider and human biology, but even if it were true, would it change my sleeping habits? Would I scour the bedroom every night like a member of the Secret Service carrying out a Presidential security-sweep, to ensure I was arachnid free? Would I set up motion-detectors around the room to alert me to these eight-legged Kamikaze creatures? Actions and history – rather than research – tell me the answer is a resounding NO.

I do have one burning question for which I would like the experts to furnish me with an answer.

……can't understand why Obi Wan dissolved when Darth struck him in Star Wars and every subsequent Light Saber strike has merely lopped off people's limbs. Was he really just a clever jelly mould? – 28 Feb 2011

I was a child of the *Star Wars* era.

The original film (whatever number that is in the new sequence) came out in 1977, when I was just three years old and – like pretty much every boy around that age – I became obsessed with the original three movies over the coming years. I'm not talking 'I really love these films' obsessed, more like 'I'm going to beg my parents for every action figure and eat, sleep and breathe the *Star Wars* trilogy' obsessed.

I collected all the figures, flew my Millennium Falcon around the lounge, and adored my AT-AT Walker in the way most children adore their pets.

I don't recall when or how I came to have access to the films on VHS, but I remember watching *A New Hope (Episode IV)* time and time again, until such time that the picture and sound quality deteriorated through overuse. Even to this day, as soon as I hear the brass-fanfare of the title-theme I am instantly transported back to my childhood. The opening music is truly epic and arguably one of the most instantly recognisable and iconic themes in cinema history.

Years later this music would form the backdrop to a much sadder moment in my life; one which left a mark on me for many years and reminded me just how precious life is and how unfair it can be.

In February 1999, as the hype surrounding the release of the first in the new prequel-trilogy was building, I returned from a three-day residential training-course to some terrible news. Paul, a friend with whom I had shared a student house during our college-years, had sadly passed away the week before. He had suffered his whole life with Cystic Fibrosis and I believe it was a bout of pneumonia which finally defeated him, ultimately claiming his life.

He was just 22 years old!

Standing at 5ft 4" with sandy-blonde hair, bright blue-eyes and a gruff voice, his tiny frame defied the powerhouse of energy, enthusiasm and positivity he truly was.

During our time together at the Welsh College of Music & Drama in Cardiff I had watched as he carried out his daily routine of exercises – to clear his chest of the debilitating mucus which would build – and listen with horror as he struggled for breath on bad days.

He was a truly amazing character, never once complaining about his condition. I don't recall ever hearing him say 'it's not fair' or ask for any special treatment and, to my knowledge, no requests for special dispensation for college assignment deadlines were ever made; he certainly didn't use his condition to shirk doing his share of the housework at home.

There were many times when I asked myself what I would do in his position? Would I have had the drive and determination he displayed to study for a career, or would I have thought 'sod it', I'm going to live every moment I can to the fullest because I know my opportunities are going to be limited?

Thankfully I'll never know the answer.

He was fully aware that the average life-expectancy for a Cystic Fibrosis suffer at this time was around 32 years of age, yet he came to college to study, fully intending to enjoy a long life and a successful career in the field he loved.

The funeral was to be held near his home on the Isle of Wight, so my wife and I made the journey, along with a few others who had shared the student house with us, to pay our respects and say our last goodbyes.

The Isle of Wight is stunning.

Once home to the famous poet Tennyson, and a place where Queen Victoria chose to build her much-loved summer residence, the island boasts a diverse landscape and a milder sub-climate – compared with other areas of the UK – thus making it a popular holiday destination. Designated as an area of outstanding natural-beauty, the dramatic coastlines, rural scenery, soft cliffs and sea-ledges are a haven for wildlife.

Unfortunately, our visit would be brief and somewhat more sombre and, coming off the back of a fairly cold-spell, the bleak weather served to reflect the purpose of our trip. Overcast skies, biting winds and a fine yet persistent drizzle of rain, blanketed this otherwise beautiful place.

In truth Paul and I didn't have a great deal in common, but one thing we shared a passion for, especially in our youth, was *Star Wars*. We had shared many conversations in the past so I knew he was an avid fan and would have been looking forward to the new trilogy.

Sadly, he would never get to see them!

The temperature in the church was freezing and, as we waited for the service to begin, there was a real sense of loss among everyone present. He was an incredibly well-liked guy and there wasn't an empty seat in the place.

I recall gazing at the surroundings, marvelling at the

interior of this wonderful building, lost for a moment in a world of my own sadness.

Then, it came from nowhere!

That all too familiar brass fanfare filled the air, sending a tingle down my spine in an instant. His parents had decided the most fitting tribute they could give their son was to be carried into church to the defiant heroic-majesty of the infamous *Star Wars* theme; a poignant touch!

My heart began racing, tears immediately began to well-up in my eyes and I gripped my wife's hand.

The sweeping, compassionate strings-section began its contrasting beautiful melody just as the coffin passed our seats and, despite the tragedy of the circumstances, I couldn't help but smile as I imagined just how much he would have loved what was happening in this moment. I had heard this music hundreds of times, but to hear it echo around the church and experience the effect of the building's acoustics was a moment I will remember forever.

It's often said that life is cruel, yet never have I felt that more than I did on this day. To lose a kind, positive and vibrant character at such a young age is awful and I have much to thank him for.

Whilst I have been fortunate, so far, in never having suffered a serious illness, I came to understand – through knowing him – the true measure of a person is not what fortune they amass during their time on this Earth, but the memories they leave in the hearts of those they leave behind.

SIX

......thinks Google must have been struggling today with the theme for their Google header - Jules Verne's 183rd birthday. What next, Hilda & Stan Ogden's 74th wedding anniversary? – 8 Feb 2011

You may be forgiven for not knowing who the heck Jules Verne is. I certainly didn't until 8th February 2011, but I do now and I guess that is one of the many things I have to thank Google for (other search engines *used* to be available).

It turns out Jules Verne was a major literary author who had a massive influence on the science fiction genre. As I took to Wikipedia to find out more about him I discovered I recognised work he had written, such as *Twenty Thousand Leagues under the Sea* and *Around the World in Eighty Days*. This man was apparently the second most-translated author in the world since 1979, ranking between Agatha Christie and William Shakespeare; both names I'm pleased to report were much more familiar to me.

I had never really taken much notice of *Google Doodles*, as I have since learned they are called. You know them, the ones where they change their logo on the search page to reflect something significant that happened on a particular day in history, or recognise a particular individual's birthday etc. However, when I sat back and realised what had just happened I was astounded. In just a few seconds I had learned something interesting about a person I had never even heard of.

I'm not saying I'll ever need this information, but I now knew something I didn't know before, just because Google chose to celebrate this man's life with a doodle. In the unlikely event I one day find myself on a quiz-show, being asked to name one of Jules' novels, I will know who to thank.

Of course, I was being flippant when I posted my comment, deriding Google for such a random birthday to celebrate, but the fact remained I had learned something new. In fact, since that day I make a point of clicking on the *Google Doodle* whenever there is one, just to find out more about whoever or whatever they are honouring.

This event caused me to think about just how amazing the internet really is. How readily information and knowledge is now available to us all and how this has happened in my own lifetime.

When I was studying for my A-Levels we had one computer in the school, situated in the library where nobody wanted to go. Even as I studied for my Bachelor of Arts degree in the late '90s, there were probably only around six computers in the whole building. My 20,000 word dissertation for my final year was typed on an electronic word-processor at home, with each word dancing its way across a small LCD, before reaching its final resting place on the 3½-inch floppy disk inside.

At this point Google didn't even exist!

We had to physically go to the library and find a book from which to plagiarise our University assignments. If we wanted to know what songs our favourite artist would be performing at an up-coming concert, we had to go! In fact, when you look at just how much the internet has changed our lives and how we live on a daily basis, it is quite frankly astounding.

As of today we can find pretty much anything we need to know, simply by typing our question into Google.

Is it a good thing?

Who knows at this stage? Are our children and the generations which follow going to be more educated as a result of having the answers to questions at their fingertips, or will they become less inclined to listen in class or seek meaningful information, because they know they can find it later, on a need-to-know basis? The answer will probably only become evident a hundred years or so down the line – by which time it may be too late.

I've had many conversations with teachers and parents in the past and there is often one thing upon which we agree; our children are often unprepared upon leaving full-time education for the real-world which awaits them. Why do we not teach our children some of the true practicalities of life while we have their undivided attention in school?

......is wondering why we don't teach our kids how to budget & deal with mortgages etc., rather than how to calculate how much grass a goat can eat if he's tied to a stake with a 3m rope. I've never even owned a friggin goat! – 23 Sept 2009

I know I'm not alone in these thoughts!

When we leave school or University we are instantly thrown head-first into a grown-up world - one in which we will need to understand how an overdraft works. A world where money is thrown at us by credit-card companies, which can lead to long-term problems for those who don't understand the consequences of not paying them off. A world where knowledge is power and budgeting is everything; mortgages, rent, bills, contracts, buying houses etc. The list of practicalities for which we leave school wholly unprepared to deal with is endless.

Of course, there will always be people who need to know how much grass their goat can eat, but they'll need to understand how to deal with the 'business-end' of their farm just as much as the 'business-end' of their livestock.

At the time of writing the teaching profession is in crisis. With Government cuts in budgets, changes in the education system and teaching staff under increasing pressure to achieve better exam results, more and more teachers are leaving their roles than ever before; vocations in which they want to remain, but find themselves increasingly frustrated.

Are we spending more time teaching our children useful information to help them into adulthood, or simply coaching them on how to take a test?

The following open-letter to Nicky Morgan MP, the Secretary of State for Education at the time – written by Zoe Paramour and published on her blog-site *The Girl On The Piccadilly Line* – was shared to Facebook, entitled Letter of Resignation, on 14 May 2016.

The sheer frustration of this teacher, someone who truly wants to give their life to the education of our children, is shared by many and for that reason, I want to share it with you:

Dear Nicky Morgan,

Please accept this as written notice of my resignation from my role as Assistant Head and class teacher.

It is with a heavy heart that I write you this letter. I know you've struggled to listen to and understand teachers in the past so I'm going to try and make this as clear as possible. In the six short years I have been teaching your party has destroyed the Education system. Obliterated it. Ruined it. It is broken.

The first thing I learnt when I started teaching in 2010 is that teaching is bloody hard work. It's a 60 hour week only half of which is spent doing the actual teaching.

It eats into the rest of your life both mentally and physically. If it's not exercise books and resources taking over your lounge and kitchen table it's worrying about results or about little Ahmed's home life keeping you awake at 2am. I've never minded this. I've always been happy to give my life over to teaching as I believed it to be such a noble cause. Besides we're not the only profession who work long hours. What I didn't realise back in 2010 is that the job would get harder each year.

First you introduced the phonics check. I was in Year 1 that year and continued teaching phonics to the best of my ability. I didn't spend much time teaching children to differentiate between real words and "non-words" because I was focused on, you know, teaching them to read. I sat and watched child after child fail that ridiculous "screening" because they read the word "strom" as "storm". The following year I taught to the test. We spent weeks practising "words" and "non-words" and sure enough our results soared.

My second year brought with it the changes to the Ofsted framework and the obsession with data began. Oh the sodding data game! The game that refuses to acknowledge how long a child has spoken English or whether or not they have books or even food at home. The data game changed things. Attainment in Maths and English was no longer just important, it would almost entirely decide the judgement made about your school. Oh and whilst we're on the judgements "Satisfactory" was no longer satisfactory – it was the far more sinister sounding: "Requires Improvement."

From then on things began to unravel at an alarming rate. The threat of forced academisation hung over each set of SATs results and the floor targets continued to rise. Gove cut the calculator paper (because calculators are cheating) and introduced SPaG. Grammar was no longer for writing – it was for grammar. Around the same time he also froze teachers' pay and doubled the contributions we would have to make to our pensions. Teachers were suddenly worse off than they had been the previous year and under more pressure than ever before.

So teaching became harder still and life in schools started to change. There were new hoops to jump through and somehow we just about managed to get through them. It meant sacrificing everything that wasn't SPaG, English or Maths but we did it – we learnt how to play the game. Outside of the safety of our schools though there was a bigger game being played – one that we had no chance of winning: the status of the teaching profession was being eroded away. There was the incessant name calling and smears in the media from "the blob" to "the enemies of promise" and, of course, "soft bigots" with "low expectations". You drip fed the message: teachers were not to be trusted and it worked: the public stopped trusting us.

As bleak as it sounds, those years look like a golden age compared to what we have to deal with now.

I was delighted when Gove went. I knew there was every chance he'd be replaced by someone equally awful but I couldn't imagine things getting worse. I figured the Tories were done playing with Education and they'd move on to something else. I was so wrong.

This year brought with it our greatest challenge to date – the new assessments. For most of the year we were completely in the dark. We had no idea what form the tests would take and how they would be scored (we're still not entirely sure on the latter.) There was also the introduction of the SPaG test for 7-year-olds (which was sadly scrapped because of your own department's incompetence.) The criteria for assessing writing has changed dramatically. Gone is the best fit approach and what has replaced it is an arbitrary list of criteria of the things children should be able to do – some of which are grammatical rules that your department have made up . Year 6 were tested on their ability to read long words and remember the names of different tenses. Whatever foundation subjects were still being taught have had to be shelved in favour of lesson after lesson on the past progressive tense.

In some ways I don't feel like a teacher at all any more. I prepare children for tests and, if I'm honest, I do it quite well. It's not something I'm particularly proud of as it's not as if I've provided my class with any transferable, real life skills during the process. They've not enjoyed it, I've not enjoyed it but we've done it: and one thing my children know how to do is answer test questions. They've written raps about how to answer test questions, they've practised test questions at home and test questions in school, and they've had extra tuition to help them understand the test questions. They can do test questions – they just haven't had time to do anything else.

At the same time you've cut school budgets to pieces. This one hasn't been widely reported yet but it will be over the next 18 months. I know of 3 head teachers who are considering having their own class next year as they can't afford to replace the teachers that are leaving. Most schools I know have already cut back on support staff (read: made valuable, hard-working teaching assistants redundant.) And this is just the start of it. I suppose the only thing schools should be grateful for is that you introduced performance related pay and, with the leap in National Expectations, there will be fewer teachers getting their pay rise this September.

In many ways I'm one of the lucky ones – I work for two smart Head Teachers in a school with an SLT who genuinely care about teacher workload. Meaningless box ticking exercises are kept to a minimum and meetings are kept brief. We only have INSET on average every other week and book scrutiny/monitoring is only carried out once a term. Demands on teachers' time are kept to a minimum but there is very little we can do to protect teachers from the unreasonable expectations being put on them by your Government, the threat of no-notice Ofsted inspections and, of course, the ever increasing risk of academisation.

I know I'm not alone in feeling like this. A recent survey found that nearly 50% of teachers are considering leaving in the next 5 years. Just within my own family my fiancé, my sister and my sister-in-law have all quit the profession in the last 12 weeks. Rather than address this issue you've decided to allow schools to recruit unqualified teachers to fill the gaps. The final nail in the profession's coffin. I don't want to stop teaching. I love teaching but I have no interest in being part of this game anymore.

Worse than being a teacher in this system is being a child at the mercy of it and to them I say this: we tried our best to fight these changes: we rallied, we went on strike, and we campaigned and made as much noise as we could. I'm sorry it didn't work and I'm sorry that I'm not strong enough to keep working in this system but as I've told many of you many times: when someone is being mean to you – you ask them to stop. If they continue to be mean you walk away. It is now time for me to walk away. I'll keep up the fight though.

Maybe in time things will change and, when that time comes, I can come back to the job I loved but until then sorry Nicky – I'm out.

>*Yours Sincerely,*
>*Zoe*

>*P.S: One last thing – if you do end up losing your job over your shambolic running of the Education System – make sure they don't replace you with Boris.*

SEVEN

......The kids are both singing along to Rhianna on their MP3 players with their earphones in. Problem is, they're about 3 seconds apart. The Chinese couldn't come up with torture like this!!!! – 31 Dec 2010

Nobody warns you do they?

When we reach that age and start to think about having children of our own, why is it nobody tells you the truth about what you're letting yourself in for? I can only assume it's a conspiracy to ensure that we continue to procreate; to avoid an otherwise certain end to the human race. Parents and in-laws clearly have their own agenda of becoming grandparents, and friends with children of their own just want you to produce a companion for their kids, so they can play together and create a distraction to give the grown-ups some peace.

I'm joking of course!

Becoming a dad is the single-most important thing that has ever happened to me and, despite the noise they create, the financial stress they bring and the mess they leave the house in, I wouldn't change it for the world.

That moment when you hold them in your arms and

they grip your finger is one that I remember fondly. That amazing feeling when you look down at your own flesh and blood and realise they are going to need you like nobody has ever needed you before is life-changing.

To be honest I never really wanted children.

I love babies, but always felt I was too selfish to be a good dad myself and at the time, would have preferred to enjoy life with just the two of us; nice holidays, a better house and the disposable income to experience some of the exciting things this luxury can offer.

More than this, I also carried a deep-seated fear that I wouldn't be any good. After all, I was only 26 years old when we made the decision to have them and I didn't feel like a proper grown-up myself.

That wasn't everything though.

I had never been particularly close to my own dad and felt he hadn't really been there for us as children, in the way other people's dads *appeared* to be. We didn't spend much time together when I was young. We had never been to a football match, tinkered beneath the bonnet of a car, or even once gone to the pub together. Hindsight tells me that this had a lot to do with work but, as a young adult I just felt he hadn't really tried. It seemed like he'd seen his role as a dad as the one who went out and worked as hard as he could to bring home as much money as he could, and that was that.

My greatest concern when my wife and I began talking seriously about having kids ourselves was that history would repeat itself. I was genuinely fearful that I would repeat the mistakes I felt had been made by my own father, and I really didn't want that.

My wife on the other hand was born to be a mom.

I don't mean that she wasn't capable of achieving a successful career if she had wanted, but there was absolutely no way she could live out her days without bearing children of her own. We talked a lot about my fears, but ultimately it became clear that there could be no *us* without children. As with any marriage or long-term relationship there had been times when we argued, but by this time we had been together for 10 years and I loved her. I didn't want that to change.

She managed to convince me I would be a better dad than I felt mine had been, and that I would learn from the mistakes I believed he had made. So that was that; it was time to make babies.

Like every other kid in middle-school I had sniggered my way through sex-education lessons and hadn't paid much attention, but after 10 years of practice I felt pretty confident I knew what I needed to do. Little did I know that there is a whole lot more to it than meets the eye?

Sorry fellas, but in my experience when a woman makes her mind up that she wants to get pregnant she assumes a whole new persona and becomes a completely different person. You may well find that the blinkers go on, the calendar comes out, and sex becomes more like a military exercise than a pleasurable pastime.

I remember her announcing casually one evening that she had been doing some reading and the book said we needed to have sex for the five days from when she began to ovulate; so basically we had a five-day window every month in which to get pregnant.

The battle plan was made!

To conceive quickly and efficiently the books will advise you to apply the kind of strategic planning that would make Rommel proud. There are clear concise-dates, during which you need to have as much sex as humanly possible without causing friction burn, passing out from exhaustion, or suffering from spontaneous combustion. As for the other 25 days each month…..forget it. If you aren't having sex to make a baby, you aren't having sex.

I don't remember the exact dates for the first attempt, but I do know that they fell somewhere surrounding the 17 November 2000. How do I know this with such clarity? Well, because I recall that particular night vividly. In fact, it is permanently etched in my mind for all the wrong reasons!

That night I tried to do my part in making a baby with Sir Terry Wogan and Gabby Roslin watching.

It's not quite as bad as it sounds, but it's not far off. After two or three days into the 'five day window', the process felt equally as mundane as cooking dinner or running the vacuum around; just another job that needed doing before the day ended.

So, with Sir Terry revealing the latest update on the amount raised for *Children in Need*, and me gazing across her shoulder – more interested in watching the cast of *Casualty* doing a song-and-dance routine – we tried to conceive.

There must be plenty of guys out there who can relate to this. I can't be the only man to feel he had transitioned from husband to sperm-donor in one swift move. I only wish I were more interested in football – at least it only lasts for 90 minutes; *Children in Need* was on for 6 hours and 25 minutes! Anyway, with the fertile period over, life returned to normal.

Now the countdown commenced until the day we could do the pregnancy test, to see if I had done my job right. When the time arrived she emerged from the bathroom looking disillusioned.

There were tears in her eyes as she announced there was no blue line; she wasn't pregnant!

'Don't worry, it was unlikely to happen first time,' I reassured her, while trying to calculate in the back of my mind how long before the window of opportunity opened again, and whether or not I'd have the stamina to survive it.

I don't know if she genuinely thought it would be so simple that we would catch on the first attempt, but she insisted she couldn't understand why, and that she was certain the dates were right for her fertile period. She returned straight to the book to check the facts.

You guessed it; the dates were wrong!

It seemed she had misread the information and the window is actually the five days leading up to your ovulation date, not following it. Basically we were five days late, hence no baby. Of course, this also meant the rest-period before another try was almost over, and we were about to enter the *true* fertile time.

Quick – pass me the spinach; I'm going to need it!

So, following another attempt and another pregnancy test, she emerged once more from the bathroom; this time she was beaming from ear to ear.

She *was* pregnant!

I don't know exactly what my feelings were in that moment, but I do know it suddenly it dawned upon me that – all things being well – I was going to be somebody's dad. It's a very humbling moment and I think at that point I realised I would be okay.

I began to think about all of the things that being a parent would entail. The responsibility that it would bring, the fears – many irrational – I would face as they grew up and began school and of course, concerns for my wife during the pregnancy itself.

We were very lucky!

Everything went without a hitch, apart from the normal bouts of morning sickness and general pregnancy-related stuff. She is a strong woman and never once allowed the fact that another human was steadily growing inside her get in the way of work. In fact, she continued to work right up until just a few days before the baby arrived.

We attended a few of the prenatal sessions at the local hospital in the hope of preparing ourselves for the birth, but we were both fairly level-headed about what lay ahead and to be honest, I felt that the classes left me with more questions than it did answers. As with many things in life, sometimes it's better not to know too much detail about what is going to happen; remember the laser-eye surgery? When the day finally arrives, whether or not you understand what to expect, mom will ultimately be placing her own life and the life of your unborn baby in the hands of the medical experts, and I think we were both confident in that.

It felt like those nine months flew by and before we knew it baby's arrival date was just a week away. My 27th birthday was also looming and, although there were no signs to suggest our little bundle may arrive early, I issued the following warning:-

'There are 364 other days in the year. Don't go having this baby early as I'm not sharing my birthday.'

She agreed to do her best, but asserted there would be no guarantees.

At one minute past midnight – just as my birthday ended – it all began. We had only been asleep around 30 minutes when she woke me up to tell me her waters had broken.

'Are you sure?' I asked, struggling to wake from the deep sleep into which I had just fallen.

She was certain!

She was standing in the doorway to the bedroom, having scurried into the bathroom moments earlier. As the light went on and I made my way across the room the answer to my question became clear. Several small puddles on the exposed wooden-flooring backed up her statement.

'Well, at least you waited until after my birthday,' I said with a smile, unsure whether it would be met with a laugh or result in a swift blow to the head.

So, with my OCD tendencies satisfied by cleaning up the bedroom floor, we set off for the hospital and arrived a short while later, having made a detour to her parents' house to let them know what was happening.

That's when it all stopped!

No contractions, no dilation…..no baby.

Mom was admitted to the ward and dad was sent home to wait for 'the call'. During those few hours at home, waiting to be summoned back to the hospital, I paced around the house trying to find something to keep me occupied; several cups of tea were drank and I watched the only half-decent thing I could find on television to keep my mind off staring at the clock – a re-run of an old episode of *The Bill* on UK Gold. In an uncertain world you can always rely on there being an episode of *The Bill* on television somewhere when you need one and trust me when I say, I needed the distraction.

Needless to say I couldn't sleep, so when they phoned me at around 5am to return I was ready and raring to go.

So much for childbirth being the most amazing experience of your life; for me the whole thing felt like something from a horror movie. After a slow start we were nearly there, but although baby was trying hard to make an appearance, mom had become tired from all the pushing and was now struggling to deliver. The decision came from the midwife that they would need to give some assistance.

'We are going to have to cut you to help deliver baby,' she announced with a calmness that simply didn't fit the words she was speaking.

Errrr, excuse me? Did I just hear that right?

It seems I did, because before you could say 'this might smart a bit', the surgical-scissors were out and approaching their destination.

The sound will stay with me forever!

I feel sure the sound-effects team for the more gruesome scenes in the *Saw* movies must have recorded audio from childbirth. Add to this the realisation somebody is hacking away at your loved one's tender bits with a sharp pair of surgical scissors – without any form of anaesthetic and precariously close to your shiny new baby's head – and you'll get the idea of how I felt. Of course this was much worse for my wife, but she did reassure me afterwards that she didn't feel a thing; I only hope she was referring to the birth and not the conception!

Within a minute baby was delivered and that heart-stopping moment, while you wait to hear your baby cry as a sign everything is okay, passed almost instantly.

As a result of complications during birth the midwife needed to attend to mom. So, with baby wrapped up cosy and warm, I was handed our brand-new bundle of joy and had the opportunity to sit for around 15 minutes and simply hold her, before passing her to mom for their all-important bonding.

I've heard stories where grown men have been reduced to tears at this point, but that wasn't to be. I just remember an overwhelming feeling of love for this baby and an incredible feeling of calmness, despite the horrors I had witnessed moments before.

Jump forward 2½ years and we were back in the same hospital taking delivery of our second baby girl. The birth was a much quicker affair this time, although we were almost responsible for giving two electricians a coronary en route to the delivery suite.

Following admission and another period of inactivity, the contractions came on suddenly and very strong. The midwife, an old-fashioned stern type with little visible compassion for the pain her subject was feeling, thought my wife was being overdramatic when she informed her she felt the sudden urge to push. Reluctantly the midwife agreed to check how far dilated she was and was met with a shock.

'Oh my goodness,' came her immediate and rather surprised response, 'you're 8½ centimetres; we need to get you to the delivery-suite now! Do you think you can manage to walk?'

Well, the missus was up and out of that bed like a *Big Brother* housemate on shopping delivery-day, waddling toward the door without a moment's hesitation, knowing full-well in her own mind that this baby wasn't hanging around.

The issue was that the contractions were now coming thick and fast – every 30 seconds or so – and it was some distance from the bed on the ward to the delivery room. After every dozen or so steps we would have to pause as another one came, and as we reached the entrance to the corridor, we were met by two guys who were repairing some electrics in the doorway. Unfortunately for them, just as we were about to pass, another contraction came.

'Jesus love,' one of them exclaimed, after watching in horror until the contraction subsided, 'I thought you were going to have it right there!'

She replied that she still might, with a smile that concealed the pain and embarrassment she must have been feeling in that moment.

She was amazing!

Just five minutes later, no sooner than she had eased herself onto the bed, our second baby-girl was born. This time there was a horrible pause of what felt like a lifetime before that reassuring cry emanated from her tiny mouth. Thankfully it came, and we now had another life for which we were responsible.

I have never once taken for granted how lucky we were to have two healthy children, and it's only since becoming a father that I really understood just how devastating and difficult it must be when your child is born with severe disabilities. Of course, in no way would it diminish the love you feel for your child, but I truly think that all every parent-to-be truly wants is for their child to be healthy. We were lucky on both occasions!

When our eldest arrived just 2½ years earlier, the advice given to us had been to sleep baby in a cot in our bedroom for the first six weeks. We had managed around four weeks before we realised that not only was this making us paranoid every time she made the slightest noise, but we were also disturbing her sleep if we got up to use the bathroom in the night, or if one of us let out a cheeky snore. Following the birth of our youngest, we were both absolutely astounded to be told that the recommended timeframe to keep the child in your room was now six months.

That was *not* going to happen!

Although this may sound awful to some, from the very first night she slept in the nursery, with the light off and the bedroom door closed. Of course we had a baby-monitor so we could hear her if she needed us, but we both believed this was a better course of action and were proven right in this case; throughout those early days and right through the first few years, she proved to be far easier to put to bed at night and slept-through with fewer problems than we encountered with her elder sister. Maybe this was pure luck or maybe it had something to do with those early choices; we'll never know for sure.

There was never any preference on my part regarding the sex of our children and if I'm honest – since I'm the least blokey bloke I know – I was really happy we had two girls.

The age gap was perfect as they were close enough to grow together and my eldest had already developed her mother's maternal nature, so she loved having a little sister. Over time they have grown to become truly lovely young adults, both with a sharp sense of humour, and have given us some truly memorable moments along the way.

I recall driving through Redditch one day with both children in back of the car. Another driver cut straight across the dual-carriageway in front of us, causing me to brake sharply to avoid a collision. As the words started to form on my lips, my youngest – around three years of age at the time – beat me to it:-

'For fuck's sake,' came a little voice from the back.

Now, you know when you have one of those moments where you can't quite believe what you've heard and you need a moment to soak it all in; this was one of those times.

'What did you say?' I questioned, trying really hard to swallow the outburst of laughter forming within me.

Naturally, she wasn't fully aware of what she'd said,

and as her parent I have to take responsibility for words they'd heard, but she suddenly shrunk back into hear seat, clearly understanding that it wasn't good. Before she could formulate a response, her sister jumped to the rescue:-

'She said for fuck's sake daddy!'

Well, at this point I nearly crashed the car myself; I couldn't hold the laughter in. She had seen her opportunity to quote her little sister, and grabbed it with both hands.

Naturally I explained the gravity of this word to them and to be honest, neither of them have ever used bad language while around us. I'm not daft – of course I'm aware they will use swear-words during their time at school, but I've always been proud of the fact that they both respect and understand the need to tailor your actions to your surroundings; to me this shows they are both very sensible and thoughtful people, a trait far more important in life than uttering the occasional expletive.

There was another incident while out walking the dogs where, completely out of the blue, my eldest turned to her sister and called her the *ultimate* swear-word. Both my wife and I almost gave ourselves whiplash turning our heads so quickly, ready to chastise her. She was now in the final year of middle-school and was naturally becoming more and more exposed to the more colourful words in the English language. It turned out she believed this was the equivalent of calling someone a dick-head, and the fact she said it openly in front of us told me that it had been a purely innocent mistake.

Moments like these, though funny for the wrong reasons, are ones upon which I often reminisce with fondness. The innocence of youth is truly wonderful and if only we were able to retain some of the qualities we are born with as we grow into adulthood, the world would surely be a more pleasant place.

For as much as I love both of them to bits, I'm ashamed to say my original fears about having children were not unfounded. Despite all reassurances from my wife that I wouldn't repeat the mistakes I perceived my own father had made, I did. I spent too many hours working and not nearly enough time with them as they grew up!

My wife was incredibly close to her sister and our niece and they would regularly take mini-break holidays together. I often took this as an opportunity to relax from work and remained at home when, in hindsight, I should have been there absorbing every possible moment I could of their childhood. I had criticised my dad for working too hard and not spending enough time with my brother and I, and now history had repeated itself.

Worse still, many years later this would play a big part in the breakdown of my relationship with my eldest daughter, with whom I had always been so close. With hindsight, I now realise that even though they may not vocalise it at the time, all children ever really want (and need) from a parent is their love and their time.

I had failed them in the worst way possible and I will regret those choices until the day I die.

EIGHT

……got instantly rejected for car insurance. I'd only got as far as saying my name, address & 3 penalty points!!! Have I been added to MI5's Most Wanted list without being told? – 30 Mar 2011

It didn't take long before I understood the two main functions Facebook is most commonly used for; bragging and bitching.

You know the bragging I mean, the posts where people present a façade of happiness when really they're as miserable as a diabetic in a cake shop. Those days when you feel obliged to tell the world just how ecstatic you are to be spending the day with your in-laws, when in reality you'd rather be sliding bamboo shoots beneath your fingernails.

We've all been there, and it is vital to remember when you're feeling miserable, the last thing you should do is scroll through your friends' pages, reading how amazing their lives are. For starters it's their life and not yours, so reading it isn't going to make you any happier and secondly, it's mostly bullshit - designed to hide the reality of their lives; work, bills, kids and housework.

I'm ashamed to say I have been guilty of these posts

myself, but far and away my favourite use of my page over the years has been the second primary-function; to have a bloody good bitch about whatever it is that has yanked my chain that particular day.

Thankfully, the country in which I live is one that just keeps on giving when it comes to providing things to complain about; service-providers, Government policies, the education system and the weather, to name but a few.

You never have to scroll far on my timeline before you'll stumble across one sarcastic post or another and, as you can see from my post, car insurance renewal was one of those things that drive me to pick up my mobile and start typing.

Now I'm not as daft as the majority of my Facebook photos make me look, yet car-insurance companies never cease to amaze me. At the time of writing this book I have held my licence for just over 24 years, so I've had plenty of dealings with them, and my personal experience has been that they offer you absolutely no loyalty. In fact, it seems most of them will bend you over like it's your first night in prison as soon as look at you. There must be some good ones out there, but unfortunately I've yet to find them.

Remember those 'experts' I talked about earlier?

Any one of them will tell you *never* to accept a renewal quote from your current insurance-provider, as it will most likely be significantly higher than if you were a new customer calling up to open a new policy.

Now I'm not a bad driver by any means. Sure, like most people I have been known to shimmy past the speed limit once or twice in the past, but in 24 years of driving I have had three speeding-fines, one of which was purely accidental because I believed Tower Bridge in London was a 30 zone instead of the 20 it actually is. So imagine my surprise when I contacted this online company for a comparison quote, to be instantly refused a policy as soon as I declared my address.

Let's be clear, I wasn't living in Baghdad or Beirut at

the time and I don't drive getaway cars for a living. I lived in an area of Redditch which had a relatively poor reputation from 20-plus years ago, but from their instant rejection you'd think I had to negotiate my way through police blockades and rocket-fire just to get to the local supermarket.

These guys had spent huge amounts of money advertising on TV at the time, shouting about how wonderful their cover was and how much you could save, yet I couldn't even get as far as being quoted a figure that would allow *me* to make that decision for myself.

Why? Because (in my opinion) most of them don't want to insure even the slightest risk.

I recall an incident from years before, where my wife's vehicle was written-off by another driver after she pulled across a road to turn around in a side-street. The insurer, who shall remain nameless, didn't seem to make any effort to support their own client when it came to judging accountability for the accident.

The vehicle was deemed unrepairable, and the amount actually paid-out was significantly less than the write-off value because she had forgotten to update the policy since receiving a speeding-fine after the policy had begun. The company quoted this as a reason to massively reduce the pay-out, despite lengthy argument from myself.

Car insurance is a necessary evil we all have to accept in life, but how these companies are allowed to make up their own rules – seemingly without any guidelines – just amazes me.

In the unlikely event I should find myself representing my local constituents as a Member of Parliament (unlikely because I consider honesty to be one of my finest qualities and I know how to complete an expenses claim-form correctly), I would make it my mission to ensure all motor-insurance companies were suitably regulated.

Since this is not an optional insurance, it staggers me

that there are no Government guidelines to protect the consumer and force clear pricing structures and visibility. I understand it's a business and, like every business they need to make a profit, but at the very least the jokers in Parliament should be protecting the hard-working public from being fleeced at the hands of these companies. After all, we elect our MPs to work on our behalf and represent our interests don't we?

I guess though, as my post from this time shows, they were clearly too busy throwing money down the drain trying to chase ghosts, in an attempt to count the number of people in the country.

......hopes everyone fills in their Census form as it has apparently cost £500m to count us all. Considering there are tens of thousands of illegal immigrants in the country who the Government have 'lost' it's obviously money well spent during a recession. POINTLESS – 7 Mar 2011

NINE

......Bike ride number two didn't turn out a great deal better than the first! I got bitten by something, stung myself on stinging nettles, got a fricking gnat right in my eye and managed to spit into my own face at high speed!!! I just love the great outdoors! - 6 Jun 2011

Dear Sir,

Please excuse Wayne from PE today as he has hurt his ankle while riding his bike.

Yours sincerely,
Mrs Spurrier

My PE teacher at school received a lot of these types of notes from my mom; she just wasn't aware of most of them.

From around the age of 11 I became a very adept at forging my mother's handwriting and signature, driven by an overwhelming desire to avoid taking part in physical education at school. It wasn't because I was lazy. There were certain things I loved such as basketball, gymnastics and track & field, but once I reached middle-school our incumbent PE teacher turned out to be a proper man's man, and all we ever seemed to do was play football, rugby or hockey; none of which floated this particular boat (and still doesn't).

Remember, I was the skinny kid with NHS glasses and absolutely no skills or interest in football. Needless to say I was the one team captains would fight over *not* to have on the team; the one always left standing awkwardly at the end. Trust me when I say they wanted me on their team marginally less than I wanted to be there, and that took some doing. It was in track and field disciplines where I excelled.

I'd always been an excellent runner when it came to short-distances. Perhaps it came from the endless hours of playing knock-door-run around our local estate, or the need to make a hasty exit from the Cranky Man's house after we had blown into his overflow pipe; an action we all believed at the time would make his downstairs toilet flush. Either way, I was fast. In fact, I was the fastest 100m sprinter in middle-school and made a bloody good dent in the scoreboard for long-jump and triple-jump too.

Despite this there was never any encouragement to develop these skills, and our PE lessons focused purely on the team activities this teacher so advocated. If my school's approach to physical education in any way reflected the norm for the UK, it's a miracle team GB have ever picked up a gold medal at the Olympic Games.

As a result of my continued reluctance to participate, on paper I must have looked like the most accident-prone kid on the planet and, in hindsight, I'm surprised my parents didn't find representatives from social-services on their doorstep on a weekly basis.

As with many things in life, when you look back it is easy to regret decisions you make as a kid, and this is one of mine. I realise now the importance of physical exercise during development and how this affects the body's shape going forward into adulthood.

At 41 years of age I'm still a 32" waist and would consider myself reasonably fit and healthy, despite years working as a 'desk-jockey', banging away on a keyboard for a living. However, my greatest physical bugbear is my lack of shoulders. I've got some obviously, they're just not as broad as I'd like and I can't help but feel that, had I been more physically active during my formative years, I would have developed a much greater span and therefore wouldn't look like I was constantly wearing oversized shirts. Broad shoulders cover a multitude of sins and even when you develop the inevitable spare-tyre in later life, you can still look okay with a good pair.

Exercise has never really excited me.

I'm one of those who will go through life having occasional bursts of fitness, never really achieving a great deal because I just don't enjoy it. I eat reasonably well and have been blessed with a halfway-decent genetic make-up, but what I really needed was motivation.

……is wondering if all the blokes at the gym getting younger & fitter, or am I getting older and fatter? Discuss! – 8 Sept 2009

I need to fall in love with exercise, but each time I make the effort I am reminded just how dull it can be, and there have been more than a few unpleasant incidents along the way which have not endeared this pastime to me one bit.

For example, imagine yourself arriving at the gym on the hottest day of the year, all geared up for a really good sweat and workout after a long day at the office. You're feeling proud you've chosen this pursuit over a drink with friends or heading straight home to sit in front of the stupid-box to eat your body weight in ice-cream. Having changed, you practically skip into the gym and onto one of the treadmills, ready to begin a 5k run in the soaring heat, with absolutely no air-conditioning for comfort. It's a heroic feeling!

Then, less than 30 seconds into your run, it hits you. Without warning you are engulfed in what can only be described as a foggy-haze of the worst body-odour imaginable. I'm not talking about an unpleasant waft, this was like an army of the great-unwashed had just marched into the room, after a month out on manoeuvres with no showering facilities. The kind of smell that could knock you off your feet and make even the most experienced forensic-pathologist gag.

It only took a moment to realise my error!

I had positioned myself on a row of machines directly behind an elderly gentleman on another treadmill, who had rather cleverly placed a large oscillating fan just in front of him while he exercised. Naturally, this was great for him; he could enjoy a swift power-walk with the cool breeze upon him while the rest of us powered through the heat. Now this wouldn't have been an issue had he not carried a scent which resembled a cross between the cartoon skunk Pepé Le Pew and a laundry basket full of sweaty sports-socks, but the fan was blowing this unwelcome mix of odours straight into my nostrils, and onto the people behind me.

I'm not certain whether it was the actual stench that caused me to hit the emergency-stop button and quickly dismount, or the sudden realisation there was a possibility the poor souls behind me may think it was my doing.

In spite of this incident there have been repeated attempts at achieving the body I dream of. Bouts of road-running which often end with me gasping for air, early morning stints at the local swimming-pool where I would be so tired I'd almost fall asleep face-down in the water, and of course the bike rides. Of these, getting out on my bike is far and away the most enjoyable, but of course the least effective. That's not to say these jaunts always passed without incident either.

I love the outdoors, but in just six miles of cycling a

beautiful route around the country lanes in Redditch I managed to completely fall out of love with nature. As if a gnat-strike straight to the eyeball and nasty nip from some unseen warrior-bug wasn't enough, I also managed to add my own calamities to the proceedings.

Having been blessed with what seems to be the world's most tiny and ineffective bladder, I soon needed to relieve myself, despite having worked up a serious sweat.

The problem was, I was so concerned with making sure I didn't accidentally expose myself to any passing children – I didn't want my name added to a special register – that I forgot to look at where I was standing. Sure enough, I walked straight into a swathe of stinging-nettles, my bare legs taking the brunt of these feisty critters. In an instant I was transported back to childhood, where on a number of occasions I had fallen off my bike or out of a tree directly into a bed of nettles, and spent ages rubbing dock-leaves into the tiny white spots.

It wasn't over yet. I was about to experience one last humiliation before I could throw the bike back in the shed and padlock the door.

On the final leg of my journey I experienced that familiar sensation of having swallowed a small bug or gnat, so I dug deep, cleared my throat as best I could, and spat it out. An experienced cyclist would have instinctively turned their head fully before unleashing this mucus-bullet, but not me.

That's right; no sooner had it left my mouth than it reconnected with the side of my face, much to the amusement of the passing motorists I'm sure.

This was like a metaphor for life, right there and then in that moment - a reminder to be careful what you put out into the world, because one day it may come back and hit you in the face. In my case, it happened in a split-second and at speed.

I returned from that ride tired, bruised, legs covered

in nettle stings and worse still, my own phlegm on my face.

At the age of 41 I have finally accepted exercise just isn't for me, so from this point forth I shall do my best to eat reasonably well and stay active, in an attempt to remain slim. No more gym memberships, no more dragging my shabby carcass out into the elements. I shall just revel in the words of Dame Shirley Bassey, and live by the motto *I am what I am*.

Well, until I get fat when – of course – I'll do it all over again.

TEN

……"Good evening Mr Bond". Dame Judy couldn't have said it any better!!! The Queen rocks! – 27 Jul 2012

Love her or hate her, when The Queen delivered those four words during the opening ceremony of the 2012 Olympic Games, you have to admit she played her trump-card.

In that one moment she did something unprecedented and it absolutely paid off. As the scene played out, I for one assumed that this was a movie-set of the palace and, if I'm honest, expected to see David Walliams' face when she turned around. In fact, the very last person I was expecting was The Queen herself.

I've had a long-held fascination with the royal family, which I think dates right back to the Silver Jubilee, when The Queen visited Redditch as part of her tour of the UK. I don't recall either of my parents being particularly interested and so unfortunately I wasn't part of the crowd who lined the streets to see her. However, the hype surrounding the visit did leave a lasting impression and a curiosity about the family as a whole, especially its figurehead.

Throughout my school years the history syllabus had been solely based on political and economic affairs, rather than social. I spent two years studying for my GCSE history qualification, which focused solely on the political and economic aspects – particularly the terms of Prime Ministers Benjamin Disraeil and William Gladstone – and how the Luddites fought to resist the Industrial Revolution of the 19th Century. None of this held any excitement for me whatsoever and to this day, I have as much interest in politics as I do in watching re-runs of *University Challenge* on UK Gold. For the avoidance of doubt - none.

Had we studied social-history however, I dare say things would have been very different. I have long been fascinated with the history of the English monarchy; the long-fought battle between Henry VIII and the Catholic Church, the incredible strength displayed by Elizabeth I and how, without her tactical planning and leadership, the English language would almost certainly have been lost forever, in favour of our Spanish counterparts. The most creative authors of our time would be stretched to weave plots with as many twists and turns as those created by some of our greatest monarchs and their trusted advisors.

It maddens me to hear accusations of irrelevance where the royal family is concerned – particularly The Queen – or to hear statements such as 'they don't add any value'.

The argument is one which has raged for at least the last 20 years and is sure to continue well into the future, but what can never be denied is the incredible work ethic The Queen has displayed throughout her reign. This is a woman who works 365 days a year in one capacity or another, in a job she never truly wanted and one she has sworn to continue until her dying day. No retirement package – no gold watch. Christ, she will even have to write her own birthday card when she reaches the ripe old age of 100.

Let's not forget that, in addition to all of her public engagements and duties, she also has to put up with the never-ending list of faux-pas from her own family; particularly those of her husband, Prince Phillip, whose cantankerous nature often causes offence during state visits around the world. I recall cringing behind a cushion while watching a television interview with him in 2011.

……loves Prince Phillip's caustic honesty and indifference. An opening gambit of "I didn't want to do this interview" is a wicked way of putting your interviewer at ease!!! – 9 Jun 2011

Whichever side of the fence you sit when it comes to the royal family, we have a lot to thank them for.

Imagine a world where *It's a Royal Knockout* never existed (anyone under the age of 35 go ahead and Google it), or the headlines of our national newspapers without Prince Phillip's racist, sexist and ageist comments plastered across them for our entertainment. Imagine if we'd never had the opportunity to witness Prince Harry making the worst fancy-dress judgement of the 21st century, or photographs of him starkers in a Las Vegas hotel (don't pretend you haven't searched the internet for the uncensored versions).

Love them or hate them, the royals have provided us with endless hours of entertainment and, through all of it, her Majesty has never faltered.

With the exception of her horrible-anus (or whatever it was) in 1992, she has taken whatever life has thrown at her without comment, and with a dignity like no other. In short, she epitomises the great British values many of her subjects can only aspire to and, I would argue, is the single most valuable asset this country has to offer.

It is well known that The Queen has a very quick-witted sense of humour and I have often wondered, given complete freedom of speech and her own Facebook or Twitter account, what caustic posts she would share with the world.

So Your Majesty, if you're reading this please get Tweeting, because I'm your biggest fan.

ELEVEN

......Oops - that moment when you walk out of your office to find security have already left, the building is locked and the alarms are now going off! #awkward – 31 Jul 2012

2011 was a pretty stressful year at work.

I was in my ninth year working for Unipart Group, and during this time I had climbed my way through the ranks from marketing co-ordinator to the dizzy heights of marketing manager. Having worked in four different offices in Redditch, Birmingham, Oxford and Coventry – sometimes driving for three hours each day to get there and back – I was reaching a point where I felt a change was needed.

The kids were growing up fast and I was regularly working 50+ hours a week, in a job where I felt no matter how hard I worked it was like trying to push water uphill. Outdated systems, multiple layers of management and what seemed like more processes in place to sell a few air-fresheners and wheel-trims than Boeing have to build the new Airbus A380. Okay, maybe that's a slight exaggeration, but you get the gist.

It wasn't all bad of course and there were elements

of the job I loved. I had a fair amount of freedom and wasn't being micro-managed, the majority of the people I worked with were absolutely amazing and, if I do say so myself, I was bloody good at what I did. Either way, with one thing or another it had been a long-arsed year already, and as spring turned to summer I was feeling very despondent and in need of a change.

As a result of the route I had taken through the company I was earning really good money for my position. However, I felt that any job which matched the salary would come with even greater stress and more travel than I was doing at the time. This would mean even less time with the family.

I felt trapped!

My wife was working part-time while she was raising the children and there were nights when I lay awake for hours, desperate to escape and find a new role but unable to reduce my income because we had a mortgage, car-loans and utility-bills to pay; not to mention food for the table and two kids to support.

……Time for change. My life has become pointless - work, eat, sleep, repeat until dead - 8 April 2011

In addition to the day job I was working almost every weekend hosting the ghost hunting experiences which left little – if any – quality time for myself. There were occasions where after a 50 hour week in the office, I would drive over 150 miles to run an event (sometimes two each weekend) and not get into bed until 8am the following morning. I wouldn't stay in bed past 11am on most occasions as this meant I wasn't spending any time with the children, so I would often arrive back at my desk at 8.30am on Monday morning, having had just eight hours sleep since leaving there at 5.30pm on Friday. I was physically exhausted!

In hindsight I realise I was being a fool to myself. I

was focusing on all the wrong things – just as I had blamed my own dad for doing all those years before – and I was missing out on so much. However, I couldn't see this at the time and I continued to work like a dog despite how I felt. I wasn't being a martyr – that's just how it was.

Then came a phone call from the owner of Haunted Happenings which would potentially change everything.

'Hi Wayne,' it was Hazel's voice at the other end of the line. 'I've been having a think and have a proposition for you to consider,' she added cryptically. 'HH is doing really well, but I have other projects I want to work on and I know you're not happy with your current job, so I was wondering if you'd be interested in talking about coming to run the business?'

In the way people tend to remember where we were the moment the terrible events of the World Trade Centre unfolded on 9/11, or the day the news broke of JFK's assassination, I remember exactly where I was when this call came; I was standing right next to my boss!

'Can I call you back?' I spluttered, with a mixture of shock, excitement and awkwardness, at the potential he may have overheard.

Needless to say I made a hasty exit from the building to find a quiet place to talk, and quickly dialled the number.

I can't recall the exact conversation, but she told me of her desire to take a back-seat from the business and that the only person she felt had the right combination of skills, along with the right personality to do it justice, was me.

Essentially what she wanted was for me to take over the day-to-day running of the business with a view to purchasing it in the long-term, once I had found my feet and *proven* I was the right man for the job.

To say I was completely bewildered is an understatement. The feelings of excitement, hope and pride were counteracted with fear, self-doubt and anxiety. Could I really walk away from a steady well-paid job, and take what could only be described as the greatest leap of faith I have made in my life? What if it all went wrong? What would we do as a family if I messed it up and found myself without a job further down the line? These questions ran through my mind like an express-train and I hoped I would never discover the answers.

I'm a naturally cautious person. I'm a Libran and as our star-sign suggests we like to weigh-up every conceivable detail before we make a decision about anything. I needed facts and figures. I needed reassurance. Most of all I needed to know I was making the right decision, but of course that's an impossible task.

Just like the Brexit referendum to determine the UK's future within the EU, no matter how much we weighed up the pros and cons beforehand in order to make our choice, we shall only ever know the outcome of the decision made, and will therefore never know if the other option would actually have served us better.

Conversations and e-mails went back and forth for a couple of months as I came up with question after question in my attempt to complete due-diligence. I pored over figures, created projections with regards to what I felt the business was capable of, and identified where I felt I could make improvements and growth.

No matter how hard I tried to tell myself it was too much of a risk to leave my job, the figures stacked up and the potential gains outweighed the risk. Ultimately that's what it came down to, but at least when I made my final decision I knew in my heart that – although there were no guarantees – it was now a calculated risk and not one based on instinct, gut-feeling or pure blind faith.

Decision made and start-date agreed, now came the moment I had waited for. It was time to tender my resignation.

My contract with Unipart Group stated that I had to

serve three months' notice, rather a long time for my position in the business, but it suited me and I timed my resignation so that my final working day would be 24th December. This meant that for the first time since my working-life began, I would be able to spend time at home with the family all through the Christmas and New Year period, before commencing work with Haunted Happenings on 2nd January.

That week was wonderful.

We spent time together as a family, enjoying Christmas Day at home together before throwing open the doors to family on Boxing Day. We played board and computer games, went into town for the girls to spend some of the money they had received as gifts and watched TV. I also did something I hadn't done in a long time; I read a book. I was in such a happy place, excited for the future and it was genuinely the best Christmas I'd had for as long as I could remember.

The New Year arrived and day one of my adventure was finally here. I signed into our new premises, just a five minute drive from home, and pushed the key into the door. The space was tiny, with bare walls, a telephone and just enough space for two desks. It didn't take long to get things ship-shape and, as soon as the phone & broadband were connected, we were off. Suddenly I was learning 'on the job' and I can honestly say I have never experienced such a huge learning-curve in all my life.

It's a simple business on paper; book a 'haunted' location as your venue for the night, sell tickets via your website or telephone, plan a team to run the event and move onto the next one. However, I discovered in those first couple of months that there was much more than meets the eye to running *any* business, let alone one with a multiple six-figure turnover.

Planning the event-calendar with venues throughout the UK, responding to guest and media enquiries, answering telephone calls, chasing and processing payments, updating the website with new content, planning teams for each event – to provide the best dynamic for the guests' experience – running the purchase and sales ledger, building our social-media presence on Facebook and even compiling and filing the quarterly VAT return. Oh, did I forget to mention going out to host at least one event every weekend too? The list was endless!

Surprisingly it only took around three months before I was flying solo, with just the help of one other person who looked after the technical aspect of the website; Hazel was also on the other end of the phone for guidance and support should I need it.

I gained so much knowledge and understanding from Hazel; how to carefully craft tricky e-mails, how to judge situations and read between the lines and – most importantly – that this was a business built on trust and respect, with the customer experience *always* being the number one priority. There was no room for an oversized ego; something I would later be accused of, but which couldn't have been further from the truth.

Everything was going great!

Ticket sales were on the increase, our Facebook presence was growing daily and I finally felt in control. That's not to say it was easy by any means.

Although by definition Haunted Happenings was a small-business, it was most definitely *not* one which would run itself. The paranormal events industry was saturated with varying-sized companies, all vying for similar locations and the same target-audience, and therefore we had to offer the best of everything; never missing a phone call, never ignoring an e-mail and always responding to comments on social media.

My typical day would see me arrive at the office at 8.30am and frequently not set foot out of the door until around 7.30pm that evening, to head home and grab something to eat, before switching on the laptop to continue working. It wasn't uncommon to receive two or three phone calls on the office mobile late into the evening and I would often still be working at 1am, researching new locations, answering Facebook queries or writing new content for the website.

The business centre in which our office was situated closed at 8pm, and I was often reminded by the jangle of keys and the rattling of door handles that the building was being locked-up and closing time had snuck up on me.

The lady who covered reception from 5.30pm until 8pm each evening would often tap on my door to give me my five-minute warning, after which I would hurriedly finish whatever I was doing – quickly tidy my desk ready for the next morning – and shut down the computer. It was a system that worked and one we both knew well; until she had a holiday and it all went horribly wrong.

As the end of another hectic day drew nearer I was immersed in a pile of invoices, trying to get through them all before the building closed.

I'd got out of the habit of looking at the time because I knew I would always hear the familiar sound of the keys jangling, or those three taps on my office door to let me know it was time to call it a day and go home. However, on 31st July 2012 I had completely forgotten that we had a stand-in security guy looking after the front desk who, as I later discovered, was not privy to our system.

8pm came and went, and by the time I'd finished my tasks and packed away it was almost 8.20pm. I had no idea what the time was and just assumed I'd done really well and was getting out early, because I'd heard nothing. I stepped out of my office, ready to lock up, and realised there were no lights on in the rest of the building. The long corridors were dark, except for the green-hue of the emergency exit signs - there were no signs of life and it was eerily silent.

Then it came!

The piercing sounds of the intruder alarm filled the air and I froze on the spot, like a rabbit caught in the headlights of an oncoming car. I had done nothing wrong, yet I instantly reverted to that feeling you have when, as a child, you are caught doing something you shouldn't be.

Although still fairly light outside, the corridors had no external windows and so I fumbled in the darkness for the flashlight on my mobile to make my way to reception, where I hoped I would find a contact telephone number to let security know what had happened.

'Hi, is that the security for The Business Centre?' I asked coyly.

'Yeah,' came a gruff voice from the other end of the phone.

He sounded thoroughly pissed off; little did he know I was the cause for his state of annoyance.

'Err,' I stammered, 'I'm not sure if you're aware but the alarm is going off and I know why. It's because I'm stood by the reception-desk on the phone to you. I'm locked in.'

Thankfully he saw the funny side, and when he arrived to set me free we laughed about the whole situation. However, despite it making a great story to tell friends and family over the coming days, it did highlight a serious point for me.

I had wanted to get away from my old job because I was working too many hours and not seeing my family, yet here I was at 8.30pm still at work. By the time I arrived home the kids would already be in bed and all they would see of me would be a quick goodnight-kiss before they were asleep.

Things really hadn't gone to plan!

Despite this wake-up call nothing changed. The business demanded more and more as time went on, and I just couldn't walk away if there was something that needed doing

......I blame a lack of effective marketing for forgetting to purchase my wife an Easter egg – 31 Mar 2013

It's easy to miss right? I mean, it's not like Easter has been around all that long.

If the confectionary companies would just give me a little more notice and start putting their products on the shelves after Bonfire Night, rather than waiting until just after Boxing Day, I feel sure I would be better prepared when the time came. Also, in my defence I never forget Christmas because they kindly keep that to the same date every year. How can a man be expected to remember an event which moves each year by up to four weeks?

Imagine the panic when I realised late on Saturday night I had completely forgotten to buy my wife an egg. Of course she had sorted something for me and, as always, had made sure the kids were dealt with. All I had to do was remember one simple task, but I'd failed.

I tried to rectify it, but it was too late. The local shops were closed and when I disappeared early on Sunday morning, in a desperate bid to find something that said 'Happy Easter' rather than 'here's some cheap chocolate to show how useless I am', I wasn't the only guy staring desperately at the empty shelves. There were others; I was useless, but at least I wasn't alone.

I walked around the shelves at least three times before admitting defeat.

They say the definition of madness is to do the same thing over and over but expect a different outcome. In this situation, it was desperation rather than madness. I think I'd almost convinced myself that if I looked just one more time, the Easter Bunny may help me out and leave one decent egg on the shelf. I was wrong, and when I returned home – empty-handed – I had to confess.

It didn't go down well, but I think deep down she understood the pressure I was under with work and I promised myself I wouldn't forget the following year. As it turned out, finding time to shop for Easter eggs would be the last of my worries 12 months down the line.

TWELVE

> ......*Will be live on BBC Radio Leeds with Liz̰ Green at around 1.20pm today to discuss all things ghostly* – 9 Oct 2012

Of course running the ghost hunting business was hard, but there were plenty of good times to counterbalance the daily grind. In fact, during my time managing the business I was gifted some incredible experiences and given the opportunity to see places and do things few others get the chance to do. I've lost count of the number of times I have turned to another member of the team and said, 'this will make for a great story to tell the grand-children one day.'

I had been managing things in the Haunted Happenings office for just over nine months when a telephone call came through from BBC Radio Leeds.

Local radio stations often feature short, topical pieces across a range of subjects, inviting 'experts' (there's that word again) in a particular field to be interviewed as part of the broadcast. With Halloween fast approaching their minds turned to all things spooky and, with a number of reportedly haunted places in and around Yorkshire – some of which our company frequented for ghost hunting events – the invitation was extended for Haunted Happenings to join the discussion.

Naturally the opportunity to talk about our ghost hunts and publicise what we did was far too good to pass up, and just a few hours after the initial call I was live on radio for the first time in my life.

I'd be lying if I said I wasn't nervous; I was petrified. Those insecurities I had always carried came rushing back into the forefront of my mind as I waited to be introduced by the presenter. All I knew before the call was that they would want to talk about haunted places in and around Leeds, but with no other information I could do nothing to prepare for the questions I may be asked.

In most cases these interviews are conducted live over the telephone. The station calls you a few minutes prior to your slot and then puts your call on hold. While you wait you hear the station's broadcast through the phone and – when the presenter brings you into the conversation – the call is switched so all you can hear is them. It's nothing more than a telephone conversation, but I still felt nervous at first.

As it turned out I had nothing to worry about.

The concern that I would freeze up or have nothing of any interest to say was unfounded, and after the first minute or so I breezed through the experience as if I'd done it a hundred times before. The whole piece lasted no more than ten minutes in total, but it did boost my self-confidence and served as a great experience for future broadcasts, of which there have been many.

One of the things I always loved about the business, even before I was more fully involved, was being able to visit the amazing places in which these events are held.

I love old buildings and I harbour a real passion for social-history. One of the first venues I investigated was a place called Tutbury Castle in Derbyshire, England. In this one location alone I was able to stand on the spot where Mary Queen of Scots had been held prisoner at the hands of Elizabeth I, lean against the very fireplace at which King Charles had pondered his next move in the English Civil War, and place my hand upon a chest which was already an antique at the time of Henry VIII's birth. The place literally oozed the fascinating history with which was the fabric of our country is woven, and I found this equally as exciting as the ghost hunting itself.

Another location which I have been fortunate to visit on 40+ occasions is the stunning Warwick Castle. I have come to know the team at the castle so well over the years I am privileged to roam freely around the building prior to the guests arriving for the night.

I often stand alone in the courtyard and marvel at the exquisite splendour of this 11th Century fortress. The Gaol (old spelling for Jail) where prisoners from the battle of Poitiers and the English Civil War were held, the rooms in which the second Earl of Warwick, John Dudley, once plotted against Queen Mary I to appoint Lady Jane Grey to the throne of England for his own gains, and a place with connections to the War of the Roses, The Gunpowder Plot and the trial of Joan of Arc. I know the building very well now, but when I first started hosting events here I unwittingly terrified one group of guests almost to within an inch of their lives.

The event was not long underway and on this particular evening the weather outside was atmospheric to say the least; distant rumbles of thunder groaned in the skies above and a hazy mist shrouded the castle as we began our exploration. All was normal, with the exception of another function in the Great Hall, but with a live band accompanying a clearly drunken soul trying to belt out Robbie Williams' *Let Me Entertain You*, we needed to find somewhere a little quieter for our vigil.

As luck would have it I discovered a room I'd never seen before which would be the perfect setting, and far enough away from the music not to disturb us. I'd found the Mirror Maze; an area adorned with wall-to-wall mirrors, severed-heads hanging lifelessly from the roof and the mannequin of a hooded-figure standing near the entrance. The perfect mix of silence and darkness, with just a little added spookiness for good measure!

With a hint of glee at what awaited us, I led a group of 12 people into the room and slid the door closed behind us.

'Keep your torch on as you move around the room please,' I warned them, 'and if you see anybody walking towards you who looks very much like you please stop, otherwise you will give yourself a nose-bleed.'

The group laughed nervously at my feeble wit.

'On a serious note though, if anything does happen and you get frightened then please turn your torch on before moving, otherwise you *will* hurt yourself.'

With the health & safety warning in place the lights were extinguished and we began calling for any spirits who may be there to make themselves known.

'If there's anybody here with us who is connected to the castle, or the land before this castle was here, can you please copy this noise to let us know you are there?'

There was no noise!

'Can you try to walk around the group and touch somebody you feel drawn to if you are here please?'

Nobody reported feeling anything!

'Can you step toward the green light on the floor if you are in the room? It won't hurt you in any way, but the lights may flash if you get very close and that way we'll know you are here.'

The static green light remained static and I could feel the group's energy and enthusiasm ebbing away, their minds drifting in favour of the hot-coffee and selection of biscuits I had promised earlier.

'Okay folks – it doesn't seem that we are going to get anything right at this moment, but we will come back later and try again as you never know when something may occur.'

That's when it came!

In the split second I finished my sentence there was a flash of bright-light, followed swiftly by two loud noises which seemed to come from the metal railing to the side of the room. Panic ensued in a heartbeat. The screams were deafening as people fumbled to find their torches.

'STOP!' I shouted, struggling to make myself heard above the hysteria. 'Don't panic. Switch on your torches and don't run, otherwise somebody will get hurt.'

'What the hell was that?' asked one of the men.

'It came from over there,' added another. 'It sounded like masonry falling from the roof onto the railings.'

'I want to get out of here,' came another, then another, and another.

Those brave enough to venture forwards searched the area surrounding the railings, desperate to find an explanation for the noise; there was nothing. Upon further inspection of the ceiling, we discovered the stonework above was covered with drapes of black material which would have prevented any small pieces of stone falling onto the ground below. The fear in the room was palpable and the lack of any apparent cause for the noise just added to the panic.

'Let's get you all out of here and have a coffee to calm our nerves,' I announced reassuringly, trying to distract them from their fear and restore some order to the chaos.

As I turned toward what I believed was the entrance, expecting to see the sliding-door through which we had crept sheepishly just fifteen minutes earlier, I was met only with my own reflection. Wherever the door was, I hadn't realised it too had a mirrored surface and I now had absolutely no idea where to find it.

'Err, try not to panic guys,' I announced, 'but I'm not certain where the door is to get back out. Can you all put your hands on the mirrors and see if you can slide them to the left please?'

Needless to say this didn't help the situation. Some of the women were cowering in groups and even some the guys were visibly panicked. No matter where we tried we could not find our exit and, after a couple of minutes, things were getting really fraught.

'Which way do they slide?' one of the women asked.

'The left', I replied. I knew I had pulled it to the right to close it, so it had to be pulled left to open it. However, in the panic and noise of people moving around, she didn't hear me properly.

'Which way do I pull it?' came the voice again, clearly terrified and getting very anxious.

'To the left; to the left' I shouted, trying to make myself heard.

Despite the escalating panic and the knowledge I had trapped a dozen people in a dark, haunted Mirror Maze – potentially with a poltergeist – the hilarity of the situation did not escape me. There we were, a group of adults stuck in a room with no mobile-phone signals, making gestures like the French mime artist Marcel Marceau and me, inadvertently dropping a few Beyoncé lyrics into the mix. If *Carry on Ghost Hunting* ever went into production this would have been the perfect opening scene.

This was not part of the plan and it was about to go from bad to worse.

'I've found the exit,' I exclaimed, 'everyone come towards the light.'

This probably wasn't the best choice of phrase under the circumstances, but they got the gist and a few of them saw the funny side, serving to alleviate the tension for a few seconds.

I pressed my hands against the mirrored-surface and began to push it toward the side, to make good our escape. The frame was heavy, resisting my intention as if issuing me a warning that this was *not* the way forward.

The group hastily made their way to where I was

standing, their shadows dancing in the light of their torches like a tribal-ritual, reflections bouncing from mirror to mirror, giving the frightening and disorientating illusion of a number far greater than we were.

'Follow me,' I instructed confidently, 'let's get you out of this place.'

But, it wasn't meant to be!

Immediately as we left the darkness of the Mirror Maze we were met with a gory scene. Waxwork figures depicted the aftermath of barbaric executions which had taken place during the Tudor-era, complete with blood-soaked chopping block and the severed-heads of its unfortunate victims; lifeless faces and bulging eyes drew gaze upon us from the spikes on which their heads were impaled.

I couldn't make sense of what I was seeing, but the rush of bodies seeking to clear the panic behind us pushed me forwards and into the room beyond. Here we were presented with a courtroom, complete with the dock and an imposing podium, from which the judge would have issued punishments to the accused.

I knew I had made a big mistake and had chosen the wrong exit, so I had to come clean:-

'Guys, can you listen for a second please?'

Trying to get their attention wasn't easy, but after a few seconds the noise subsided and I broke the news.

'This isn't the way we came in,' I informed them, 'but this is clearly part of the Dungeon attraction and therefore must lead to an exit. Follow me and let's see where it takes us.'

My hopes of discovering a brightly-lit doorway, marked clearly with an 'exit' sign, were dashed within seconds. Instead, what lay in wait was a dark passageway leading deeper into the castle. As we rounded the corner our eyes were met with a horrific sight; the room was adorned with implements of torture, a cage and a terrifyingly authentic waxwork of the torturer himself, complete with blood-soaked leather apron and a menacing smile. Then, at the worst possible moment, the noise came - without warning.

A blood-curdling, anguished scream; a man's voice.

My heart skipped a beat. The whole scene slipped into slow-motion; that feeling survivors of life-threatening accidents experience as they career towards certain death. In a split-second I imagined something terrible had happened to one of the guests, or somebody had just stumbled across a real-life corpse, slumped in the passageway with its throat slit and blood pumping from the gaping wound. Had *Carry on Ghost Hunting* seamlessly morphed into *Murder She Wrote*? Would Jessica Fletcher suddenly appear from the stairwell to gleefully announce whodunit?

Thankfully not!

Chaos broke forth once again and people grabbed each other in a desperate bid to find comfort within the confusion. As I turned, my gaze fell upon a man's face behind a set of iron-bars, eyes pleading for mercy; the figure of a prisoner awaiting his appointment with the torturer in the room beyond. We had triggered a sensor which is carefully positioned to frighten the daytime visitors as they wander unwittingly through the Dungeon attraction, which had then activated the scream we had just heard.

The corridor before us led to a tiny spiral-staircase and I made the decision we would have to go back the way we came, as I feared any further surprises may just tip us over the edge altogether. So, with hearts racing and with more tension than an *X-Factor* sing-off, we retraced our steps and re-entered the Mirror Maze in which this adventure had all began.

In reality it had been no longer than ten minutes since we had heard the noise which had led us to flee in the first place, yet it felt like a lifetime. Thankfully it didn't take long to find our way to the correct exit, and the nightmare was over. Needless to say there were a few reluctant faces when I suggested returning to this area later in the evening to carry out another vigil, but it gave the group plenty to talk about while they settled their nerves over a coffee and a chocolate digestive.

A key part of my role while managing Haunted Happenings was to discover and research potential new locations for our ghost hunts. At the very heart of the business lay the desire to deliver guests a variety of buildings to explore, from castles and inns, to old prisons and asylums. We even ran some events at a haunted windmill in Thaxted, Essex.

Discovering places with reports of ghosts and hauntings was never the issue, but finding locations which would provide the necessary facilities, combined with sufficient areas to explore and enough evidence of paranormal activity, was much tougher. For as much as it seems like a great idea to explore abandoned buildings, the priority was *always* to provide a safe and secure environment for the guests to enjoy; one which offered – at the very least – somewhere to have a wee during the night.

For a number of months we had been trying hard to find an old asylum which was in good enough condition to be of use to us, but the search was failing to yield anywhere with the necessary attributes and facilities. Then, out of the blue one Sunday night at around 11.15pm, I received an e-mail to our enquiries account which would change everything. The message comprised just one photograph and one sentence.

Would groups like yours be interested in this building?

The photograph, a dimly-lit hospital stairwell with peeling paint and ominous doorways leading onto now empty wards. The location, a Victorian orphanage which later became a hospital; abandoned since 1997.

A rush of excitement surged through me as my fingers raced across the keyboard, quickly typing a response to the mysterious message. Within moments it was arranged. By 10am the following morning – less than 12 hours since opening the e-mail – I would be stood outside the now infamous Newsham Park Hospital in Liverpool, to meet with the owner and hopefully thrash out a deal to get the doors of this imposing institution open once more to the public.

It was a cold spring-morning in early March. The bare branches of trees lined the approach to the hospital, along the aptly named Orphan Drive, and morning birdsong carried effortlessly through the still air. Daffodils scattered the grass verges of the lake in the centre of Newsham Park and, as I gazed up at the vast and imposing building before me, the thick mist of my breath hung as heavy as a dense fog.

'Hello Sir.' A heavy Liverpudlian accent which would become very familiar to me over the coming months, broke my reverie. 'Are you ready to have a look around?'

One of the owners of the former-hospital, and the source behind last night's cryptic e-mail, was to be my guide. Over the coming hour, as we ventured through the many wards, basements and corridors of this sprawling location, he delighted in providing me with literally hundreds of facts and figures about the history of the place.

It had begun life in 1879 as an orphanage for children whose parents had been lost at sea, becoming home to over 1,000 children by the time the great-war ended in 1918. But, with new laws which prohibited young children living in an institutional-school and great expansion of the country's social-services schemes, the Orphanage closed in 1949, making way for a new hospital which opened its doors in 1954.

The hospital had officially stopped taking new patients by 1988, and by 1992 all patients and staff had been relocated. However, with the closure of the nearby Rainhill Lunatic Asylum, the inmates were moved to

Newsham Park Hospital – taking up to 90% of its space – and around £1.6m was spent on making the facilities suitable for its new patients.

The place was staggering!

I wondered to myself whether the barbed-wire which adorned the perimeter fencing had been added to keep unwanted visitors out, or to keep the patients in.

Daylight broke through the cracks of the boarded windows, casting much-needed shards of light upon darkened rooms and breathing life into the now desolate space. Crackled paint peeled from every wall and the cubicles in the wards, once a place of rest and recuperation, now stood empty - with privacy curtains hanging lifelessly from the rails.

Down in the basement the empty lockers which had once served the hospital's staff still contained a few items – left behind some 16 years previously – including a single shoe and a roll-on deodorant stick. Throughout the building a number of wheelchairs stood, like broken-down vehicles, abandoned on the spot where they had delivered their last useful means of transport many years before.

'This place is amazing!' I enthused, 'If we can make it work and open this building up for people to explore, it will undoubtedly become the most sought-after location we have.'

'Well, we'd better talk business then,' came the reply, with a glint in his eye and a knowing look which said 'gotcha'.

It didn't take long to work out the detail, and that very afternoon a few of the photographs I'd taken that morning were released to our Facebook followers as a teaser of what was to come. No member of the public had set foot in this place for over 15 years and as expected, the reaction was immediate.

'Where is this? I need to go!' came one reply.

'Please let me know as soon as you are going to

release tickets for this event, as I definitely want six places,' came another.

In less than a week since the initial e-mail we released two dates for Newsham Park Hospital and, in less than 24 hours, both had sold-out. Since this place had never been investigated before we had absolutely no knowledge of who or what we might encounter when darkness fell, but that didn't seem to matter; people were desperate for a location such as this and now they could finally gain access.

Further dates were added to satisfy the demand and tickets continued to sell, but with just 10 days until our first event I received a phone-call which made my heart sink and would potentially jeopardise everything.

'Hello,' the voice sounded very official and unwelcoming in its tone, 'I'm calling about your forthcoming event at Newsham Park Hospital.'

Since we had begun marketing the events here we had received literally hundreds of enquiries which began in the same way, but something about the tone of this gentleman's voice sounded different, and I just knew it wasn't good news.

'A prohibition notice has been posted on the building today and I regret to inform you that, should you or any of your guests cross the threshold, you will be liable for prosecution.'

My heart stopped.

My brain struggled to make sense of the words which had just been spoken and I began to panic.

'I don't understand,' I spluttered, 'we have 40 guests booked to attend in just over a week's time and I cannot let them down. What is the reason for the notice?'

He went on to explain he was from the Fire Department, and they had tried to get in touch with the owners to carry out a fire risk-assessment for public events at the building, with no success. Without the audit and subsequent implementation of any required measures, there would be no public access to the building and therefore, no ghost hunts.

This was a nightmare!

All the hours which had already been put in to get this far were about to go out of the window. Worse still we were just 10 days away, and if we couldn't resolve things quickly we would disappoint almost 100 people who were already counting down the days to their experience.

Anyone who has ever ran a small business – closely in touch with its clients – will understand the weight of responsibility you feel for your customers. On average around 40% of the guests attending our events were regulars, loyal to the business and very supportive of everything we did. In some cases customers had become acquaintances or even friends, but this just served to add further pressure in making sure we always delivered the very best experience possible for them.

During my time in the business the very last thing I would do at night, after climbing into bed, would be to check my e-mail for any late enquiries and – before even putting a foot on the floor in the morning – my phone would be back in my hand to check for any problems which may require immediate attention. Social functions were often interrupted with bookings and enquiries via the office mobile, and there was absolutely no respite whatsoever. The pressure and responsibility I felt was enormous.

The weight of the ten days which followed that fateful telephone call was crushing. Not only would we upset a number of valued customers if we couldn't run the events, but the business would stand to lose a significant amount of money in lost-revenue, refunds and administration costs. We had to pull out the stops to get things resolved, and quick.

As it turned out, it seemed the fire department hadn't tried quite as hard to get in touch with the owners as they had first made out, but following a few phone calls a date was set for the inspection and Hazel and I made our way back to Liverpool.

The atmosphere was tense.

The fire-officer arrived with a team of eight firefighters and what felt to me like the most officious attitude imaginable. You could have cut the atmosphere with a knife and Hazel, a trained psychotherapist, stepped in immediately to diffuse the situation in the hope of getting everyone onside, so that we could deal with the matter in hand and come to a resolution.

She did an amazing job!

We spent almost three hours trawling the entire building, explaining in detail what the activities would be and coming to agreements regarding the areas we would use and limitations we would put in place in order to protect the safety of the guests attending. The firefighters were great. In fact, on the whole they were really encouraging and were genuinely intrigued about the paranormal element of the building, but of course we were there to get the job done and time was slipping away fast; plus the fire officer was a stickler for detail.

Following an additional two-hour meeting back at the fire-station, a set of measures were agreed which, subject to their implementation and the production of a minutely-detailed risk-assessment, would mean the events could go ahead as planned. Some of the requests seemed petty, but at least we were all agreed they were achievable and we were prepared to jump through as many hoops as it would take in order to make this happen. However, the pressure wasn't off just yet because the re-visit to sign-off the measures wouldn't happen until just two days before our event was due to take place.

Thankfully, with just 48 hours to spare we received the e-mail to say everything was resolved, and on Saturday 18th May 2013 – after months of preparation – Newsham Park Hospital finally re-opened its doors and ghost hunting groups across the UK could now begin to explore this phenomenal building.

None of the guests would know the grief we'd experienced and the hoops we had jumped through to make it happen, and the first night was a roaring success.

Since then, as predicted, the location has gone on to become the most in-demand ghost hunting venue in the UK. However, before we got underway there was one final surprise in store.

During my return journey from the safety-inspection the previous week another driver had shunted my car at a roundabout near my home, and as a result I was driving a courtesy-car when I arrived to run the first event. The Vauxhall Corsa was brand new and gleaming white; an immaculate car which I was so paranoid about causing any damage to, I had driven with more care and attention all week than I had for the past 20 years.

I made my way cautiously through the rusted wrought-iron gates and into the compound, taking great care over the speed bumps and avoiding the overgrown brambles, their gnarly branches reaching forth as if attempting to wrap themselves around me.

As the car rounded the rear of the building and approached the small hatch which gives access to the mortuary, my eyes were astounded by what they saw. The blood was first to catch my attention, followed immediately by the torn clothing, exposed jaw-bone and wide-eyed, lifeless stare.

As the car edged forward, I drew closer and closer to the most gruesome scene I have ever witnessed.

Two figures – one male and one female – began moving toward the vehicle, their arms reaching outward with purposeful intent. The man was dressed in a police uniform, his white shirt soaked with thick gooey-blood and his jaw hanging loose, completely ripped apart to expose the muscle and bone beneath. His companion, dressed in a white wedding gown – complete with tattered veil – looked equally as horrific with blackened teeth, a damaged eye-socket and open sores upon her face; the bride of Frankenstein being the closest mental association I could summon in my mind.

Both stared wildly at me through the windscreen of the vehicle, moving closer and closer to the car while emitting a guttural, groaning sound.

Had I been delivered into the hands of the undead? Was Newsham Park Hospital really a compound for Zombies and this whole thing was a front to deliver them some fresh meat to tear open and disembowel? Is this how it would all end?

In a word, no!

I wound down the window as they drew nearer.

'If you pair get even as much as a drop of blood on this car I will kill you myself,' I shouted through the opening. 'By the way,' I added, 'you're looking a bit off colour!'

The unearthly gurgles turned to laughter and what ensued was the most surreal conversation of my life. They followed us into the courtyard and we talked for ages about the ghost hunt, as daylight yielded itself to dusk. They had just wrapped after filming a music-video, and as we chatted my eyes were fixated upon the severed flesh hanging loosely from his exposed jawline.

They were two of the nicest people I have ever spoken with, but it occurred to me later that – should I ever find myself in a real-life Zombie apocalypse – I might want to re-think my strategy and consider my own safety first, instead of my car!

THIRTEEN

......You can always take comfort that you were good in Gladiator Mr Crowe – 24 Jan 2013

I don't watch many movies; I never have.

When conversation turns to classic films it's rare that I can add any value. I often wonder if I'm the only guy on the planet who has never seen *The Godfather* and, even when I do manage to sit still long enough to settle down to a film, it has to be a real corker in order to capture my imagination and keep me interested for a full two-hours or more.

I generally turn to the big-screen or television purely for entertainment and escapism. For me it's a form of switching-off from the world, and to achieve that I just want something I can stare at for a couple of hours and then leave, feeling no more educated than when I arrived. Complex storylines, subtitles and deep messages aren't for me; give me a *Die Hard* film or something similar, where good always triumphs over bad and the protagonist runs around in a white vest, and I'm as happy as a seagull with a stolen chip.

However, despite the increasing workload I made

myself a promise I wouldn't miss the opportunity to see the much-anticipated screen adaptation of *Les Misérables* on the big-screen, when it finally reached the cinemas at the end of January 2013.

I've loved musicals ever since my parents purchased me tickets for my 16th birthday to watch *The Phantom of the Opera* in London's West End. I already knew some of the music and, since beginning to learn piano for my GCSC music course, I had begun to take an interest in this and other West-End scores.

I remember the night like it was yesterday.

The buzz within the auditorium of Her Majesty's Theatre was electric. The show had already been running for four years by this point, but the anticipation within the audience felt like the opening night of a brand new spectacle.

'This is my third time,' I heard one lady say to another while sipping from a champagne flute and looking down her nose at a less well-dressed fella, who was happily glugging his way through a beer.

'I saw Michael Crawford play the lead role,' came the other lady's response, seemingly desperate not to be outdone by her companion. 'Nobody will ever be able to better his performance,' she added with a look so smug I doubted even a baseball bat could shift it.

I remember being completely staggered by the demographic in the room. Ages ranged from small children of around seven or eight years, right up to those in their 60s and 70s, and seemingly from all types of background. I'd never been to the theatre before, other than the Palace Theatre in Redditch as a child – for the annual Christmas panto – so was quite taken aback at the sheer diversity this show attracted.

As we took to our seats in the stalls my attention was drawn to a guy in his early 20s, taking his seat just a few rows away and creating quite a stir. As I looked more closely I also recognised the older gentleman with whom he was talking; the mystery duo was Jason Donovan and his father Terry, who'd had roles in *Prisoner Cell Block H*, *Sons & Daughters* and the same daytime soap in which Jason had become famous, *Neighbours*.

By this time Jason was at the height of his singing-fame as one of Stock-Aitken & Waterman's prodigies, so he was a pretty big-deal. In hindsight, it was most likely no coincidence they were here at an Andrew Lloyd-Webber show, for less than six months later Jason hit the stage himself in the 1991 West-End revival of *Joseph & The Amazing Technicolour Dreamcoat*, to rave reviews.

The show was staggering!

From the opening line to the very last notes from the orchestra the audience was transfixed. You could hear a pin drop and I recall looking across at one of the younger children's faces, completely mesmerised as the Phantom and Christine drifted effortlessly across the stage by boat, surrounded by candles – which appeared from nowhere – and a swirling mist, further adding to the magical illusion.

The whole thing was a spectacle and from that day onwards I was hooked. I might struggle to sit through a two-hour film from the comfort of my own home or an air-conditioned cinema, but you can squeeze my 5'11" frame into a West-End theatre seat – knees wedged somewhere near my ears – for three hours and I'm a happy man.

Since then I have seen dozens of shows, from Sondheim's dark and menacing *Sweeney Todd*, to the Ken Russell classic *Blood Brothers*.

However, without question my favourite is the epic *Les Misérables*; a thumping, triumphant and tragic story where all but two of the 33-strong company are dead by the time the curtain falls. Set against a backdrop of the French Revolution, with a score capable of purging tears from even the most hardened heart (I speak from experience), *Les Mis* has been running to packed theatres for over 30 years now - and still going strong.

When I heard a film adaptation was in the making I was thrilled. I began to consider all the amazing things they could achieve on the big screen and, although you cannot best the experience of a live orchestra, I could already imagine the effect of the rousing music in glorious Dolby Cinema™. There was absolutely no doubt in my mind this would be an epic production, taking what had already been achieved on the stage to a whole new level.

How wrong I was!

If Jimmy Saville's *Fix It* was still on TV (minus Jimmy of course), my dream would be to have a crack at the role of Javert, the menacing and determined police inspector who relentlessly hunts Valjean and who, in my humble opinion, has the best role of any West-End musical currently running. This is a man absolutely driven by duty to the law and his unfailing vision of right and wrong – later compromised in the show – is the basis for his pursuit of his nemesis; prisoner 24601.

I was dubious when I first discovered the casting for Javert. Russell Crowe is undoubtedly a major Hollywood name and of course, a big-budget movie was bound to attract some even bigger actors.

I knew Crowe had sung in a band before and, after the surprise performance by Meryl Streep in the film version of *Mama Mia*, I trusted in the casting-team to make the right choices for *Les Mis*. Surely when making a film in which the whole story is sung, they would be absolutely focused on ensuring the cast were able to carry it off right?

The lights in the cinema dimmed and those familiar notes began. The heavy driving-beat that sets the opening scene, in which the chain-gang haul a gargantuan ship into dry-dock, boomed throughout the theatre - and then it happened. Russell Crowe opened his mouth and in my opinion it all went horribly wrong.

The disappointment for me was akin to that moment

when you tear open the lid of a delicious-looking dessert, one which you has sent your saliva glands into overdrive with the anticipation of what was to come, only to discover the taste is blander than the walls of a new-build house.

For me, Russell Crowe was magnolia!

Worse than that, I felt he was single-handedly destroying the very essence of the character I loved. He was to Javert what Pierce Brosnan was to Sam Carmichael in *Mama Mia*. If you've not seen Brosnan's performance get yourself on YouTube and you'll soon understand my thoughts.

I've seen Crowe on many chat-shows and I think he is a great guy; funny, decent and without question an incredible actor. It's not that he can't hold a tune, but this just didn't work and if I'm honest, this one poorly-cast character ruined the whole film for me. In fact, to this day, I have never had the desire to re-watch the movie and probably never will. The saying 'you're only as strong as your weakest link' was never more apt.

I guess sometimes people get things wrong!

In our everyday existence we all make choices based on our gut instinct. Job roles are often awarded to candidates with less skill or experience, but who display characteristics which the employer feels will bring more to the business. Often we make decisions ourselves based on our heads rather than our hearts, such as accepting a job we know will make us less happy, because it offers us greater financial reward. We all weigh-up the pros and cons when we make choices and most certainly don't get them right every time.

Russell Crowe did the absolute best he could, he just wasn't up to the role in my opinion and it wasn't his fault.

As bizarre as it sounds this whole experience taught me something valuable. It made me realise that we are often too hard on ourselves when things don't go to plan, and what we should really do is ask have I done my best.

Did I do everything I possibly could to make this opportunity work? If the answer is yes, then sleep easy at night. If not, then pull your finger out of your arse, stop blaming others for life's little hiccups and move on; we all fuck-up sometimes!

FOURTEEN

......Doing exciting things — at ODEON Leicester Square – 15 Jul 2013

Darkness fell upon the auditorium. The babble of voices which had filled the air just seconds before became hushed in anticipation of what was to come. My heart raced faster and faster like a speeding train, careering out of control, unable to slow its pace.

'When you have finished your bit we need you to introduce the director, who will in turn introduce the movie by video message. His name is James Wan.'

These words, spoken by one of the PR team managing this special preview-screening, coursed through my scrambled mind.

Why had they not told me this earlier?

Would I even remember his name with 800 faces staring at me from the darkness? How would I fill the next two minutes? A dozen or more questions raced through my head all at once, jostling for attention as if I were a celebrity walking the red-carpet, with news-crews and journalists seeking to have their question answered next.

'Ready?' he asked, with a firm but reassuring hand on my upper back, guiding me toward the steps leading to the vast stage before me.

I lifted my head and drew a deep breath, as if I were drawing in the first fresh air I had breathed for years, then gave a confident nod.

The moment was here!

A spotlight appeared on the stage, indicating the place from which I was to deliver my speech, and I walked towards it with a façade of confidence – completely faked – designed to hide the overwhelming nerves I felt. An internal battle raged inside me; part of me desperate for the stage to open up and swallow me so this would all be over, and the other ready to absorb every second of what was happening in this surreal, once in a lifetime moment.

There really had been no time to prepare.

What had begun a few weeks earlier as a simple request from Warner Bros. to provide our services after a preview screening of the new movie *The Conjuring*, had escalated at the very last minute to delivering a two-minute speech about 'haunted London' to an invited audience of 800 journalists, bloggers and competition-winners at the historic (and intimidating) Odeon in Leicester Square, London.

I felt the warmth of the spotlight on my skin as I emerged from the darkness into its glare and the next two minutes of my life became a blur. I remember those dozen steps as I made my approach; the pep-talk I had given myself to speak slower than my mouth would try to make me, to grip the microphone so those at the front of the audience would not see it shaking in my sweaty hand and, most of all, to trust in my head that I could do this.

I recall telling myself that whatever happened next, this was the equivalent of a nano-second in life's great journey and, even if it all went wrong and I made a complete tit of myself, nobody in the audience would remember this moment in a few weeks, let alone in a year's time.

I knew I'd be fine if I could just get the audience onside from the start. Nobody was here for a lecture and I wasn't about to give them one.

'I feel like I'm about to audition for the *X-Factor*,' I quipped - my eyes darting between the darkness before me and the dazzling circle of light around my feet. 'Which one of you is Simon?'

They laughed, and in that second my nerves vanished.

I went on to talk about some of the ghost stories I knew of from West End theatres and the surrounding buildings and, just as I began to feel that I could talk forever, I saw the hand-gesture from the wings to let me know I was good to wrap-up. Before my final task of introducing the video-message from the director, I added one last thought for them to consider during the movie.

'The very building in which you are seated began its life as a London theatre,' I informed them, 'and has its own ghost who haunts this very auditorium. So before you settle down to enjoy the film, you may just want to give the person either side of you a little prod, to reassure yourself you're not sitting next to him tonight.'

I'd done it!

The sense of achievement was overwhelming as I made my way from the stage to the sound of applause. In that moment I realised I had just faced up to a fear of public speaking and chalked up an experience which could only make me stronger and more confident.

The feedback from the PR team was good, and just a few days later I received a call at the office with an unexpected request.

'We would like to invite you back to London to carry out a few radio interviews,' came the voice at the end of the line. 'We have eight radio stations lined up, each with a five minute slot, wanting to talk about the film and discuss your ghost tours. It'll be a great opportunity for you to talk about the business. What do you say?'

There was only one possible response and, less than a week after standing on that stage, I found myself seated in a sound-booth – headphones in place – speaking to one interviewer after another on live-radio around the country.

Two things occurred to me.

Firstly, this was an experience very few people would ever have the good fortune to be a part of and secondly, there was no way I would ever have thought myself capable of doing what was being asked of me.

I realised in that moment that life is a journey and none of us know where our train is heading, or even which platforms it will stop at along the way. From that moment I vowed to take every opportunity, embrace every moment and make the most of each and every one. After all, you only live once and what doesn't kill you makes you stronger right?

I told myself that whatever came my way, I would now approach life with a 'go for it' attitude. Whether things went the way I wanted or not, at the very least I would pick up a few great anecdotes along the way.

FIFTEEN

......Just clicked my 'Year in Review' button. When one of the highlights of your year is going for a bike ride and getting a sore bum, you know you need to get out more! - 11 Dec 2013

2013 was a tough year and one which saw the hopes and dreams I'd had for my future with Haunted Happenings come crashing down.

The year had begun well; ticket sales were up, a few new locations had come on board which were starting to gain traction, and we had a number of media-related projects which had either come to fruition, or were in the pipeline. I'd even managed to get away with the family for a few days over the Christmas break for a much needed rest, albeit with the company mobile in-tow. I had been as sick as a dog for three of the four days we were away but the break still did me good, and I arrived back at the office in January feeling fresh and revitalised.

In addition to the successful promotion of *The Conjuring* and the subsequent radio interviews, throughout the year we worked with a project for a Ukrainian TV channel, featured in a music video for *X-Factor* finalist Sam Callahan and went ghost hunting with China's equivalent of Lady Gaga. We even found time to spend the night in a haunted house in Essex, terrifying Louise Thompson – one of the stars of the reality TV show *Made In Chelsea*.

Despite all of the amazing projects we had already been involved with, nothing quite prepared us for the scale what was to come.

During a ghost hunt in Shropshire a few months earlier, one of the event hosts had recognised a member of the group as the actress Kelli Hollis, whose roles had included the mouthy shop-keeper Yvonne in the gritty drama *Shameless* and who was currently playing a leading role, as lesbian Ali Spencer, in ITV's *Emmerdale*. During the event Kelli had talked about a Huddersfield-based charity for which she was a patron, and the idea of a charity ghost hunt – with some of the cast-members – was born.

The business had helped a number of charities in the seven years since its creation, but this would be different. With the popularity of the soap and some of the names in the mix to attend, we could really make a difference with this and so we headed off to Leeds to meet with Kelli and a lady called Nicola, who would play a fundamental part in helping us to organise the details and maximise its potential.

The meeting was a huge success. Kelli was really up for it and filled us in with more detail about Ruddi's Retreat; a local charity which had been created to offer holidays for families with children suffering from cancer and other life-limiting illnesses. Its founder, Ali, had been through an incredibly tough journey herself after her son Ruddi was diagnosed with a rare form of cancer, aged just six months. Her goal was to give families in real need of a break a one-week holiday at the Primrose Valley Caravan Park in Filey, Yorkshire. By the end of the meeting we were all in agreement and fired-up, ready to make this happen.

The last time I had watched *Emmerdale* a plane had just parked itself on top of the village and Seth Armstrong was still trailblazing the style of moustache which would not see a comeback for at least another 20 years.

I had a lot of catching up to do!

Over the coming months, as preparations continued and ticket sales for the event were snapped up like hot-cakes, I made sure I watched a few episodes. At the very least I wanted to give the appearance that I knew some of the people we would be working with at the event. I recognised Gaynor Faye from another ITV soap, *Coronation Street*, and as the winner of the first series of celebrity ice-skating show *Dancing on Ice*. As a fan of the prison drama *Bad Girls* I also recognised Alicya Eyo, who had played the character Denny Blood and now played Kelli's partner in *Emmerdale*. Nicola Wheeler was familiar from her role as the stroppy Nicola King, but the rest of the cast I would need to brush up on – fast.

The night was a huge success and when everything was tallied up Haunted Happenings had raised over £3,500 for the charity, thanks to the support of some amazing guests and some sponsored raffle-prizes from our locations. It felt good to know we had made a difference, but the best part for us was yet to come.

On 27th September we made our way north once more, following an invitation from Kelli to present the cheque in style, on-set in the actual *Emmerdale* village. After a tour of the studio and the opportunity to watch some of the scenes being filmed, we made our way across town to the village itself, rubbing shoulders with the super-handsome Matthew Wolfenden (David Metcalfe), the very funny Chris Chittell (Eric Pollard) and the feisty Charlie Hardwick (Val Pollard) as they filmed scenes outside the infamous village pub, The Woolpack.

Tensions were high within the crew that day. Filming had taken much longer than planned and the whole cast and crew were tired and agitated, trying hard to complete the day's shooting schedule so they could all begin their weekend. We didn't know what the storyline entailed at the time, but later discovered the scenes in which the Woolpack came under siege – and the cellars flooded – had been filmed just days before, so most of the cast had spent the week working late at night, constantly doused in driving rain. This explained how the Woolpack came to have boarded-up windows and why there was a completely new interior back at the studio.

'Cut,' yelled the director, 'well done everybody. We're all done!'

Before coming down into the village we had been instructed to make sure our mobile phones were switched off, to avoid any interruptions in filming. So, knowing there would inevitably be e-mails coming through thick and fast while we were out of the office, I reached for my phone and pressed the button to turn it back on as soon as I heard those words.

Then, in the instant that I pressed it, his voice returned.

'Remain still and silent for a moment,' he shouted, still sounding agitated and short-tempered, 'we're just going to record the sound of the car driving through.'

My heart stopped!

It was too late – I'd already pressed it and there was no way of me preventing that familiar sound of the HTC One start-up. What's more, as soon as it had loaded there would be ping after ping of e-mail notifications and potentially texts or voicemails too. My instant reaction was to quickly move into the Woolpack building, as far away from the sound-boom as possible, but he'd specifically told us to stand still and I couldn't make the move without creating a scene, as we were stood right at the edge of the road and directly next to where the car was heading.

There was only one thing for it. I grabbed the phone from my pocket and stuffed it quickly into the fleece hoodie I was wearing, clasping my hands around it tightly in a desperate attempt to muffle the inevitable sound.

I felt the vibration just as the car was about 10 feet away, praying hard that my attempts to silence the noise would suffice. Then, just as the car pulled up alongside us, I heard it. The faint call of my mobile, trying hard to make its presence known despite my best attempts to conceal it.

I froze on the spot.

Had he heard it? Had I just put the nail in the coffin of this already stressed director's bad day? I held my breath as they listened back and then he spoke:-

'Thank you everyone.'

Relief flooded through my body faster than the spam e-mails and missed calls reached my phone. I'd got away with it!

I'm not sure if the sound was picked up at all or not, but if you heard the faint noise of a HTC mobile phone in *Emmerdale* sometime around Halloween 2013, it was probably me.

With the Ruddi project finally complete it was back to the grind stone. Endless hours behind a desk paying invoices, booking locations, planning teams and marketing the events – predominantly through our Facebook followers, since our audience had grown massively over the past six months. The workload was still relentless and, despite the realisation some months earlier that I was working harder than ever and seeing even less of my family, I forged on.

Ever since I had joined full-time, the plan had been for me to prove my worth and to purchase the business. Hazel had stepped back to a purely advisory role and was working on other projects and everything was going to plan; a fairy-tale ending was in sight and my dreams of owning my own business, doing something I really loved, were all set to come true.

But life has a way of kicking you in the teeth and a

fairy-tale happy ending just wasn't to be.

Haunted Happening had been born from a dining-room table in Nottingham and the blood, sweat and tears which had gone into making it the largest ghost hunting business in the UK were not merely metaphorical.

Everyone involved in those early days had worked incredibly hard; weekend after weekend they had ran events and ploughed money back into the business to ensure its growth, while working late into the evenings during the week to develop the website and promote the events.

By the time I joined as an event host two years later the hard work was already done, and Haunted Happenings' reputation was firmly established. My new task had been to build upon this success.

As with any company, where the team are all passionate about its success and the quality of the experience delivered to its guests, we didn't always agree.

I was running all of the day-to-day aspects of the business, but it seemed some of the original team felt I wasn't taking full advantage of the experience and knowledge which had been gained from those early years.

If I'm honest this was probably true, but not for the reason you may think; it had much more to do with having to make decisions on the spot and trying to keep up with the demanding workload, than being bloody-minded or determined to make my mark. All I really wanted was to make the business work and I can say, hand on heart, I did everything I could.

The workload was relentless as always, but with differing opinions regarding a number of details surrounding the following year's plans and a number of other issues, more and more time was taken with discussion and debate – trying to make the right decisions for the business – and I found myself struggling to cope with everything required of me, whilst also fighting my corner on those things I felt strongly about.

Long days became even longer, with many additional hours spent going over tiny details. The business had been going well but I felt that things were beginning to unfold, and it became harder and harder to resolve differences surrounding a number of matters. I guess everyone was doing what they believed was best for the business, but it's human nature that people won't always agree.

Small businesses are built from passion and determination and this one was no different. I will never forget the conversations Hazel and I had before I became more fully involved; the ones where she stressed how important it was to *never* forget what the purpose of the business was – to deliver an outstanding experience for anyone who chose to spend their money with us, rather than one of the other companies out there offering the same type of event.

She also stressed the point that, until you have delivered the event, any monies you hold from customer bookings have not yet been *earned*, and therefore should not be used for anything else. Her integrity and desire to protect the customers who placed their trust and money in her hands is the real foundation to the success of the business, and there have been many larger companies – across a number of sectors – who have failed, simply because they have not followed this simple practice.

Hazel's intention had been to work on other projects and eventually exit Haunted Happenings for good, but she was becoming more and more involved again, in order to ensure the best decisions were made for the long-term good of the business.

It was becoming increasingly more stressful.

At times the situation would get the better of me and there were days I would break down with tears of sheer frustration. I was working harder and harder but could feel it all slipping away.

I think it was around early December when I realised

the inevitable. The business didn't need two people leading from the front and, with Hazel back to the extent she was, changes needed to be made.

Something had to give and that something was me!

I don't blame her for the decision she made; she had to do whatever was necessary to protect the longevity of the business, but it didn't make it any less hard.

On Thursday 2nd January 2014 she took back the driving seat; I was made redundant and left Haunted Happenings with immediate effect.

I felt like a failure!

SIXTEEN

......*Sloth 1 - Motivation 0* – 14 Jan 2014

Numb!

There is no other way to describe the feeling. I had gone from working 18 hour days, my mind in a permanent state of warp-speed, to nothing. I have never lost a loved one or close friend in sudden circumstances, but the empty lost-feeling which consumed me on 3rd January was – I believe – akin to suffering a bereavement. That zombie-like state people sometimes display when their body goes into shock following a traumatic accident is the only way I can describe the vacant expression I wore.

I had fought hard right to the end and never given up, but although I had known in my heart that something was coming I hadn't been prepared for *this* outcome. I remember drawing similarities to reaching retirement; endless years of hard-work, long hours and tireless dedication to a job which becomes your purpose for getting out of bed in the mornings, suddenly ends. It's like slamming on the breaks and, even though you know the end is coming, the change in pace is difficult to adapt to.

The first few days were a blur. What made the situation worse was the fact my wife had left her part-time job several months earlier to support me in this venture in the belief that it was our combined future. In one fell swoop we *both* found ourselves lacking an income. I would rise from my bed each morning and wonder, what next? What are we going to do and, more significantly, how were we going to survive?

There were no tears; they had all been spent.

I was physically, mentally and emotionally exhausted. The toll of the past two years' workload weighed heavily on me physically and now that my purpose had been taken away I went into shutdown. I slept for hours, probably my body's way of dealing with the situation, and as the end of the first week of unemployment came we began to make some decisions.

Thankfully, the financial situation wasn't dire.

I came away from the business with some money which would allow me some breathing space while I worked out my next move. I knew I needed some time. I just wasn't in a fit state to even consider presenting myself at my best for job interviews and, after much discussion with the missus, we agreed that I needed to take a breather. So that's what I did. I would take a couple of months of guilt-free recuperation before commencing my job search. It was time to do some healing and focus upon getting back to my normal self.

The effects of the past 12 months ran much deeper than needing some rest. I felt enormous guilt for having taken a risk which hadn't worked out. The potential impact on my family could be huge and the blame I placed upon my own shoulders for not making it work weighed heavily. Why hadn't I been strong enough to make it work? If only I'd done better, we wouldn't be in this situation now.

These thoughts, and more, ran through my mind on

a daily basis, like a juggernaut gaining momentum and careering out of control.

It's fair to say that the pressure I felt as a husband and father – to get things right and provide for my family – are common among men. Whether those expectations derive from external sources or self-imposed thoughts, they *were* tangible. Once I made that commitment to start a family, I felt a greater and greater burden to make sure I could provide them with everything they needed; not just for the children, but for my wife also.

We were a unit and I had to play my part! *My* wants and needs in life were secondary to my duty as a husband and parent.

It's a sad statistic that anxiety and depression in men (particularly in their 30s) has been steadily on the increase for a number of years. You could argue that we simply need to 'man-up' and get on with things; after all, our grandfathers and great-grandfathers had it much tougher didn't they?

Perhaps; but to compare a person's ability to cope with situations you really need to measure eggs with eggs. While life was undoubtedly tougher for our ancestors, the problems faced were very different and in many ways, far simpler. Jobs tended to be for life, people worked much closer to home – compared to the average commute of one hour and thirty-eight minutes in 2015 – and the cost of living was less, with fewer aspirations and expectations.

In short – life was hard, but arguably less *stressful*.

The ideology of the perfect family unit one-hundred years ago seems near-impossible to achieve in today's society. The 40-hour week is almost unheard of in any job paying above the 'average' annual salary, and with greater and greater pressure in the workplace, it is inevitable that home-life will suffer. The increase in separation and divorce rates is a sad reflection of this in the 21st Century.

I – as I'm sure many men do – absolutely felt that my role in life was to provide for my family, and that had now gone horribly wrong.

Perhaps the greatest long-term issue I would come to face was the enormous impact the experience had on my confidence going forward.

For years I had felt I was blagging my way through my career and that one day a hefty finger would tap me firmly on the shoulder and say 'you've been sussed.' It had nothing to do with my confidence to do a good job on a day-to-day basis, just that I had worked my way through the company at Unipart and, being brutally honest, hadn't felt I really had enough knowledge to qualify for the job. I'd never taken any marketing qualifications and my BA in music history and performance wasn't going to save my ass when the heat was turned up in the monthly marketing meetings.

In joining Haunted Happenings I had finally felt completely at home with both my ability and my knowledge. Sure, there were times when I felt out of my depth with particular situations, but there was not a single moment throughout the whole period I worked there that I didn't feel I could overcome those issues. That is why it hit me so hard when I didn't succeed. After all, if I couldn't make it work having given 110% all the way, then how would I ever succeed at anything? It wasn't self-pity. I wasn't determined to hate or blame myself, but that's just how I felt.

Breaking the news to friends and family was tough. Naturally my mom had expressed reservations from the start.

'It's such a big risk to leave a well-paid job,' I remember her saying, 'especially when you can't be certain it'll work.'

My response had been simple:-

'There's a very good chance I'll be made redundant from Unipart within 12 months and this is something I know I can do - and want to do.'

Admitting things had gone horribly wrong wasn't

going to be easy. I didn't think for a moment I'd hear the words 'I told you so', but the embarrassment of failure was still unbearable to speak aloud. To make matters worse I had developed an exceptional poker-face over the course of those two years. To the outside world everything was rosy. Nobody was even vaguely aware what was going on behind closed doors, so from mom's perspective this had come completely out of the blue.

……Lie-in, breakfast & dog walk all done. Now having lunch with 4 loose women before doing something…………maybe – 17 Jan 2014

Days merged from one tiresome drawn-out effort into another. No focus, no purpose and no motivation. Even the smallest of tasks felt like climbing the tallest of mountains. Walking our two dogs became my only real need to venture into the outside world and those crisp wintry-walks became something I would use as a crutch over the next few months; an outlet to help cleanse my mind of the negativity I felt about myself and the situation I had allowed us to be placed in.

My wife had found another job relatively quickly and by the end of January she had returned to work – her first full-time position for many years. Of course this was great news and helped to relieve some of the pressure I was beginning to feel about our immediate finances, but it also came with a downside.

It sounds self-indulgent as I look back, but I had always been the breadwinner; the one who could be relied upon to earn money and ensure our finances were in good order and now, the shoe was on the other foot. The relief I felt now one of us was working was tainted with the shame that she had picked herself up, dusted herself off quickly and was out earning again. I berated myself every day but in all honesty, I just didn't feel ready to put myself back out there yet. I guess I was more damaged than even I had realised.

Daytime television became my best friend.

This Morning and *Loose Women* were both on the list of daily activities; less to do with what I may learn and more about the fact that I could stare at the stupid-box for hours and not have to think about anything. Another favourite was *Homes Under The Hammer*, a house-renovation programme in which they follow properties purchased at auction, through development and back onto the market for rent or sale. I've always loved home-renovation programmes and this one was on every weekday morning so, after getting up sometime around 9.30am, I would be ready – cup of tea in hand – for 10am when the titles would begin to roll.

There was an upside of course. The roles had been reversed and although it was killing me inside that I couldn't contribute in the way I felt I should, this situation meant that I spent more time with the children than ever before.

Their school was within ten minutes' walking distance and on some days I would walk the dogs over to meet them. We would often ride our bikes, walk the dogs, or just spend some time together. Cooking meals, while not my favourite pastime, provided some respite from the boredom which began to take hold, and household chores were always calling to keep me busy.

One of the girls' bedroom finally had the redecoration she so desperately wanted, the garden was always neat and tidy and I spent many hours immersed in music, playing the piano which had otherwise been silent for so long.

Time ticked on and I had some decisions to make. We needed money and whilst it would be difficult, the door had been left open for me to continue hosting events for the business at the weekends and this would – at the very least – provide us with a small additional income while I continued to search for a job.

I was still in touch with Hazel. The handover of the business had required us to keep in contact and despite the hurt I felt when the axe fell, deep down I knew the decision had been taken only for the good of the business and was nothing personal and therefore, I held no grudge.

However, swallowing my pride and returning to the business after everything that had happened just a short time before would be hard.

I have always maintained what I believe to be a good work ethic and been in continuous employment since leaving college at the age of 23. As a couple we'd both worked for everything we had and I always said that – if push came to shove – I would pack boxes in a warehouse if I had to in order to pay bills. Work is work and I wouldn't consider myself above anything.

One of my biggest peeves has always been to hear people complain there are no jobs out there; there are, and there always have been. They may not be the jobs you want for a career, but for anyone truly willing to work and get their bills paid there will always be something available to anyone who is able to work.

In recent years, with immigration becoming a greater issue in the UK, the excuse that people from nearby shores are coming over and stealing our jobs has become more and more common among the bone-idle. Many would argue that it is the Government's fault for making the benefits system so easy to abuse. Why would anybody bother going out to work when there is the option to sit at home watching the *Jeremy Kyle Show* on a 46" plasma TV at the expense of the tax-payer?

The time had come to suck it up and return to the events. The poker-face which had served me so well for the final nine months of my time with Haunted Happenings would be dusted off and I returned to hosting.

In truth, standing before 30 guests with a smile on my face was the last thing I wanted to do at the time. My mind was still all over the place but I needed to work and I knew this was something I could do, regardless of how I was feeling inside. As for the guests they would never know anything was wrong, because what I presented to them was a happy, friendly and warm façade; no less than they deserved.

It had been my experience with the business which had destroyed my confidence and brought me to this place yet ironically, it was getting back into the saddle which also began the healing process. Those voices in my head, telling me every day that I had messed up and would never achieve anything, had been taking hold and gaining momentum.

Every passing day reinforced this negativity in my own mind, repeating over and over again that I was a failure, so returning to the one thing I fundamentally believed I was good at helped me to begin turning that around and would – in time – boost my self-confidence sufficiently to do what was necessary to tackle the issue of my next career-move.

The biggest problem I faced was fear. I was frightened because I didn't know what I wanted to do; afraid of trying something new, but failing again. Then it came.

During my morning ritual of tea, toast and *Homes Under The Hammer*, I had an epiphany. I wanted to be an estate agent. In a single moment it all became clear. I had an interest in property, a background in sales and most importantly, a good rapport with people, which is the key to becoming a success in any sales-related role. In that moment I made my decision. I wanted to pursue this, a complete change in direction, and was determined to make it happen. The problem was that nobody was advertising for new staff. I trawled the local papers, scoured the internet job sites and there was nothing.

Undeterred, I decided to go back to basics.

As with any town Redditch was blessed with at least

a dozen different agents, and so I drove into town and hand-delivered a speculative letter to them all.

If the mountain will not come to Muhammad, then Muhammad must go to the mountain!

This was the attitude I adopted, and as luck would have it I received a phone call a couple of days later from the area-director for a leading estate-agency group. An interview followed swiftly, then the offer of a role in their Redditch branch and – just a few weeks after my initial decision – I was back in full-time work; a new career and something to sink my teeth into.

The relief I felt was amazing.

Not only this, but I felt a certain amount of pride in having taken the bull by the horns, creating an opportunity where others may have just accepted there wasn't one.

I had turned a corner. Months of financial worry were at an end, and finally I felt I had started the process of rebuilding my confidence. I was ready for a new adventure.

I've never been one to judge without having walked in another person's shoes and the same applies to the assumptions often made about other people's careers.

The teaching profession is always an easy target for derision; resentment from the masses for the amount of annual-leave they enjoy has always been a grumble for those with 'real jobs'. It is easy to forget that for the majority of teachers the day doesn't end at 3.15pm when the pupils leave. Open-evenings, plays, after-school activities, marking homework and planning lessons all happen outside the normal school hours – all additional work which is so easily overlooked when criticising the profession.

Oh and let's not forget they also 'enjoy' the privilege of extended holidays; paying literally double the price that most of us pay, simply because the travel companies and airlines hike their prices for any weeks which fall outside term times.

Estate agents have traditionally been high on the list of most-hated professions in the UK, coming a close second only to traffic-wardens and rubbing shoulders with bouncers and motorcycle couriers. In recent years the top-ten has shifted somewhat, making way for politicians, bankers and call-centre workers, but you can always rest assured that – for anyone who has ever bought or sold a house – your local estate agent will be high on your priority hit-list. It's just the status quo.

Revealing my new career to people clearly invited some choice comments and gentle banter on my Facebook timeline but, of course, my friends and family wished me well and were very encouraging.

It soon became apparent to me that, as most of us do, I had truly underestimated the work that goes into estate-agency and this would be far from an easy ride.

There was a lot to learn!

A common misconception has always been that the agent is there to help the buyer find the right place, but in reality they are *always* working for the one who pays their commission when the sale finally completes; the vendor. Little white lies about the level of interest in a new property are common in the industry, to create some urgency and encourage potential purchasers to get their offer on the table quick. It's just part of the game but something I'm pleased to say the company I joined didn't advocate.

It didn't take me long to settle into the routine; morning meetings, setting your daily and weekly targets for viewings, sales and mortgage appointments and of course, trying to sell the damn houses. Unfortunately for me – but not for my colleague and direct competition in the branch – I actually wasn't very good at the job, something which became apparent fairly quickly, despite a decent couple of months' initial sales.

My approach, while great for the potential buyer,

didn't fit with the hard-nosed methods required to pin-down those who showed interest, but were hesitant. As a result the other sales-negotiator in the branch, who was much more experienced and a far stronger character than me, often beat me to the sale with her clients.

As is probably the case in most towns, the competition between agents was fierce. Canvassing properties for new listings was essential, because with so many agents to choose from you simply couldn't sit back and wait, in the hope that potential vendors would offer you the opportunity to list their house.

Likewise, booking appointments for the in-house mortgage advisor was a vital part of the role too, as this would bring much-needed income to the bottom line of the branch's profit, as well as provide a nice boost to the agent's payslip at the end of the month.

I had gone into a sales role with my eyes wide open, so none of this was a surprise. I'd sold computer systems before with ridiculously expensive support-packages and warranties, so I knew the score. In sales every customer comes with a set of £ signs above their heads and it is up to the advisor to see how many they can shake from you.

That aside, what I didn't expect to find was the level of care the team I was working with would apply to the customers we had. In my relatively short time there I witnessed outbursts of anger, frustration and even tears from other team members, simply because they really cared about the people they were dealing with; vendors and purchasers alike.

This agency was – and probably still is – one of the most expensive in town for fees, and we therefore faced an uphill battle before the race had even begun. When you charge a higher price for your services there is only one way to make yourself stand out and that is with your service.

My competition in the branch was a Rottweiler when it came to her job; loud, determined, passionate and knowledgeable, but most of all, caring. Beneath the veneer of the brash exterior she presented this was a girl who really gave a damn about the customers she worked with. When some of the agents would play tricks to win business for their own gain, often at the expense of the client, she would fly into a rage on the customer's behalf at the injustice of the situation.

Her fiery character was often the cause of both tension and amusement in the office, but she and the rest of the team worked tirelessly to get the best results possible in a tough market.

I was proud to be part of that team!

Over the years I've worked in a number of different environments and positions but I can honestly say, hand on heart, I thoroughly enjoyed working with these people and have fond memories of my time there.

One of the biggest challenges in any work-environment is getting a team to gel, and in this instance we had it nailed. Everyone had everyone else's back and the banter was second-to-none. In fact there were so many Tena-Lady moments in the short time I worked there, I'm surprised we didn't need the carpets cleaning more often.

……Managed to get through the day without squirting Yorkshire Tea from my nasal passages #Result – 20 Jun 2014

I had been working in the branch for less than two weeks when I made an absolute show of myself in the morning meeting.

Seated around the manager's desk every morning the team would run through potential sales, new listings and any other information which may help us to achieve the day's required results. On this particular morning the guy who was responsible for listing the properties and bringing them onto the market for us to sell was seated to my right. As always, he would run through the good and bad points of any new properties, and that's when it happened.

'It's a really good house,' he began, pitching his latest listing to us with enthusiasm. 'There's a bit of redecoration required and the outside it a bit tatty, but otherwise it's a winner'.

As he ran through the layout of the property and its key benefits I sat attentively, making notes and sipping my morning brew of choice, a piping hot cup of Yorkshire Tea with two sugars.

'What work is required on the outside?' my nemesis chipped in, already scribbling down potential viewers who would probably be walking around the house before the end of the day.

'The guy said he was going to replace the facia-boards,' he replied, 'but I've told him that isn't going to add any value and not to bother.'

The manager nodded in agreement and, just as he began to utter his next sentence, I tipped the final mouthful of tea into my mouth.

'He does have a wonky soil-pipe though and I've suggested he gets that straightened before it leaks.'

I couldn't stop myself!

As the words rolled from his tongue my mind went into innuendo-overdrive and the outcome was inevitable.

In an instant I could feel the explosion of laughter rising from within me and, catching the eye of the manager – equally as quick and filthy-minded as me – certainly didn't help. There was no going back. Despite my best attempt to clamp my lips together the tea began to burst free, like the first cracks of a dam about to succumb to the growing pressure behind its walls. As I felt it leave my mouth the rest of the team reacted with more laughter; it was about to get worse.

With my mouth now firmly shut, the physiological response to fighting back an involuntary second-wave of laughter was to let out a snort through my nose.

Under normal circumstances this wouldn't have such devastating consequences, but having just tried to swallow back my drink to prevent any further escape there was only one possible outcome; there, in front of my brand new work-colleagues – less than two weeks into my new job – I squirted Yorkshire Tea from my nose, dousing the paperwork, contracts and diary on the desk before me.

This was most certainly not the impact I'd intended to make on my new workplace, but it did act as a great ice-breaker and let's face it, once you've sprayed tea from your nasal passages in front of your colleagues there really aren't many other boundaries to knock down are there?

SEVENTEEN

......Staggering! Just heard one woman say to another waiting to see the doctor "I don't mean to be rude, but do you think you will be long when you go in?" You may not mean to be rude lovely, but it doesn't appear to be stopping you! – 6 Feb 2014

I love people!

What a complex, mixed-up and fascinating bunch of individuals we are. I've often pondered upon what makes a person who they are; is nature really stronger than nurture, are we pre-disposed to grow into the people we become or do the experiences we encounter along life's journey and the people we meet really shape our personalities and characteristics?

I suspect it's probably a combination of both.

No matter how far back in history you travel (maybe you can ignore the Dinosaurs), there have always been divisions within society. Wealth and power have been at the heart of this separation since man began to form civilized societies and it's fair to say the two go hand in hand, fuelling each other's growth exponentially, each one fanning the other's flame.

Travel back to ancient Rome and you will discover a

tiered hierarchy, one which you could argue still exists today throughout many of the world's countries.

At the very top of the tree were those who attained wealth and power merely through ancestry - a comparison in today's society would be those born into a country's monarchy, where status and ruling is a right of birth and nothing to do with democracy.

Close on their tails were the Equites (a rank akin to Knights), followed by those who formed the Senate, the equivalent of today's Politicians. Noblemen, known as the cursus honorum, held public office positions – often aspiring to become politicians – and these were placed higher in superiority than the Roman citizens who lived in towns surrounding Rome and were awarded varying rights and privileges.

The lower-classes might hold citizenship but not necessarily have the right to vote, and at the very bottom of the masses were the slaves – considered property by the upper-classes – who often had no rights whatsoever. Sound familiar?

You could argue that little has changed over the last 2,000 years, and that even today this basic structure still exists. Almost every country on the planet has either a monarchy or republic – democratic or autocratic – and without some form of leadership society would descend into an unlawful and unruly mess. Whether we think it or not, we all require leadership of some level in order to grow and exist.

What I find most fascinating is how leadership develops within a person and this, for me, is where the argument of nurture over nature loses valuable ground. Take Richard Branson for example; arguably one of the leading entrepreneurs of our time and certainly one of the most successful businessmen the UK has ever seen.

Born into what would generally be considered a wealthy family – his father was a barrister and his mother a flight attendant – Richard's early life was blessed with educational opportunity beyond that which the majority of the country enjoy, but he was by no means guaranteed success in life.

He struggled with dyslexia, had a tough time settling into the educational institutions he was placed in and, by the age of 16, had dropped out of school altogether. Whilst his family had the means to provide their son with a top-quality education, he simply didn't have the capacity to maximise what was on offer. However, what Richard had was something completely intangible and most certainly not learned from a book, or even from the example set by his parents; he had vision. A determination to succeed and a quality sometimes referred to as the x-factor.

The same can be said for Alan Sugar, once a Sir and now a Lord. Sugar was born into a family who accepted their place in society, worked hard, and who actively discouraged their son's entrepreneurial nature, in favour of a more 'traditional' career.

The *Sunday Times Rich List* cited a combined net worth of these two men as £5.5bn in October 2015, just shy of 10% of the total net worth of Microsoft founder, Bill Gates, yet another self-made billionaire. Sure, all were fortunate to be born into families with loving parents and opportunity, but none would be where they are today without that indefinable, entrepreneurial-quality which burns inside and drives everything they do.

What sets these men apart from the average? It can only be genetic. Some element within the makeup of their DNA which made them pre-destined to think differently in some way from the norm.

In contrast, you don't have to look very far in order to find plenty of examples of people born into families with self-made fortunes, earned through the same entrepreneurialism as Gates, Branson and Sugar and exposed to the incredible work-ethic they display, who simply don't think in the same way.

If nurture were solely responsible for everything we do and achieve in life, how could a child born into wealth and exposed to those things required to emulate such success end up failing in business or, worse still, go off the rails altogether, making their debut TV appearance in a mug-shot on the national news channels?

In many ways, I wish I were different.

For years I berated myself for not having the confidence to speak my mind, to take risks or even believe in myself. It saddens me to hear people diminish their own abilities and yet, for the majority of my 20s and 30s that is exactly what I did.

I never felt confident in work, despite having achieved what many would consider a very good salary, and I suffered in many ways with a low self-esteem about the way I looked. Much of this I believe was the result of those big ears, NHS specs and skinny frame, but in all honesty I also believe it is just part of who I am.

Watching my children grow I witnessed many of the traits I considered failings within myself materialise in them and, of course, never saw them as failings in my own children. Instead, I saw their consideration for others above themselves as a trait which deserved praise, and accepted their quiet nature within a crowd as politeness, rather than a lack of confidence to speak up.

However, having realised the importance of asserting your place in the world and believing in yourself, I have always tried to instil this within them and I'm proud to say – as they have grown into young adults – they most certainly seem to have achieved what I never did in my younger years.

In her final year of middle-school my eldest displayed this quality, following a falling out with her art teacher over a trivial matter. Having forgotten to pack her pencil-sharpener for school that day, she told me of how she had approached her teacher during the lesson with a request:-

'Excuse me Miss,' she (allegedly) began, 'could I borrow a pencil-sharpener please?'

'Where is yours?' came the teacher's curt reply, disregarding the question which had been posed to her.

'I must have left it at home.'

'Well you can borrow it but you'll be given a behaviour point too, for not bringing the right equipment to school,' her teacher added, handing her the sharpener.

Behaviour points are awarded to pupils for lapses in behaviour and, if a pupil received three points within a certain time-frame, this resulted in an after-school detention.

She was clearly not impressed:-

'That doesn't seem fair Miss. I usually have all the right things and I must have accidentally left it at home,' she answered. 'I won't borrow it if it means I'm going to get a behaviour point and I'll just do the work without it, but it won't be as good,' she added - most likely with a flick of the hair or a typical teenage-pout.

'You *will* borrow it,' the teacher asserted, 'and you'll also receive another point for answering back.'

With an incredulous sense of injustice rising within her, she came straight back at the teacher.

'I didn't answer back rudely Miss,' she responded, 'I just said it doesn't seem right and I don't want a behaviour point.'

The teacher, most likely becoming more and more infuriated with her refusal to accept the sharpener and the punishment, issued another warning:-

'Take the pencil-sharpener, get on with your work and you *will* be receiving two points,' she insisted.

However, she wouldn't let it go.

'You're not being fair,' came her reply, 'and if you're going to give me two points you might as well give me another and I'll have the full set.'

Needless to say she spent the following afternoon in school detention, surrounded with children who had been fighting, swearing and caught breaking a number of other school rules throughout the previous day.

Now I'm certainly not one of those parents who believes their children never do any wrong, and I absolutely believe that discipline and example are equally as critical as each other in helping youngsters to develop into good human beings. Listening to her side of the story I read between the lines; somewhere within the exchange she had described would be the truth and I feel sure that there would have been a level of teenage-attitude in her responses, but I couldn't help feeling proud.

The whole scenario seemed as ridiculous to me as it had to her and, whilst I supported the teacher's right to issue a punishment for being challenged by a pupil, I completely disagreed with the original issue. The situation was worsened by the fact that, on a different occasion, she had made a similar request to another teacher and he had allowed her to borrow something, without question or punishment. There was no consistency, resulting in mixed messages to the kids.

I reiterated to her that, providing she had been polite and respectful during the exchange, she was absolutely within her rights to question the teacher's ruling and that in a few months this particular incident would be long-forgotten and would have absolutely no bearing on her life going forward. More than anything I was proud that she'd had the guts to stand up for herself - a quality I most certainly never had at school.

I didn't express my annoyance to her, but was quietly seething that an otherwise polite, friendly and 'outstanding' pupil had been thrown into detention with a group of outwardly naughty kids, and therefore exposed to the very behaviour the school was trying to stamp out. As far as I could see the only lessons learned from this detention were a few new swear words she hadn't yet encountered and a masterclass from her peers in how to disrespect authority.

The penal-system has long suffered a similar problem and one for which it seems there really is no solution. With overcrowding in our prisons at an all-time high, petty criminals often find themselves incarcerated with those serving time for violent crime, drug addiction and even murder.

Recidivism, whilst down almost 2% since 2003 is still a major issue, with 26% of all those having served a custodial-sentence reoffending between 1 July 2013 and 30 June 2014 (according to the *Ministry of Justice's Proven Reoffending Statistics*).

I've always believed in punishment where due. All this new-age crap, where parents refuse to smack their child because it's a violation of their human rights, is a load of bollocks as far as I'm concerned. Sure, there's a line between a swift smack on the arse to jolt their attention and remind them who is boss versus the ill-treatment we see flashed across the news, but as a child of the '70s I received my fair share of slapped arse, and I've turned out pretty well.

Sometimes words just don't cut it with children and I would argue that a well-timed swift connection between hand and arse is just what is required to remind them they need to take heed of what they are being told.

Every action has a reaction.

Of course I'm not advocating violence towards children, and believe corporal punishment should only be employed where all reasoning has failed. As with any form of learning and development, raising children is much more about setting the right examples; respect for others, an understanding of right from wrong and a strong work ethic.

Demonstrate these qualities to children and you will raise decent human-beings who will add value to society and other people's lives. Fail to live these values yourself and you will nurture your little ones into those very people who feel the world owes them something and who will drain the country of its resources, rather than add to them.

In my opinion smacking a child is, despite what the new-age nutters believe, a critical and valuable part of teaching them consequence, and that failure to follow rules as you grow will result in serious repercussions.

It is for this very reason I believe a short prison sentence can be far more effective in rehabilitating first-time offenders than a lengthy one. If the primary goal of prison reform is to reduce recidivism and rehabilitate offenders, then fear is surely the greatest weapon in the justice system's armoury.

I have met people who have served time. I have spoken with both former and serving prison-officers and I know people who provide services into prisons; I've also watched all 692 episodes of *Prisoner Cell Block H* so I'm pretty much an expert on the subject.

One thing on which they are all agreed is that, for a first time offender the initial 28 days are a nightmare. Alien surroundings and unfamiliar routines combine with the loneliness of missing family and friends and the fear of other inmates, to make this first month a very difficult time for new offenders.

Once an inmate begins to feel comfortable within their surroundings the shock-effect of the punishment begins to lose impact and, after a while, most will begin to see prison as a relatively comfortable place. Had they only been subjected to that initial period, their associations would predominantly reflect fear and upset, whereas once they have settled in and begun to make acquaintances, the negative associations begin to fade and a prison sentence becomes less of a deterrent.

Essentially, a short sentence which shocks the inmate and leaves only negative connotations is surely more powerful a deterrent than one in which they begin to feel comfortable in their environment.

I don't think I'd survive a week inside for the very

same reason I have to be careful when I'm out for a drink at a pub; I'm a people watcher. Not the kind who hides in your privet-hedge with a pair of binoculars and watches you get undressed at night, but the type who can't help but observe people's body-language.

The difficulty is, often I find myself staring at people and, if caught, it can become very awkward. Not only that, but it's often the dickheads who catch my attention and I'm not the world's greatest at hiding what I think; my facial expressions say everything my head is secretly thinking.

……finds people who don't swing their arms when they walk, very, very scary! – 12 Jul 2009

It's fascinating to me when you hear reports of a murder and the neighbours are interviewed on the local news.

'I never suspected he/she could do something like this,' they say, 'they were always so kind and polite.'

Well, they do say it's always the quiet ones you have to watch eh?

My greatest pet-hate is a lack of consideration for others. It drives me nuts. I'd consider myself a tolerant guy and will allow most things to float over me without a reaction, but what really grinds my gears is people who fulfil their own needs in life with absolutely no thought for anybody else. Even the small things like not parking within the lines in a busy car-park get me angry and, as for one person keeping a whole group of others waiting just because they can't be arsed to arrive somewhere on time – or haven't bothered to read the instructions properly – don't even get me started.

Just have some decency and realise that the world doesn't revolve around one person and we'll get along just fine.

So, to the woman in the doctor's surgery, I'd like to

whole-heartedly apologise for the dirty look I gave you when I heard you harass that poor, elderly woman you made to feel so uncomfortable with your aggressive and inappropriate tone of questioning.

I do hope it didn't take the doctor longer than your allocated 10 minutes to diagnose you as rude and self-absorbed.

EIGHTEEN

......Need someone to take me out, get totally steaming drunk, dance like an arse and leave me in the gutter with sick in my stubble - please apply within – 18 Aug 2014

I honestly didn't see it coming!

Maybe I'd been too caught up in getting myself back on track after Haunted Happenings and finding a new job, but after 24 years with the same person – 17 of those married – my wife dropped a bombshell.

Seemingly from nowhere, she announced that she wasn't happy with our marriage.

The words hit me like a truck. I didn't know what to say.

She went on to add that she felt we were simply two people living under the same roof and had nothing in common any more. The coolness of her demeanour didn't sit comfortably with the gravity of the words she was speaking.

It was a very awkward conversation and one which led to many more awkward evenings ahead over the coming weeks.

In truth, she was absolutely right. For years, we had

both been very independent of each other socially, each with our own friends and quite different in the things we enjoyed doing.

As I'm sure is the case for the majority of parents, when children come along all of your focus turns to them and it's easy to lose touch with your partner. Social activities were few and far between and, as I mentioned before, holidays even fewer. She had often taken the children away at weekends for mini-breaks with her sister and our niece and I had remained at home, either enjoying some much needed time to myself, or working.

Now that she was back at work full-time we had made the decision to stagger our annual-leave, to cover as much of the children's school holidays as possible without having to ask for too much help from family during the seven week summer-break.

The week after the bombshell I was due to be off work and, with that in mind, I booked a last-minute holiday for just myself and the children at a caravan-park in Lincolnshire; a decision taken partly to spend some quality time with the kids and also, to give she and I some space from each other to think.

The holiday was amazing!

Four days of sunshine on the east-coast of England with just the girls and me. We played ball games, spent a whole day at a local fairground riding the rollercoasters and ate chips by the sea; perfect in every way and, although things were clearly going awry at home, I felt more at peace and closer to the children than ever before.

As we packed up for the return journey we made one final walk across the vast, empty beach which lay behind the caravan-park, to see the sea for one last time and that's when something special happened — a memory I will cherish forever.

'What's that out there in the water daddy?' my eldest asked, indicating a point just beyond where the waves were breaking onto the sand before us.

'Where?' I responded, expecting to see a plastic bag or some wood floating on the surface.

'Just there,' she pointed again, 'something keeps poking up out of the water.'

Then I saw it; a large Grey Seal was bobbing up and down in the surf, seemingly looking straight toward us at the water's edge. Then, her sister shouted excitedly.

'There's another over there daddy,' pointing further to the left, 'and another. There are loads!'

She was absolutely right. Within a matter of minutes there were more than 30 seals of varying sizes, all floating in the water less than 20 feet from where we stood. I couldn't believe what I was seeing and as we walked just a few feet into the breaking waves, they would disappear beneath the surface – all at once – before reappearing a few feet further away. I was reminded of the Hasbro '*Whac-A-Mole*' game, where moles would pop up out of holes and you'd have to hit them down with a toy hammer, before they popped up elsewhere.

We must have watched them for around 30 minutes before heading back. It was truly magical. Seeing the children's faces, hearing the excitement in their voices and the sheer joy of being able to witness these creatures up-close in their natural habitat, was a moment I'll never forget. As we set off along the sand to begin the long journey home my heart was full.

Things were no better when I got home. I felt completely unable to talk to my wife. I knew she was right and, for as much as I didn't want our family torn apart, I didn't know how to react.

Over the coming weeks I suggested doing things together, to spend more time with each other and see what happened. A theatre-trip to London for just the two of us seemed like a great suggestion; something we both had in common and which would give us some time away together, but nothing was forthcoming from her and things were becoming unbearable. There was an elephant in the room and it continued to go unnoticed.

It was a Thursday evening, the 14th August to be precise, when our marriage ended.

That evening she was at her parents' house when I returned from work, as the children were going to be staying there overnight. I sat alone at home and, frustrated with the fact we were stuck in limbo, I wrote her a letter. I can't remember exactly what it said but basically I told her that she had raised this issue and now didn't seem willing to try to do anything to find a resolution. I ended the note with a demand that she either make an effort to fix things, or we should call it a day. Placing the note on the kitchen worktop, I then left the house.

I drove around for hours, aimlessly following the roads, devoid of any real purpose other than trying to clear my head.

I felt vulnerable!

I was fearful of what the outcome might be and unable to think clearly about anything. I have no idea why I went back, but something drew me to return to the place I had grown up.

I parked the car and stood for several minutes, leaning against the wall opposite the house in which I had been born and raised, where my happy childhood had played out. In hindsight I think I was grasping for comfort; something familiar and a place where I had always felt safe. I noticed a slight movement from the window of the room in which I had slept for the first 18 years of my life and then something very strange crossed my mind.

I was taken back some 35 years, to that moment when I stood on the inside of the very window at which I now found myself gazing, looking out upon a mysterious figure against the wall upon which I now leant myself.

That moment had always stuck with me and now, as if in some weird Déjà vu reality, I felt that I had lived the whole experience before.

How was it that I had seen that figure in the darkness when my father – standing right beside me – could see nothing? I had always believed there was some purpose or reason it had been visible only to my eyes, but the thoughts now entering my mind seemed crazy.

Was the strange apparition from all those years ago actually me right now; standing alone in the darkness, seeking solace and comfort in my own-self from many decades before?

I'm not a conspiracy-theorist and don't buy into many of the nonsense discussions surrounding photographs from the past which appear to show people ahead of their time but, through my interest in the paranormal I have come to believe that we may just have it wrong when we assume time to be a linear model.

In lengthy conversations with my good friend Carolyn – a psychic-medium – we have laboured over the concept that time is a much more complex affair than simply a journey from A to B, and is perhaps a cyclical journey.

In my uneducated mind it is a theory that would offer some explanation for the many Déjà vu moments we all encounter at some point in our lives; the feeling that we have already lived a certain moment before, to such extent we seem to recall exactly the words which were spoken. It would also support the argument of those who believe they have seen a ghost.

For example, could it be possible that the very moment we are living now is actually the past, the future and the present, all existing in the same time but on different layers?

If that were the case then those who claim to have seen a ghost could possibly have merely witnessed a slip in time, like a jump in the grooves of a vinyl record, and effectively time-travelled for a few seconds. What if somebody from the future (or the past) were witnessing you in *your* moment of reality and believed you to be the ghost?

Could that be exactly what happened to me while leaning against that wall? Had I become a real-life Marty McFly from *Back to the Future*? I suspect not, but somewhere deep within me I felt those two moments were intrinsically linked and it afforded me great comfort.

Before returning home there was one other place I felt drawn to visit.

Something inside me needed to physically connect with my past and I walked the short distance from my old home, to the place where I had spent many hours as a kid; the local slide. It wasn't there anymore, having been removed many years before, but I sat for a while – on the spot where it once stood – and allowed my mind to drift back to the many warm, summer evenings, during which we had played here.

I had never really considered myself a spiritual person, but on this night I needed some reassurance from somewhere, and I lay my hand upon part of the brickwork which had once edged the curve of the slide itself. In some bizarre way, touching something which had existed for my whole life and formed part of my youth gave me strength and reassurance. I felt like I was in touch with myself - a person I had temporarily lost along the way.

As I sat there I received a text from asking where I was and when I was coming home. I had a feeling that she had already made her decision and was just trying to find the right moment to tell me and so, rather than wait until I returned, I asked her if she had come to any conclusion. She said she wanted to talk face-to-face, but I returned that talking had got us nowhere until now and, after some prompting, the text came through.

I don't want to try.

By the time the message came through I had pulled over at the roadside, just a short distance from home. I felt numb. I didn't even respond. I sat there for a few minutes before completing the journey and, as I walked through the door, the reality hit me.

In that very moment I realised this was no longer a family home.

Whatever was about to happen and however it ended, the four of us would no longer be living under this same roof. Everything was about to change and my whole world was falling apart around me. She spent the night in one of the kids' rooms that night as I lay in our bed, crying, trying hard to contemplate what was happening.

By the time I went downstairs the next morning she had already left. I showered and dressed for work, with no idea how I would get through the next eight hours, let alone the rest of my life.

It was a nightmare, and throughout the day I broke down several times.

The team at work were amazing and gave me the support I needed to make it through until 5.30pm, when I could go home and lock the door for some quiet contemplation. I received a message from my wife explaining that she had already arranged with her parents for her and the children to move in with them for a while, so I could stay in the house. She had told them we were not getting on very well and would be spending some time apart.

Even though it turned out there were much darker times ahead, the next morning I faced – without question – the hardest thing that had ever been asked of me.

She returned to the house along with the children to pack some things, so they had everything they needed for the immediate weeks. For the sake of the children I had to hold back the tears and keep myself in check. I couldn't allow them to see me cry as this was no-doubt difficult for them too, and I didn't want to add to their worry. In their minds this was just a temporary thing, but I knew different.

I sat in the conservatory – staring into space – as they packed their things upstairs and, after what seemed like an eternity, they finally walked back into the room. They both came over to me and wrapped their arms around me and my heart broke. I felt a physical, debilitating pain deep within me and I summoned every ounce of strength I had, just to hold back the tears.

'We can still come and visit daddy,' they reassured me as they held their arms around me and squeezed my waist tightly. 'We're only just up the road.'

Their words, despite the best intention, cut into me deeply.

'We love you,' they added, before finally letting go.

I took a deep breath, determined not to allow my voice to crack and reveal my anguish.

'I love you both so much,' I replied, and then it happened.

I stood and watched as the three of them left the house; my whole world and everything I had known for the last 24 years disappeared right before my eyes. On Thursday evening I had a wife, two children, two dogs and a cat. Now, on Saturday morning, it was just the cat and me.

I don't even recall what I did next.

I remember vividly the thoughts which ran through my head though. I thought about how I would no longer be able to just walk upstairs in the evening and kiss the children goodnight, or peek my head around the door for a second and watch them sleeping. I began to wonder how I was going to survive financially, with only one income and ultimately the sale of the house. I started to fret about how quickly I would need to find another home and, like a tidal wave, it all came crashing down on me.

To make matters worse I felt I had nobody to turn to. Mom was the only person I could confide in, but she and her fella had flown out to Cyprus for two weeks the previous morning, just as it had all happened, so she wasn't around and I didn't want to disrupt their holiday with my problems.

I couldn't face the thought of life without the children and, even though they would be nearby, I knew deep down it was inevitable this would change everything. Hours later I found myself sat at the top of the stairs with the loft-hatch open, to expose a beam sturdy enough to carry my weight.

The hopelessness was overwhelming and those feelings of complete failure I had felt six-months earlier rushed back with such force I was physically sick. The tears were streaming down my face. I knew what I was contemplating was wrong, but I didn't have the strength to stop myself. I needed somebody to talk to and I picked up the phone and began to text:-

Hi. I need to see you. Would you come over please?

It was only about 15 minutes before she arrived.

Bizarrely, the very person who had created the situation was the only one I could turn to in that moment. I think I needed some familiarity; someone who knew what was happening and who I didn't have to explain anything to.

We talked for around 30 minutes before she left and during that time we agreed some basics. I would remain in the house, the children would continue to come around straight from school on some of the days and have their evening meal there, and she would carry on paying half of the mortgage, until such time as we sold the house. I didn't tell her what I had been contemplating but that afternoon, just by coming over, she saved my life.

In all honesty it didn't take me long to get myself together and begin picking up the pieces.

Although I'd never had anything to do with the finances (I trusted her implicitly and didn't see the point of two people dealing with those things), I soon took control of my own accounts and got to grips with bills etc.

I saw the children regularly, still cooked tea for them on the days when they came over from school and began to get used to life on my own. Of course it was horrible returning to a three-bedroom house every night alone, when I'd been used to a constant hive of activity for the previous 12 years, but I soon got used to it.

I realised soon after that I didn't miss her at all.

She had been absolutely right; we were no longer right for each other and were both just plodding along in a loveless marriage for the sake of the children. In honesty I had felt the same, but I had resigned myself that I would never make that move, at least until the children had grown up and moved out of the family home. I guess she was braver than me.

Over the coming months I began to surround myself with friends and, to avoid too much time alone at home, I began to socialise more. I loved my new-found freedom, but as time went on something began to weigh heavily on my mind.

All of my immediate friends were now aware of the separation, but it would be only a matter of time before people began to ask questions. Photographs on Facebook would show only me and the girls, never the family, and with my social life expanding it was becoming more obvious something had changed.

Facebook is a curious place!

An army of 'virtual' friends sharing information about their day-to-day lives, posting comments, sharing funny moments and wishing each other well in new jobs, anniversaries and birthdays. I consider many of the people on my Facebook page to be friends, even though we may not see each other from one year to the next – if at all – and although you could argue it was nobody's business but mine, I felt I needed to let people know what had happened.

I wasn't seeking sympathy or attention, but

Facebook had become an integral part of my life, and I believe if you make that commitment to bring people into your life, you should share the good with the bad. Whether they be friends you see regularly, or people you simply converse with from afar, they are still friends as far as I'm concerned.

It was partly a selfish move too.

If I posted something to let people know it would save me having to explain time and time again as I bumped into them further down the line. I didn't want to have to think before every post, taking care not to say the wrong thing and invite questions. Not only that, but the house had been put on the market and, with a buyer agreed, would hopefully complete around the end of November.

So, I decided the time was right and I began to type:-

I've thought long & hard about posting this and very nearly didn't, but I've got a lot of people on here who I consider friends (even those I don't see from one year to the next) so have decided to make it public knowledge that for the first time in 24 years I'm single again.

Because we all share photographs and exchange comments on Facebook, it is inevitable that sooner or later somebody would notice, so I thought it would just be easier to write a post and put it out there.

I'm a pretty private person and I'm not posting this for attention or to see a long list of sympathetic comments below, but equally I don't want to pretend to be something I'm not going forward or have to consider every post I write in future to avoid somebody asking the question or putting their foot in it. I've got so many changes in my life coming up that it would be hard to hide them and to be honest - I don't have the energy or inclination to be bothered to do that.

Its human nature to want to support people when shit happens to them, but I really want to stress that I don't want anybody to post anything negative in any way, shape or form towards my ex. People change and life goes on and the most important thing is that our kids aren't affected so please, if you do post anything - remember it's possible they could see it. To be honest - the last couple of months have proved to me just how many good friends I have and for those just finding out, you don't need to post a comment for me to know that you give a damn.

So - onwards & upwards. They say life begins at 40 so here goes............ Watch this space – 5 Nov 2014

The response overwhelmed me!

118 people 'liked' the post and there were 93 comments, ranging from simple messages of sorrow for the situation to much longer expressions of support and encouragement.

Some of the words these people wrote were truly moving and gave me great strength and validation of the person I am.

I found that, although spread far and wide, people did care and I had much greater support network than I realised. In many ways it was a relief to finally have it out in the open and sharing this post with my friends effectively drew a line in the sand for me.

It was time to move forward with my life and broaden my horizons.

NINETEEN

......Well, the suits have officially been put into retirement and tomorrow starts a new career adventure. Have some great memories & made some brilliant friends but can't wait to get started at my new job – 22 Feb 2015

Christmas was an incredibly tough time!

I had been settled into my apartment for just over a month when it arrived and was loving my new home, but the thought of spending Christmas morning alone, for the first time in my life, had been weighing me down. When I woke that day I had a choice; wallow in my own misery until the children arrived, or get out and do something I enjoyed to fill the time. So, with the sun shining and the crisp-frost now beginning to fade, I pulled on my boots and set off for a long walk.

It was during this time that I made some decisions.

Whilst I loved the people I worked with and would be sad to leave them behind, I needed to find a new job. Now I was on my own, I needed to think seriously about my financial future and at the forefront of this was a desire to get back onto the property-ladder.

Renting was a good short-term solution, but I felt

that if I wasn't working towards owning my own property again, in 25 years' time I'd be no further on than I was now and have no equity to serve as a nest-egg for my retirement.

The estate-agency business is heavily weighted by commissions; you need to sell lots of houses to generate a good income and I just wasn't that great. Not only that, I realised if I wanted to get back on the property-ladder I would need a steady, reliable income on which to base a mortgage.

I needed to know – every month and without fail – that I could make the repayment and felt the ever-changing estate-agency market was far too risky a business on which to rely. So the decision was made and I began to scout around for a new challenge.

It didn't take long and, on 23rd February 2015, I joined a small company situated in the picturesque village of Henley-In-Arden, in Warwickshire.

The company's purpose was to help small businesses achieve their dreams, offering advice and solutions where a business owner may have hit a wall with their progression. My role would be to provide copywriting services to the clients, writing e-mail sequences and sales-pages for their campaigns and wow, what a different environment it was.

The average age in the business was around 24 years and, at 40, I was the oldest there. That said, I've never really acted my age (I tried it once and didn't like it) and always felt more comfortable around younger people, so it suited me to a tee. That aside, the dress-code was casual and the start time in the mornings was 9.30am, meaning I wouldn't have to part myself from my duvet until much later; a definite plus for someone who struggles with early mornings.

I settled into the new role quickly and thoroughly enjoyed the challenge. Although I knew I had a natural ability with words I had never worked in this field before, so I loved learning a new trade and completely immersed myself in the role. The pay wasn't great, but it was fixed and I could survive.

Shortly after joining I was asked to assist with the next company conference, to be held in Heathrow, London. The event would bring together key business speakers from across the world, with over 500 delegates in the room, across three action-packed days. Needless to say these conferences were exhausting, but as a team we always managed to have some fun.

The days were long, beginning with a briefing at 7am and – more often than not – would not end until after 9pm in the evening, following a drinks reception with the delegates. Of course, the team would then hit the bar to wind-down before doing it all again the following day and, it was during these moments that the team really bonded. At this first conference, myself and one of the delegates were the last men standing and, having only achieved 1½ hours sleep that night, I vowed never to repeat my folly.

Of course, that was until the next one!

I've always loved socialising. Never the kind to be out every weekend clubbing, but one of those who – on those occasions I did hit the town – would go hell for leather and really make the most of it. I didn't have great track record though, not even making it beyond the champagne-reception at one work's Christmas party and sustaining an alcohol-induced pole dancing injury in a club in Malta; a twisted knee which still gives me problems some 10 years later.

The trip to Malta had been a last-minute thing for work; a promotional campaign funded by one of the suppliers when I worked at Unipart. As part of the marketing team I had been asked to attend and there was no way I was going to pass up such a great opportunity. Three days in Malta, accommodation at the 5-star Radisson Blu Hotel in St Julian's – overlooking St

George's bay – with all meals included and the opportunity to relax around the pool among other things. The hotel was just a 10 minute walk from the main strip of bars and clubs and of course, where there's a bar there's mischief to be had.

The team organising the trip had warned us on arrival that we had a full itinerary planned for the following day and, although they wouldn't tell us what was in store for us, they urged us to take it easy with the drinks. Needless to say a handful of the group (myself included) ignored this advice and sought out the bars. I can't be sure what time we rolled back into the hotel, but I do know that across the three nights, I slept in my room for around 5½ hours in total.

There were a few slightly pale faces around the breakfast table that morning and it was about to get a whole lot worse.

'Right gang,' one of the organisers announced, trying to attract everyone's attention, 'hopefully you didn't have too much to drink last night as we have organised a boat excursion around the bay and a visit to Valletta.'

My heart sank!

What on Earth had I done? How was I going to survive the motion of the sea when I could barely keep my breakfast down on dry land?

As we boarded the boat the sun was beating down upon us and dehydration began to take hold of my already delicate body. Malta is a stunning place and, despite my hangover beginning to take full effect I marvelled at the idyllic surroundings; the craggy rocks against which the crystal-clear Mediterranean ocean crashed, the gargantuan vessels which floated in the great harbour of Valletta and, the somewhat understated (far from it) yacht belonging to Roman Abramovich. It was all there, along with a rich tapestry of history as its backdrop.

The whole three-day adventure was a bit of a blur, although I do recall one incident, after another drunken night, which created much amusement for the group when I shared the story.

Following a pretty heavy night in the clubs we were due to enjoy some free-time on the second full day and, while most of the gang were outside enjoying the sunshine, I decided to grab a short power-nap in my room in a vain attempt to recharge my batteries. After a quick shower I set my alarm for one hours' time and flopped, stark naked, onto the luxurious king-sized bed.

My head had barely hit the pillow before I slipped into a much needed sleep; a loss of consciousness so deep the hotel could have been raided by the SAS and I probably would have woken afterwards, wondering why the windows were broken and bullet holes peppered the walls.

I reached out for the alarm, now screaming for my attention, and hit the button to silence the incessant buzzing it emitted. I headed for the bathroom to take a pee and, as I stood there relieving myself I looked around the room.

I was puzzled!

I was absolutely certain I had dropped my towel onto the floor following my shower. I was equally as certain I hadn't re-folded it and placed it upon the shelf where it now sat, looking as fresh as if the room had been turned. Then it hit me. Somebody had been into the room as I slept and had changed the towels.

I was horrified.

The poor maid must have innocently knocked my door for housekeeping and, receiving no answer, assumed the room was clear. Upon entering she would have been greeted by the sight of my skinny white-arse sprawled across the bed, balls sticking-out between by legs and not a stitch of dignity in sight. I'm surprised I didn't wake to find a paper swan placed carefully on my butt cheek and am thankful to this day that the incident occurred before the existence of Facebook. Otherwise, I feel certain that my bottom would be out there in cyberspace for the whole world to see and trust me when I say, you'd need a long course of therapy to help you get over the sight of that.

I wish I could say I learned my lesson that night, but of course I didn't. Many years down the line, at another business conference, I would encounter one of the most surreal and bizarre moments of my life, following another drinks reception at the Ibis Hotel in Earl's Court, London.

With the party over and most people heading somewhat sensibly for their beds, a few of the team and a handful of delegates decided to seek out a bar for another drink or two. One of the guys, a handsome fella in his early 20s, assured us he knew the area and he could lead us straight to a pub that would still be open. If you've ever been to the Earls Court area of London you'll probably already know that he was talking shit.

Central London is renowned for its nightlife, but once you stray east of the river, or further afield than the West End, you'll find most places are closed by 1am and that's exactly what we discovered; unfortunately, not before we had walked over a mile to find them in the first place. Disheartened, we had returned to the hotel and settled for a coffee in the foyer, before heading off to bed ourselves.

Had it not been for some of our exhibitors walking through the hotel doors just at the moment we were about to retire to our comfy rooms, that's where the story would have ended; but alas, it was about to get very strange.

'Hey guys, how you doing?' one of them asked. 'What you doing drinking coffee?'

'There's bugger all else on offer,' one of our group grumbled in reply. 'The hotel bar is closed and there's nowhere open around here to go for another drink.'

'Sure there is,' came the reply, 'we've just come back

from a bar about 100m down the road.'

'You've got to be kidding?' I replied, 'we've just walked over a mile and back looking for somewhere and you're telling us if we'd turned right instead of left then we'd have saved ourselves a long walk and got a drink as well?'

We all looked at each other in disbelief.

'I don't suppose they're still open are they?' I continued.

'Well, yeah,' he said, 'but it's a bit of a strange place. It's a gay bar and you'll have to tap on the window to get in because it's locked.'

'Sounds dodgy to me,' one of the guys added.

'Yeah, it does, but could be a laugh,' came another.

'Are you guys going to come back down if we go and take a look?' I asked the four who had just returned.

They looked at each other for confirmation and, with just a little coaxing, agreed to get us through the door of their secret establishment.

'What are we waiting for then?' I asked my group. 'There's a bar open down there and we're sat here drinking coffee. Let's go!'

In less than 10 minutes we found ourselves standing at the doorway of a shabby looking terraced-building on a corner, somewhere in London.

The brickwork looked well-weathered and the door itself had peeling paintwork, with a net-curtain of all things restricting the view of the inside. One of the guys who had brought us here knocked on the glass and, a few seconds later, a face appeared at the door.

'We've come back and brought a few friends,' one of the group announced, 'can we come back in?'

The guy inside smiled and unlatched the door. We were in!

'Heyyyy, I knew you couldn't stay away for long brother,' came the greeting. 'Come on in.'

My eyes darted around the room. It was the smallest

club I've ever seen. Half a dozen chairs, a small bar and a big screen on the wall. I've been in some 'spit & sawdust' places in my time, but this was something else. If the Wetherspoon chain were Tesco Finest, then this place was value-brand at best; but I liked it. No frills, decent music and most importantly, the bar was open.

With the exception of our group of nine, there were just three other people in the place. The owner was shimmying around the place without a shirt, his toned muscular-physique completely defying the 50-something years he claimed to have behind him. He had a friendly demeanour; chatty, full of fun and very flirty with the guys in a cheeky, non-offensive way.

The other two were much different.

The guy seated to the right of the bar looked like he had just stepped off the catwalk of a fashion show in Milan, or somewhere equally as exotic. Trendy jeans, a crisp-white shirt with dark chest-hair sprouting from the open collar and tanned, good-looks. With jet-black hair, brilliant-white teeth and perfectly manicured stubble, he cut a handsome figure and oozed the sort of confidence one can only carry when completely at ease with your appearance.

It was the third guy, the one behind the bar, who put me slightly on edge.

In stark contrast to Mr Milan his appearance was scruffy and his face somewhat unfriendly. With eastern-European features and an accent difficult to place, there was something very unnerving about his presence. His teeth were stained and uneven, his beard unkempt, and his eyes held a vacant stare, giving the impression the workings of the mind behind them were somewhat sinister. In short, he wouldn't have looked out of place in one of the *Hostel* movies, wearing a blood-soaked apron and wielding a junior hack-saw.

No sooner had we ordered some drinks and begun to chat among ourselves than the scent of weed began to waft around the place. My head spun to the right, towards Mr Milan and there he was, joint in hand, smoking openly as if it was nothing out of the ordinary. In typical English style, the first thought to cross my mind was that he wasn't allowed to smoke indoors and I was instantly reminded of a Victoria Wood sketch I had seen some years before.

'Last time I went Intercity there were a couple across the aisle having sex. Of course, this being a British train, nobody said anything. Then they finished, they both lit up a cigarette and this woman stood up and said, Excuse me, I think you'll find this is a non-smoking compartment.'

I don't have the best sense of smell. Ever since I conquered an addiction to Vicks Sinex nasal-spray several years before (I'm not kidding), my ability to detect odours has deteriorated significantly and therefore, I knew this must be a fairly strong 'cigarette' he was smoking for me to have smelt it so quickly.

Thankfully, drugs have never featured in my life and I've never really been exposed to them, but fuelled by the alcohol I seized my opportunity to be cheeky. I didn't need to speak a word; one knowing look and he handed me the joint.

I raised it to my mouth and inhaled deeply. The herby taste coursed through my senses and deep into my lungs and I held it there for a few seconds, before breathing out. There was something truly calming about it and after a long and stressful two days' work at the conference it was most certainly good timing. I turned towards Mr Milan to hand it back to him, but to my surprise he was already in the process of rolling himself another and he motioned for me to keep it.

I declined!

The craziness of the situation suddenly dawned upon me. Here I was locked in a gay pub in the middle of

London, Vodka in one hand and a joint in the other, surrounded by delegates attending a conference at which I was working. In my defence, having spent the previous few hours with them all I knew it wasn't an issue and there was nobody in the group who would be offended or concerned, otherwise I wouldn't have done it.

I was definitely right about the strength of the joint though and within minutes, felt thoroughly relaxed. The owner continued to flirt shamelessly, at one point grabbing the front of his trousers to reveal a pretty significant bulge inside.

'Bloody hell,' I exclaimed, with a surprised look on my face, 'you could get arrested carrying that around.'

My reaction seemed to confuse him. I think he expected me to run a mile or be shocked.

'You're not…' he paused for a second between the words, '…are you?'

I'm a natural-born flirt myself, I always have been, so couldn't resist winding him up and enjoying the sheer confusion in his eyes. I simply raised my eyebrows and smiled in response but, as open-minded as I am, I really didn't expect what happened next.

As I turned to walk away I felt a tap on my shoulder and turned around again. One hand was pushing down the waistband of his jeans and in the other, the biggest willy you've ever seen in your life. Before I could even react he began to swing it around like a helicopter propeller, before stuffing it back inside its holding pen. The look of sheer horror on my face must have said it all and I turned heel quicker than I have ever done before and made towards the rest of my group.

1-nil to him!

We finally returned to the hotel sometime around 3.45am and, after the morning briefing, the reality of the night before began to kick in. Why can I never seem to say no to a party? With yet another nine-hour stretch ahead of us, followed by the breakdown of the equipment, a re-load of the van and a 2½ hour drive home, a hangover was certainly not the best way to begin the day. I think it was only the camaraderie of the team I worked with that got me through, but I made it.

The team were great and I made some truly good friends there, but over time I began to feel that I didn't quite fit. The business was quite unique and the guy who owned it was all about positivity. Meetings always began with each person giving a positive-focus, something about which they were feeling good, either work-related or something happening in your personal life.

This was all well and good until you found yourself in your third meeting of the day, struggling to come up with anything more than 'I just had a nice sandwich for lunch.' It all felt a tad contrived and began to grate on me a little.

One of the practices at the very heart of the business was the use of metrics. Everyone had at least three personal metrics to report on, by which they were measured, and even the lady who packed envelopes and ordered stationery had to report her numbers during the Monday morning meeting. The theory was, if you can't measure it, don't do it.

Sometime shortly after I started working there the boss decided we should do more as a team and a 'social' metric was introduced, with someone allocated to take responsibility for ensuring there was a social-event every month. To me it seemed crazy that you would implement such a rigid measurement for having fun, and kind of defeated the object; if people want to socialise with each other then they would surely arrange it themselves wouldn't they?

Anyway, following a vote the first team social was announced; a night in Birmingham for a Chinese meal and Karaoke. My heart sank. Two of my least favourite things. I'd only ever sang karaoke once before, in Malta, so I wasn't enamoured at the thought of a repeat performance in front of my new work colleagues. The problem was, I knew that both of the guys who ran the business would surely get up there, as would the majority of others, so I wasn't going to be the only one to sit it out.

The night arrived and before leaving the apartment I decided to lubricate the vocal-chords in preparation for the shenanigans ahead.

Two shots of Apple Sours and two decent-sized glasses of Pinot later, the taxi arrived. One of the guys with whom I was sharing the taxi had some Budweiser with him so, en route to Birmingham, this was added to the already precarious mix of alcohol in my system. As we arrived at the venue we were ushered upstairs to the function room above the main restaurant and I could already feel the effects of this bizarre cocktail. Next on the hit-list was Magners Cider, followed by some more green stuff, a Jack Daniel's shot and a large glass of Merlot.

Despite all of my previous groaning about not wanting a Karaoke night, it turned out to be one of the best evenings I'd had in a very long time. It would seem that, if you get me drunk and put a microphone in my hand, you'll struggle to get it back.

First up for me was a performance of the 4 Non Blonds track *What's Up*, along with a guy called Jack and the boss. Between us we absolutely slayed it, or should I say slaughtered? It was one of those typical Karaoke performances where somebody was off-key throughout the whole thing and, even if one or two of us could sing, nobody could get it back on course properly.

A bad start!

Other songs from the team included *Crazy Little Thing Called Love* by Queen, Lou Bega's infamous *Mambo No.5* and a word-perfect rendition of Will Smith's *Miami* by Nick, the other boss. Expectations were high following a promise from Alex, one of the nicest guys in the office and renowned for his dry sense of humour, who had signed up to perform the Flo Rida track, *Low*. Everybody was on their feet as he smashed his way through the song, complete with some dad-dancing and the occasional slut-drop for good measure.

I don't know for sure what the key driver was; the atmosphere, the other guys' wicked song choices or the alcohol, but I was wracking my brains, skimming through the thousands of options in the book, looking for something they just wouldn't expect from me. I wanted a song nobody would think in a thousand years I would get up and do.

Then, as I turned the page, there it was.

The slip of paper was duly completed and submitted without anyone's knowledge and we sat back and waited. The plan was for two of us to perform it, but that's not quite how it worked out.

The first they knew was when the song-title came up on the screen and, when the opening notes of the intro began to boom out, the confused looks on people's faces was priceless. Myself and Tim headed swiftly for the stage and grabbed the microphones.

A massive cheer went up from the team.

I'm a huge fan of Eminem's first three albums and must have sung along to *The Real Slim Shady* a hundred times or more over the years, so I felt pretty confident the words were lurking somewhere deep within my memory. Thankfully they came; one after another every single lyric flowed as if I'd written the thing myself and people's mouths began to drop in complete and utter shock.

Unfortunately for Tim it seemed he had completely misunderstood the song we'd agreed to sing and it became apparent very quickly that he knew precisely none of the words. So, after the first verse he bowed out, leaving me up there alone.

I was loving it!

When the chorus dropped everyone was on their

feet, breaking out their best moves on the dancefloor and singing along. It was, without question, a moment I'll never forget. I hadn't given any thought to what I would sing before going out that night but somehow, I'd delivered.

Something had changed.

If you'd asked me six months before this night to stand up and sing in front of twenty people, I'd have laughed in your face and flatly refused. My inhibitions would have served as a brick-wall through which I would stand no chance of breaking. I had always been crippled by the fears of what others may think of me and this had limited me throughout my life. I realised that night I was a completely different person to the one I'd always believed myself to be.

I'm unsure if I had been holding back until now, or if time had just rewarded me with more confidence in myself, but I was definitely more outgoing and prepared to try new things than ever before. Maybe I was having a mid-life crisis? Perhaps I was finally living the life I felt I had missed out on in my twenties? I'm not sure what it was but, for the first time in my adult life, I felt free!

"To get back my youth I would do anything in the world except take exercise, get up early or be respectable" - love this quote from Oscar Wilde's 'The Picture of Dorian Gray'. Great book! – 16 Jul 2015

TWENTY

……So - not washed the clothes I need, not packed my suitcase & not sorted holiday insurance yet. Oh, and got some work to finish before I go anywhere #ALittleBitLastMinute – 16 Apr 2015

The breakdown of my marriage prompted me to think long and hard about my life. What had I actually achieved for myself? Where had I travelled? Could I say with all honesty that I was happy with how things had played out, even prior to the break up?

As the dust settled and I began to come to terms with it, I made a promise to myself. Within the next 12 months I wanted a holiday.

My passport had expired eight years previously and knowing that we had no plans for a foreign holiday at the time, I didn't bother to renew. It seemed crazy to do it straight away and effectively waste a full year, since it wasn't going to get used. As it happened, if I had renewed it I would have wasted the majority of the 10 year lifespan, so it was most definitely one of my better decisions.

I had no idea where it would be, but with the

promise made to myself I set about the process of applying for a new passport and, in less than 21 days, it arrived. Now all I had to do was decide where its first use would be and with whom. I considered my options. Did I want to travel to see new places, or should my first priority be to find somewhere hot, complete with crystal-clear waters and soft, white, sandy beaches upon which to relax and reflect?

Money was, of course, a consideration. By the end of 2014 I was earning less than half the salary I had enjoyed just three years before and now, having sold the family home and renting a place on my own, finances were becoming increasingly tighter.

To rent a one-bedroom apartment (nothing flashy) I was spending almost my entire salary every month, purely on the essentials and maintenance payments for the children. I budgeted just £100 per month for food and had no budget in place for any unexpected problems.

I was far from being in trouble for the immediate future as I had the equity from the sale of the house in premium-bonds, but that was there to act as a deposit for a new property when I eventually came to buy again. I was absolutely determined that I was not going to touch this money, whatever happened.

I had never been extravagant with money; cars were never flashy and the most expensive item of clothing I owned was a pair of Nike trainers at around £50. Brands had never interested me and the vacations, when they happened, had only been beach holidays to Europe. However, with circumstances as they were and feeling weighed down by the insecurity of being alone for the first time in my adult life, I became very frugal with money and cut everything down to the barest minimum I could.

Weekly shopping bills were usually well under budget, sometimes surviving a whole week on just £14 and meals were carefully planned. Sunday evenings became food-preparation nights, usually something like a Lasagne or Cottage Pie, providing meals for the following three nights. Everything was value-branded with the exception of baked-beans which, in my humble opinion, must have the Heinz logo on them.

I became obsessed with checking my online banking and would log in every day, just to be certain no unexpected payments had left my account.

Always in the back of my mind was the thought that I needed to save, save, save as much as I possibly could, just in case something happened as there was nobody to fall back on; no second salary to act as a buffer if I were made redundant or if the washing machine just gave up one day. It was stressful at times because inevitably things did crop up, and every time I felt I'd managed to save a little it had to be allocated somewhere. I felt like I was doing everything I possibly could and getting absolutely nowhere.

That said, getting away somewhere was a priority and at the beginning of 2015 a long-term friend suggested a week in the sun. Andy had a mate who owned an apartment in Albufeira, Portugal, and if we could find a week where he wouldn't be using it himself, we could have it at no cost whatsoever. All we would need to find was the money for flights and a little spending money.

I couldn't believe it!

A free week in the sun, in a luxury-apartment. Somebody was smiling down on me and, with the flights booked for early June, I finally had something to look forward to. I was going abroad for the first time in eight years and I could not wait; the countdown had begun.

In the meantime I continued keeping my spending to a minimum and, although the change in career from estate agent to copywriter didn't yield an increase in salary, at least I knew for definite the net-pay figure which would be printed at the bottom of my payslip each month. That alone gave me a greater feeling of security and eased some of the worry I felt.

Shortly after beginning my new job I was asked to write some copy for a client who offered life-coaching services, at the heart of which was a principle called *The Law of Attraction*. I'll admit, when I was first introduced to her and learned the basis of her business, my first thought was 'what a load of old nonsense' and the ensuing conversation did little to change my preconceptions.

The lady in question was lovely.

I'd have placed her somewhere in her early 50s, with a friendly demeanour and clearly very well educated, asserting an air of authority which belied the fluffy nature of her business. I've always been respectful of others people's beliefs and opinions and, although ours differed greatly when it came to this particular area, I had learned many years before that one should never judge a book by its cover. To make assumptions about a person's character based upon their beliefs is a high-speed route to making an arse of yourself and that was a road I didn't wish to travel.

The Law of Attraction is essentially a new-age belief that, in some higher consciousness 'like attracts like'. The philosophy suggests that by focusing upon positive or negative thoughts, a person will attract positive or negative experiences into their life; in short, you reap what you sow. On a deeper level, practitioners of this principal believe that people and their thoughts are made up of pure energy and therefore believe that energy attracts energy.

In the same way I'm very sceptical about many of the paranormal experiences people report, I also struggle to buy into this stuff. However, on a much broader and more general level I'm totally on board.

Imagine for a moment you're in the canteen at work, waiting for the kettle to boil for your well-earned afternoon cuppa. You're generally in a good mood; not quite the kind of day which sees you skipping around the office, but you're feeling pretty good. Then, in walks Colin, carrying the weight of the world on his shoulders – like Eeyore's gloomy cloud – and you just know he's going to start complaining about how much work he has and how nobody works as hard as he does. What's your gut instinct when he walks in? Do you engage in conversation or quickly grab your mobile phone from your pocket and deliver an Oscar-winning performance of 'person on phone'? You'd probably avoid him like the plague because you just know that any conversation with him is going to bring you down.

In contrast, when Jenny comes shimmying into the room carrying a smile wider than Jim Carey in *The Mask*, you will most likely feel your own energy lift and be much more likely to want to share in whatever has created this good mood.

It is human nature to instinctively surround ourselves with like-minded people and that stretches beyond casual acquaintances, into friendships and relationships. The only people who are likely to want to surround themselves by the energy-vampires who suck the fun out of every situation, like a Dementor from the *Harry Potter* books, are other energy-vampires.

Where it all falls down for me is the belief that our thoughts can directly influence our health.

Authorities in this area assert that worry, stress, fear and other negative emotions make people sick, while positive thoughts of love and wellness can not only sustain a person's general health but even *cure* illnesses. Although it has been proven many times before through scientific study of the placebo-effect, where patients see an improvement in their health simply because they believe they are receiving treatment that will work, it's still too far-reaching for me to accept that simply visualising yourself as healthy and well can produce the physical equivalent.

Little did I realise at the time that, in less than 12

WHAT'S ON YOUR MIND?

months, I would test this theory for myself.

Henry Ford, the American Industrialist and founder of the Ford Motor Company famously said, 'Whether you think you can, or you think you can't, you're right.'

Here was a man who believed that hard work alone was not sufficient to achieve a person's dreams; asserting that belief was a major factor in the determination of achievement. Essentially, if you created a positive belief in your mind that your goal *was* achievable, then you could achieve it. In contrast, those who carry the mind-set that they can't do something, won't.

Ford didn't invent the automobile, but you could argue it was his absolute belief it could become an affordable, practical and viable option for many middle-class Americans, which led to his ultimate success. He once said, 'If I had asked people what they wanted, they would have said faster horses.'

He was a visionary!

Despise as I do those phrases such as 'think outside the box' and 'blue-sky thinking', heard so often in today's corporate environments, one thing is evident throughout history. Anyone who ever really achieved something significant shared one thing in common, a positive attitude.

Where all of this becomes infuriating for me is the way many people today seem to have forgotten that it's not all about positive thought and that, somewhere down the line, you actually have to *do* something.

Whether you consider your glass to be half-full or half-empty, the only way you're going to get it full is to get off your arse and pour something else into it. In my opinion, too many people blindly believe in the power of the universe and that, just by thinking something and believe it to be true, it will come.

You can visualise yourself stepping off the edge of a skyscraper and floating gracefully in mid-air all day long, but Newton has proven categorically that this won't be the outcome and you're going to hit the deck - hard.

If I were to sum up my thoughts on this subject, my quote would be:-

'Without ambition and belief you have nothing to aim for, but without hard work, you will have nothing.'

During our conversation we had talked very generally about life and work and, in response to a question about my personal goals, I had mentioned my desire to travel some more. There are certain places I'd love to experience and whilst I was in dire need of a week in the sun, lounging around the pool and simply relaxing, I told her of the buzz I get from visiting places with some historic background; Rome was, and still is, on my list of places to visit. I remember the conversation as if it were yesterday.

'What has prevented you from having travelled to these places already?' she asked, curious to understand more about the obstacles which had blocked my journey so far.

'Life got in the way,' was my reply. 'I married fairly young, had a family and fell into that age-old trap, where my sole purpose simply became supporting *those* choices.'

'So, what will you do differently now to allow you to achieve what you want and visit some of the places you've mentioned?' she quizzed.

I went on to explain a little about the breakdown of the marriage and how, at 40 years of age, I was now in a position – for the first time in my adult life – to think about myself and the things I would like to do.

'The only difficulty is,' I explained, 'although I now have all the freedom in the world, my financial situation as a result of living alone is likely to prevent me getting anywhere, at least for quite a few years.'

It felt quite odd, discussing my financial and personal situation with a complete stranger, but something within me felt that by sharing openly, there would be something to gain. It was completely intangible, yet quite powerful.

'You just need to believe it will happen,' came her reply. 'Picture yourself boarding that aeroplane, feel the sensation of your passport in your hand and most of all, visualise yourself doing it. It will happen!'

'Okay,' came my half-hearted reply, 'I'll definitely do that.'

The look on her face told me she knew I didn't really believe it and, throughout the consultation and subsequent conversations over the coming weeks she made reference to it a few times, gently reminding me that visualisation was the key to achieving what I wanted.

Picture it and it will come!

I did try. There were a few nights when, lying in bed, I chose to let the sheep count themselves in favour of trying to imagine some of the far-off places I'd love to visit. Since I have only ever seen photographs of places such as the Colosseum and St Peter's Basilica I found this difficult, so instead I tried to visualise the types of buildings I would love to visit and imagined myself standing before them.

I tried to feel the heat of the sun I longed to feel upon my skin, to smell the heady scents of local cuisine wafting through the air and imagine the excitement I would feel, gazing upon some of the world's most amazing and historic landmarks.

Alas, for as much as I tried I have never been great at visualisation and besides, my common sense kept telling me that, regardless of how much I thought about these places, I wouldn't be able to afford them for some time – if ever – and therefore I settled for looking forward to my sun holiday in Portugal, now less than 12 weeks away. Then, something unexpected happened. One afternoon while eating lunch at the office, I received a phone call from Hazel.

'Eh up,' came the familiar greeting, 'I wanted to ask you if you'd be interested in joining myself and Carolyn for the Transylvania Tour in April? I wasn't sure if you'd be able to get holiday from your new job, but if you can I'd love it if you could come.'

There was absolutely no question in my mind; I wanted to go!

'That would be amazing, let me speak to my boss and check that I can book the time off and I'll call you straight back.'

It took me less than 15 minutes to complete the holiday request form, get it signed and call her back.

'I'm in,' I chirped, already excited at the thought of the trip. 'Thank you so much for asking me.'

This was second tour of Transylvania that Haunted Happenings had undertaken, but would be the first time I had ventured outside the UK with them.

As I drove home that night, excited to read more about the planned itinerary, something dawned upon me.

Despite having gone through the motions of those visualisation techniques, I hadn't thought for one second about actually travelling anywhere, other than my forthcoming trip to Portugal. I hadn't believed for a moment that I'd have the means or the opportunity to get away anywhere else and yet, here I was being offered an all-expenses paid trip to Romania, to help with the running of a ghost hunting weekend-break.

The client's words rang in my ears.

She had been absolutely right when she said 'it will happen' and as hard as I tried to brush that off as pure coincidence, I couldn't help but smile. Perhaps the universe was listening when I said I wanted to see new places? Maybe there really was something to this positive thinking and visualisation? Whatever the answer and however it was that this opportunity came to me, I was thrilled and the anticipation as the trip approached left me feeling great.

We landed at Henri Coandă International Airport in Otapani, situated 16.5 km north of Bucharest's city centre, on the evening of 17th April 2015. In addition to Hazel, Carolyn and myself, the trip would be shared by 24 excited guests who turned out to be truly lovely people. The temperatures were unusually warm for April and the airport, Romania's busiest, was still teeming with activity despite the lateness of the hour. The cases arrived with a speed *never* enjoyed upon arrival at any of the UK's airports, and we were soon on the coach for the very short transfer to the hotel, at which we would spend our first night.

The Rin Airport Hotel in Otopeni was stunning. Ornate, sparkling chandeliers hung gracefully above the foyer, casting fragments of multi-coloured light upon the polished marble-floors beneath. Light-oak coloured columns rose from the ground like giant monoliths, contrasting sharply with the gleaming stainless-steel railings of the upper floors.

The bedrooms were well proportioned, with comfortable king-sized beds and ultra-modern bathroom suites. If this was what Romania had to offer, I was absolutely sold on the country already. However, we had a packed itinerary ahead for the next three days and so an early night (and an early start) were required.

The following morning we were joined at breakfast by our Romanian tour guide, who would be with us every step of the way for the rest of our stay. At just 25 years of age he carried with him an air of confidence and professionalism you wouldn't expect in a man of his age. That's not intended to patronise; simply that the fine-line between arrogance and confidence is often only crossed with the passing of years and, with more life experience than you would generally have been exposed to by his age.

He was a handsome guy; not traditionally good-looking or blessed with the chiselled-features you would expect to see on the cover of Vogue magazine, but a friendly face with ruffled brown-hair, blue/green eyes and a wispy beard. He had the type of smile that could put a person at ease in an instant and what struck me most about him was his sense of humour.

Despite being born and raised in Romania he truly understood the strange nuances of British humour. Over the coming days Hazel, Carolyn and I spent a lot of time with him and, with the marriage separation behind me and the divorce already underway, I laughed more than I had done in a very long time.

There are very few times in your life when you meet somebody new and instantly click. I don't mean romantically, but those people who – despite vastly different backgrounds and even different first languages – you find a connection somewhat above the norm. For me, he was one of those people.

As our first day evolved it became apparent very quickly that we shared a similar sense of humour, and by the end of the trip there had been a number of occasions where words were not even necessary; somebody would say something unintentionally funny and a simple exchange of eye contact with a sly smile would suffice, to let the other know that the innuendo hadn't gone unnoticed.

The journey from Otopeni to our next hotel in Bran, Transylvania, was broken by two planned visits, affording us an opportunity to see some of the amazing places this country offered.

First up, we would visit the final resting place of the legendary warrior Vlad the Impaler. The location, a monastery on a remote island in the middle of Snagov Lake is accessed only by boat or footbridge. Built somewhere around the time of Vlad's grandfather, the monastery is now surrounded by idyllic gardens and is, without question, the most tranquil place I have ever encountered.

On arrival my mind was cast back to those nights during which I had visualised imaginary places of historic value and now, here I stood right before one, the glorious afternoon sun glistening on the surrounding lake, its warmth matched only by the feelings of happiness and peace this isolated place evoked.

Inside the small building were just two rooms. Colourful-frescos adorned the walls and columns – some dating back to the 15th century – and beyond them lay Vlad's tomb, marked only by a marble-edged stone slab at the foot of the alter and a small portrait of the man himself. His headless body is said to have been discovered in the woods around Bucharest by the monks of Snagov Monastery and brought here to be buried, since both Vlad and his father had donated money to the church.

I had no expectations before travelling to Romania.

If I'm honest, before looking on the map I really wasn't sure exactly where the place was let alone what to expect, and I suspect it to be the same for many of those who venture here. The landscapes are phenomenal; picturesque houses in a variety of architectural styles sit comfortably against the exquisite backdrop of the Carpathian mountain range and, but for the occasional rural village – where wild dogs roam freely – I was astounded by the sheer beauty of the place.

I've never been one to take things for granted in life, although perhaps it could be argued I didn't apply that attitude to my own family, and throughout this whole trip I felt hugely grateful for the opportunity I'd been given. Yes, I was there to work and it should never be underestimated just how hard the guides work during these kind of excursions.

You have to be completely focused upon the customer, after all they're the reason you've been given the chance to be here yourself. Whether it be a single night's ghost hunting in an old pub or a three-day trip around Romania, the customer must always be at the forefront of your mind. You're always looking out for anybody who may have become isolated in any way, especially those attending on their own, and are constantly watching people's body language for any developing issues. After all, it is human-nature for people to rub each other up the wrong way and, since we're all different animals, if you put a group of 24 people together for three whole days there are bound to be some clashes.

Careful and discreet management of these situations is what lies at the heart of making such an excursion a success and where the true skill of any tour-guide lies.

Our tour guide was amazing at this and to be gifted with somebody who skilfully combined charisma, charm and wit with the ability to keep 24 people engaged – while sharing insights into the history of the places we were visiting – shows a true professional at work.

Following lunch and a welcome introduction to the Romanian beer, Ciuc, we headed to the stunning Peleş Castle, a Neo-Renaissance royal-palace, situated high in the Carpathian Mountains, near Sinai. Completed in 1914, the castle comprises over 170 rooms, mostly Baroque influenced, and houses over 4,000 pieces of arms and armour – accompanied by a collection of paintings numbering more than 2,000. The palace, surrounded by woodland and nestled high above a valley, blends romanticism and opulence and attracts almost half a million visitors annually.

It was breathtakingly beautiful, and for me one of those moments in life where you can completely lose yourself, immersed in the surroundings.

However, at the heart of this trip was the impending overnight ghost hunt at the home of the title-character in Bram Stoker's *Dracula*, the imposing and allegedly-haunted Bran Castle.

I'm somewhat ashamed to say I'd never read the novel (I have since), although I was fully aware of the legend of this infamous Vampire Count's wicked, bloodthirsty ways and – for the first time in ages – I was truly looking forward to getting underway with a paranormal investigation in this vast fortress.

By the time we made this trip I'd been ghost hunting with Haunted Happenings for almost six years so, as with any repetitive thing in life, the excitement of it had begun to wane.

Visiting the same locations time after time, albeit with different guests, it is easy to forget how exciting it can be to explore somewhere completely new and now, here was something totally different. Not only were we on foreign soil, in the very heartland of the myths and legends of vampires, werewolves and spirits, but we would have this vast castle completely to ourselves for the night, in which to carry out our own experiments and discover some of those said to still inhabit it's walls.

I was truly excited and had high hopes that something may happen. That phrase 'be careful what you wish for' has never been more apt, for that night I most certainly wasn't prepared for what awaited us.

The early part of the evening had been fairly uneventful. Some knocks and bangs had been heard for which we could find no explanation, and some of the ghost-hunting equipment we had taken registered high EMF (electro-magnetic field) readings, but there was nothing concrete or outstanding to note. However, it was later in the night that something truly terrifying happened.

The castle houses a collection of medieval torture-equipment, some original and some replica, in a series of rooms on the upper floors, directly above the chapel. The group I was working with at the time, most of whom had ghost hunted many times with us before in the UK, were standing in a circle – with our hands connected – surrounded by these barbaric instruments of torture and death.

A short while into the vigil, many of the group became aware of a noise from the corner of the room, seemingly emanating from one of the pieces of equipment.

The Rack, considered one of the most feared methods of torture in England, was employed as a method of extracting information during medieval times. The poor victim would be strapped upon a huge piece of wood, arms and legs tied with rope to the four corners, which were attached to two giant rollers. A handle at each end would turn the wheel, thus tightening the ropes and stretching the limbs, causing excruciating pain. Ligaments would tear, muscles would rip apart and limbs would literally be pulled from their joints, dislocating arms, legs and shoulders with each slow, agonising turn.

The greatest misconceptions of The Rack are that the victim would ultimately die from the injuries they sustained at the hands of their torturer. In truth they would be left crippled and in agonising pain, but not dead. If they continued to withhold the information sought, the next stop was often a visit to the executioner's block and, since many of those subjected to The Rack were innocent, they could not provide the information their captor was trying to extract.

In short, once strapped to that contraption your days were numbered regardless.

Another misconception, perpetuated by television dramas such as *The Tudors*, is that it was a common form of torture; it wasn't!

The Rack was reserved for those believed to be withholding information pertinent to issues of treason; crimes or plots against King and country. Either way it existed and here, in the very room in which we were carrying out this night-time vigil, we were standing right beside one, convinced we could hear a noise which sounded like the creaking of a tightening rope, emanating from its position.

'Shhhhhh,' came one of the voices from within our group. 'I can hear something.'

We all listened, our hushed voices creating a deafening silence. *Creak…creak…creak*

'Did you hear it?' came another.

'Yeah, it's coming from over here, right behind me,' came one of the men's voices, standing with his back to the equipment in question.

It went silent!

We waited with bated breath for a few seconds, before calling out to the spirits.

'If there's somebody here with us who's connected to this place, please could you make that noise again?'

I'll admit now, the sceptic within me didn't expect it to happen, assuming it had just been a random noise, misinterpreted by our eager senses.

Then it came again.

'Oh my God,' it's definitely coming from over here, came the man's voice again, 'right behind me.'

We listened intently for a couple of minutes, asking for the noise to be repeated and each time we asked, it was heard again by the majority of the group. There were however a couple of people standing farthest away who couldn't hear the sound so, having suggested we all change positions within the room and re-form the circle, we released hands and started to move.

As a company Haunted Happenings carry out risk-assessments for every location and take great care to advise guests of the potential hazards they may encounter, and in all my years nobody has ever been hurt. However, it was that decision to move places at that moment which prevented a potential accident that night.

In addition to The Rack there was another piece of equipment – around which our group had form the circle – consisting of a rectangular base, upon which two vertical frames were positioned. One merely had a carved-out semi-circle, over which the victim's arched back would rest and the other contained two holes – through which their feet would be locked into place – resembling the stocks through which people's heads and hands are often placed at village fetes.

The main difference here was there were no soggy sponges being launched at the poor souls who found themselves subjected to this ending. Instead, they were positioned into the equipment and water pumped into their stomach, until such time as it could take no more and would rupture, causing certain and agonising death.

We had spent quite some time in this room already, moving into position and conducting our vigil, yet at no point had there been any indication either of these uprights were loose, or even that they could be moved. However, literally seconds after one lady had stepped from within the framework of the base, there was a deafening crash.

Screams and confusion filled the room in an instant.

'Stand still,' I shouted at the top of my voice, desperate to be heard and prevent anybody hurting themselves in the darkened room. 'Turn on your torches and stand still.'

As the room began to illuminate with the reassuring glow of torchlight, the source of the noise became apparent. One of the vertical pieces had come crashing down and was now resting against the base-frame, exactly where the lady had been standing merely seconds earlier. Horror consumed me as the realisation of how close this encounter had been dawned upon me and the potential damage it could have caused.

People's faces dropped; genuine fear and confusion etched across them – mine included.

'Did any of us touch the frame when we moved?' I asked, convinced we must have caused this in some way. 'It's not a problem if we did,' I added, 'I just need to know if *we* caused that to happen.'

I chose my words carefully, using 'we' and 'us' instead of 'you', to avoid anybody feeling accused.

Everyone said no and the lady who had been closest

to it confirmed she had stepped in the opposite direction, and had been the last to move.

With people beginning to calm a little I stepped forward to re-position the frame and was astounded by what I discovered. My scepticism wouldn't allow me to believe this wasn't an accident and that, inadvertently, somebody had brushed against the frame causing it to fall; they were probably just too embarrassed to say.

However, when I tried to lift the wood back into place, the sheer weight of it took me by surprise. I had to bend my knees and use all of my strength just to lift it. Reluctant to cause any damage, I chose not to recreate the incident, but once back in place, we applied pressure to the upright and concluded it would have taken a deliberate push – with some force and determination – to make it fall in the way it had.

With the combination of the cranking noise we had heard from The Rack and the near-miss we had just encountered, we were thankful it was time to re-group with the others and end the night. Bran Castle had most certainly given us all something to think about!

Back at the Hotel Dolce Vita, our base for the weekend, the team and a few guests congregated in the hotel's reception foyer.

It was now 3am and the bar had closed long ago, but now we were finally off-duty and only had the return journey to deal with the following day, we needed some time to unwind and headed straight upstairs to raid the mini-bar stock from our rooms, which was then laid out on the table in the foyer.

We had a great time sharing stories, telling jokes and really getting to know each other; some ongoing friendships were forged that night.

During the ghost hunt Carolyn had expelled a deafening scream during a vigil in the chapel, causing the whole group to react with further screams, frightening the group I was working with in the torture room above. As we laughed about this I was reminded of an incident at the London Tombs many years before. Sited beneath London Bridge at the edge of the River Thames, this is a scare-attraction by day but at night, one of the many terrifying locations at which we conducted our paranormal events.

Once again, the beginning of the night had been uneventful, and by the time we reached the break the team had realised we were losing the guests' interest. So, I suggested to the host for the night that we create two larger groups and see if we could raise their energy and enthusiasm a bit, before continuing with the vigils. Having agreed it may help we separated into two groups, each with two of the team members.

Our host and medium both headed down to the sewers area, while the other team member and I took a group into a very dark corridor, commonly referred to as the Carriage-Room due to the presence of a Victorian carriage and genuine taxidermy horse.

With the whole group standing in a circle in the darkness of this room, all holding hands, we began our séance. The energy was low and, in a desperate attempt to encourage the spirits to come forward and show some interest in us, I suggested we create some noise.

'Does anybody know any good jokes?' I asked. 'Maybe a bit of laughter from us will help to raise everyone's energy and attract them nearer.'

There was a pause, I presume while people tried desperately to come up with a joke worthy of sharing with 20 other people; then something happened.

With no prior warning the lady immediately to my right let out an ear-piercing scream.

My immediate reaction was to reach for my torch, but consumed with fear at whatever had just happened she clutched my hand with a vice-like grip, from which the great Houdini himself surely couldn't escape. Naturally, in the darkness of the room and with the anticipation of potential paranormal activity, the situation escalated quickly. The screaming became louder as, one after another, people began to join in.

I was mortified!

Why the fuck is everyone screaming?

In desperation I began to shake my arm to release myself from the constraints of her grip and, finally free, I turned on the torch to calm the group down. After a few seconds, I managed to speak.

'What happened to make you scream?' I asked the lady, still visibly terrified by her ordeal.

Her eyes were wide and her hands shaking as she spoke.

'I felt something hit me in the stomach, right here,' came her reply, indicating precisely the point on her body at which she had felt this contact. 'I know it wasn't anybody messing around as I was holding the hands of both people beside me.'

I reassured her and checked she was okay, then addressed the rest of the group.

'What else happened?' I asked, intrigued to discover if anyone had felt something similar, as they had all been screaming.

They looked blankly at me.

'Didn't anybody else see or feel anything?' I urged.

Still nothing - just empty gazes.

'Why were you all screaming down that end of the room then?' I asked.

Finally, they began to speak:-

'We thought the screaming was part of the energy raising, so we just joined in.'

I tried my hardest not to laugh but couldn't help myself and, pretty soon the whole group were in stitches over the whole episode. I remember thinking this would make a great story and have recounted this anecdote on a number of occasions since.

Among the merriment of the hotel's reception foyer

in Transylvania, surrounded by friends and new acquaintances, I realised just how big a part of my life ghost hunting had become. Not the events themselves, although I do still enjoy hosting them and meeting new people, but the places I have had the good fortune to visit and the people I have met along the way, many of whom have become genuine and loyal friends.

You can never be sure where life will take you. Which roads will guide you effortlessly down a smooth carriageway and which ones will become dirt-tracks, riddled with pot-holes and obstacles. However, one thing I have come to believe is that everything happens for a reason. The people we meet and the choices we make are all part of a greater plan, of which we have no conscious control.

I believe I was destined to meet Hazel that night at the Station Hotel!

During that conversation with my client about *The Law of Attraction* I regret to say I had been quite dismissive of her beliefs. However, whilst I don't attribute the trip to Transylvania solely to my visualisation of travelling, part of me feels it was destined in some way and maybe, just maybe, the universe heard my plea.

However, it is yet to yield me a fortune playing the Lotto, so the jury is still out on that one.

TWENTY ONE

......Just when you least expect it. Just what you least expect – 14 May 2015

Since the separation I had begun to enjoy living alone and had absolutely no intention of actively looking for another relationship for quite some time so, it was as much of a surprise to me as it was to anybody else when I found myself falling for somebody; least of all because it was a man.

I'm not able to pinpoint exactly when I first realised I was attracted to men, but have never been homophobic or even judgemental of others' choices, beliefs or opinions – especially where sexuality is concerned. The very fact that as a human race we are all different and unique in some way is what makes us more interesting and creates variety and diversity in the world. Besides this, I wholeheartedly believe sexuality isn't a choice people make. If that were the case, who on Earth would choose the ridicule, prejudice and even physical danger that many same-sex couples, particularly homosexuals, are often subject to?

Some people like cheese, others don't. Some like

spicy food and others can't tolerate it. Some men like men and some women like women - some even like both!

It's not shocking and it's not even new.

The morning of 11th May 2015 had begun like any other. The alarm was set for 8.30am as I was working from home that day, studying some copywriting techniques for a course I was completing to hone my skills for the new job. The weekly company meeting was due to take place at 9am, as it did every Monday, so my first job of the day was to Skype-in and report my personal metrics for the week.

It was a pleasant day outside.

Seated at my dining table, nestled in the corner of the room where the lounge area opened into the kitchen, I could look straight out of the window and gaze at the beautifully manicured lawns opposite. The grounds were maintained by a landscaping company and therefore always looked perfect, with neatly-trimmed grass and perfectly sculpted shrub-borders. It was a view I appreciated greatly, although I often found myself gazing out into the landscape rather than concentrating on the work I should be doing.

Despite the distractions I ploughed ahead with my work that day, getting to grips with the tiny nuances of expert copywriting, discovering killer-phrases and words which could make the difference between thousands of pounds to a client, or absolutely no engagement whatsoever. Having always harboured an interest in words and the tricks employed to get people to do what you wanted them to do, I found the whole experience fascinating.

In the same way supermarkets utilise background music to subliminally influence their customer's buying choices, or increase the tempo and urgency of the tracks to move them more quickly around the store, words can be hugely powerful if used correctly.

I was coming to the end of the final module when I

heard a familiar tone from my mobile; the notification sound to alert me of a new message from a dating-app I had been using for some months.

It was early afternoon and, having ploughed through the course since the end of the Skype call, I felt I had earned a well-deserved break. I filled the kettle, popped a tea bag into the cup and reached for my phone. Curiosity had got the better of me and I wanted to see who had messaged me.

I had created a profile at the beginning of the year, not because I wanted to find a partner, but I was now single and had the freedom to explore my sexuality and – for want of a better phrase – I was curious. My ex-wife and I (the divorce was well underway by now) had been together from a very young age and well before I ever had any inkling I was attracted to men.

For a long time before our separation neither of us had made the effort to maintain the physical side of a marriage. As she had stated, we were just 'two people living under the same roof'. Now, as a single man for the first time in the whole of my adult life, I was free to explore and enjoy new things and – since I had known for a long time I was now more attracted to men – it meant I could do what single men do. A whole new world was open to me and it was one I enjoyed discovering.

When I first joined the site I genuinely didn't know what to expect, or even what I wanted. I knew with absolute certainty I wasn't looking for a relationship and openly maintained this with anyone I chatted to on the app. In truth, I was lonely and wanted to meet new people.

Neither my wife nor I had retained friendships from school and, having moved around many times with work, I had a number of acquaintances but only a very small number of *actual* friends. Worse still, many of those I would genuinely enjoy the company of lived too far afield to call or message for an impromptu drink or trip to the cinema, so evenings were often spent alone in the early days which was no fun at all. I wanted new friends and I wanted a social-life so, since I also wanted to explore my sexuality, a gay dating-app seemed the obvious way forward.

As anybody who has a gay friend or has encountered such a site themselves will testify to, it's not always easy to sift out the wheat from the chaff. Unlike dating websites such as Match.com and eHarmony.co.uk, where its members make the commitment of a monthly fee in the hope of finding a long-term partner, this was much more direct in its approach – and free. That's not to say there aren't many hundreds, even thousands, of guys on there who would like to meet somebody for more than a quick fumble, but it takes some doing to find them.

As with anything in life, these kind of apps are what you make them. If you are looking for no-strings meetings then you'll find them. If you're looking for something more then it's going to take time, but you'll find it.

The truth is, if you're honest about what you're looking for and act in a decent, friendly and polite way then it's a doddle. Treat everyone with the respect they deserve, in the same way you would when talking to them face-to-face, and if all else fails just hit the block button and move on. After all, if you block the nutters then fresh profiles will appear for you to say hi to.

This I believe is where many people go wrong. Not just on dating websites, but with social-media in general. While the internet has given us so much freedom and delivers unprecedented levels of information at our fingertips, it also provides a voice for anybody who chooses to use social-media.

Unfortunately, while freedom of speech is undoubtedly a positive thing, the way in which we air our opinions often requires careful thought and consideration and, as a result of this faceless medium – where consequence is just a word – basic good manners are sadly becoming a thing of the past.

Facebook and Twitter, being the two largest social-media sites, are rife with messages of hatred, homophobia and bigotry; a place where anybody can voice their opinion with no consideration for the feelings of others. I often read comments online and ask myself, would this person be so free in vocalising their opinion or their abuse of another if they were standing with them face-to-face?

In most cases, the answer is no.

The rise of social-media undoubtedly has a huge part to play in the erosion of common decency and manners, which also extends to dating-apps, where one can be downright rude or abusive to another, with no fear of retribution.

I was once contacted by an Asian guy whose profile didn't include a photograph and made no mention of his ethnicity. I always tried my best to retain my morals and good-nature while using the app and, after a fairly lengthy conversation – in which he seemed a perfectly decent and kind person – he eventually sent me a photograph.

I don't have a racist bone in my body, but from an attraction point of view I only like white guys and therefore this wasn't going to work for me. From the conversation it was clear he was looking for someone to have some fun with rather than friendship so, rather than waste his time, I addressed the point.

Taking great care not to offend him I explained my position and therefore, although he seemed like a really nice bloke, I wouldn't be interested in meeting up for anything more than a drink as friends.

What happened next astounded me.

He launched into an abusive rant, accusing me of wasting his time, asserting that I was a disgusting racist and calling me just about every conceivable swear-word in the English language.

He was duly blocked!

I considered whether I should point out to him that I had not wasted his time, it being he who had chosen not to include a profile picture in the first place, or make mention of his ethnicity in his profile. Why not be open and honest right from the start about who you are? It seemed to me the issues were his and not mine.

Attraction is different for everybody and something you cannot easily define, but I'm simply not attracted to black or Asian guys. It's no different to not liking ginger hair or tattoos, it's just who I am and why should he feel he has the right to question that? Should I date somebody I don't fancy just to avoid being branded a racist? It wasn't going to happen.

What I did discover during the time I used this app was that, despite all of my self-deprecation I was actually incredibly confident when it came to meeting other people.

Following a long conversation with a guy shortly after registering on the site, one in which we talked about everything from what we did for work to the kind of music we liked, we agreed to meet up for a drink at a local pub. I guess you'd call it a date, although I had been pretty clear in our conversations that I wasn't on the hunt for a partner. Either way, we made plans and I arrived looking smart, but casual; not wishing to appear as if I was trying too hard.

I was the first to arrive so, rather than the awkwardness of him having to walk into the bar and find me – based only upon the profile picture he'd seen – I waited at the entrance. As each and every car pulled into the car-park, I peered into their windows to see if it was him; I'm surprised I didn't get arrested.

Eventually he arrived, and as he approached me I opened my arms to give him a hug. It felt totally natural for me to do this, rather than extend a hand for a more formal handshake. After all, we'd already chatted lots and knew a fair bit about each other, so I decided to just go for it. Later, over a glass of Pinot, he admitted he'd been petrified about that moment; unsure of what to do.

This was my first ever date and to me it seemed both natural and comfortable and, although he had been on many dates before and been 'out' for many years, it was me who took control and led the way.

The night was very enjoyable. We seemed to get on really well and had plenty in common. The conversation was easy, like chatting to an old friend, although I became aware as the night went on that I'd led much of it. I felt hugely at ease being out with another guy and not in the least bit conscious of the conclusions people may draw; I didn't care!

I hadn't planned to invite him back, but I was enjoying the night and to be honest I wasn't quite ready for it to end. Coffee made, we settled on the sofa and chatted some more. He told me about some ex-boyfriends he'd had and I told him more about my marriage and children and how it came about that I was now on a gay dating-site.

Then it happened.

Like a scene from a *Mills and Boon* novel we made that eye connection which requires no words to know the other's thoughts and, we kissed.

I won't go into detail about what happened, but that night was an eye-opener and I loved the thrill of being able to do whatever I wanted. He and I didn't have another date because I soon realised he was looking for more than I wanted to give and we eventually lost touch.

During the course of the next few months I met a number of guys. Some involved nights out for drinks and even a meal and some were for one purpose and one alone. I had never been promiscuous in my life, but I'm not ashamed to say I enjoyed every moment of those few months and actually did make a few new friends along the way with whom I've kept in touch, despite living in different counties and, in one case, on different continents.

Although I was enjoying myself there was still absolutely no part of me that could envisage me having a relationship with a man. Bedroom antics were one thing, but I just couldn't conceive ever having the type of feelings for another guy that lead you into a full-blown relationship; I certainly couldn't ever see me falling in love with another fella.

However, on 11th May that was all about to change.

The message on my phone was from a guy called Johnny. His profile revealed little more than his age, and that a guy with a good personality was more important to him than one with great physique (phew).

At the time neither he nor I were revealing our faces in our profiles. My reason for this was because I hadn't told anybody I was gay and it was important I wasn't accidentally discovered before such time as I wished, if ever, to tell people. It had nothing to do with shame – I felt none – but it was absolutely nobody else's business who I was sleeping with and most importantly, I had two children to whom I may want to explain it one day, in my own words. The problem with these kind of sites is that you never know who may be on there and what their agenda may be.

Conversation with Johnny was very easy.

We chatted for quite some time about our jobs and interests and I told him straight away about my marriage and children. He revealed that his reason for not displaying his face in his photo was due to his work and it was important to him to avoid being compromised. He needed to be able to filter out guys who contacted him and never to accidentally engage in conversation with anyone who may compromise his career.

The conversation somehow felt different to many of the ones I'd had before. Either he was playing a long game, still heading for the same goal as most but softening the approach with general chit-chat, or he was genuinely a nice bloke who was more interested in meeting up and getting to know me as a person.

It was impossible to know at the time but he certainly appeared genuine and, having exchanged photographs by this point, he was most definitely my type.

We arranged to meet that night at 9.15pm, in a pub just a couple of miles down the road from my home.

Johnny was a handsome fella and as I approached him at the bar the warmth of his smile and demeanour struck me instantly; dark stubble framed that friendly smile and his eyes were deeply captivating. Before we had even been handed our drinks and found a seat I knew I liked him. He exuded confidence, a trait many of the other guys I'd met had lacked – despite their good looks – and I felt instantly comfortable in his company.

Conversation flowed easily, both as eager to discover more about the other as to reveal information about ourselves. We eventually realised we were the last two people in the bar and the staff were getting ready to close the doors. We said our goodbyes in the car-park, exchanged a hug and agreed we'd both like to meet up again.

I've never really given credence to love at first sight, predominantly because I don't believe you can truly love somebody without fully knowing them, but as I drove the short distance home there was a flutter in my stomach I had never felt before and the smile on my face was so wide the corners could easily have been in different postcodes.

Despite the lateness of the hour, no sooner had we both reached our homes than we began messaging each other. I lay awake for ages, going back over the night's events and eventually fell asleep around 1.30am, feeling content and happy.

Messages were exchanged constantly from that point

and, with the exception of one night – where we both already had plans – we saw each other every evening that week. I struggled to make sense of the feelings I had. Constant butterflies and a churning stomach mixed with excitement and happiness; absolute joy whenever I was in his company and unsettled, even nervous, when apart. I knew deep inside this was different and, just ten days after meeting this man, I made a confession.

'You do know, don't you?' I was looking into his eyes and he nodded. 'You do know I've fallen for you?'

I could sense the feelings I had experienced over the past week were reciprocated and somehow this gave me the courage to speak honestly about what was on my mind:-

'I love you Johnny!'

As the words formed on my lips I felt completely at ease, despite the gravity of the declaration and the speed at which I had reached this point. I had no idea whether he felt the same, but something inside me was telling me he did.

'I love you too,' came his reply. 'I've never said that to anybody before, other than family,' he added. 'There's never been anybody I've wanted to say it to, but I really do.'

I couldn't believe what was happening. I'd known for a few days before this conversation that I felt completely different.

When we met I had no expectations whatsoever and hadn't been looking for anything more than friendship. However, this had been completely different, and until this point we hadn't done anything more than talk and kiss. I'd genuinely been more interested in learning more about him than getting him into bed. Of course the attraction was there, but more than that I truly enjoyed his company.

I found him engaging, intelligent and interesting, and through hours of conversation we discovered many of our thoughts and opinions – though in the minority – were similar.

I was reminded of the following quote from English essayist and juvenile novelist C.S. Lewis.

'Friendship is born at that moment when one person says to another: What! You too? I thought I was the only one.'

Johnny had never had a long-term relationship. In fact, he always maintained he'd never really had a proper relationship at all, which seemed crazy to me considering he was a good looking, intelligent and caring guy.

How had he never been snapped up before?

He'd led an interesting life and had travelled widely, but maintained he'd always enjoyed his own company and had never felt lonely, hence he had never settled into a relationship before now. He insisted that meeting me had changed everything and he was the happiest he'd ever been.

Falling in love was a new thing for us both.

Although I'd been married for almost 17 years, we had known each other for many years before becoming boyfriend and girlfriend; the same class at school from the age of 11 and in the same circle of friends from 14. That stomach-churning feeling which consumes you when meeting and falling for somebody had never happened between my ex and I, as our relationship had evolved slowly from friendship into something more.

The excitement of falling in love was just as alien to me as it was to Johnny and had a profound effect on me. I struggled for a while to come to terms with the feelings I had, but I also really enjoyed those crazy emotions too.

Saying the words 'I love you' just didn't seem enough, so in order to further express how I felt I turned my hand to poetry for the first time since I'd left school some 22 years before, and penned the following words for him:-

For Eternity

Worlds collide; Universe expanded.
Stars align, a perfect storm.
Oceans once explored with fearless independence, become vast in solitude.
A chance encounter, gifted for two,
Not seeking, but secretly yearning.

Souls intrinsically connected,
Minds in unison, bodies entwined.
A tapestry woven with common beliefs and ideologies.
Two stories, one ending,
A language often studied but never before deciphered.

Soulmates; kindred spirits......
Making memories.
Fears, uncertainty and self-doubt dissipate,
Absorbed in the protection of loving arms;
Blanketed in the warmth of unconditional love.
The searing flame of solitude suffocated and extinguished forever.

Worlds collide; Universe expanded.
A new day dawns and peaceful tranquillity envelops.....
For eternity.

Since the moment I first began exploring my sexuality I had maintained that the catalyst for me to reveal my choices with family and friends would be if I ever met somebody I could see myself forging a relationship with.

I felt certain being gay was my future and 'coming out' held no fear for me, but until there was something to say other than 'I'm having sex with men these days', I would keep it to myself. However, I knew without question that I wanted to be with Johnny and I honestly believed he felt the same so, not wishing to keep such an important part of my life a secret from those I loved, I decided it was time.

I had already told a couple of very close friends a few weeks prior, but on 23rd May 2015 (ironically, the date of my ex-wife's 40th birthday) I told my mom and her partner that I'd met somebody and it was a man.

'You're joking?' came mom's immediate reaction, her eyes searching for some hint within me that this was nothing more than an elaborate hoax. 'Are you serious?'

'It's not a joke,' I maintained, 'his name is Johnny.'

It was that simple; no dramas, no tears and bizarrely absolutely no nerves whatsoever. I had accepted who I was and wanted the people I cared about to know.

'Well, I can't say I'm not shocked,' she continued, trying to take it all in, 'but as long as you're happy, then I am too.'

I don't know if she truly believed her own words in the moment but, whatever she was really feeling at the time she covered up and kept to herself. She did struggle initially which I guess is a natural thing for any parent, later admitting she'd been concerned I might just be 'going through a phase' or that I'd had my head turned by an 'experienced' gay guy. However, after meeting him some weeks later, she began to adjust to the idea and everything was fine.

It felt strange!

I'd just gone through this huge experience, one which people have been known to take their own lives rather than deal with, and I felt nothing; no wave of relief and no life-changing feeling of finally being myself. It just passed by and life carried on.

Monday morning arrived, kicked off by another of the weekly meetings at which everyone in the business was present. I'd had no thoughts before arriving at work that day of sharing my news with anybody but, as we sat around the room and my colleagues began to narrate their positive focus from the weekend, it suddenly crossed my mind that I might just tell them.

There were 20 people in the business at the time, including the two guys who owned it and I didn't register a single one of their stories that morning. As my turn crept closer and closer I was too busy debating in my own head whether or not this was either the time or the place.

Chris, a larger-than-life character and an incredibly funny guy, had just finished his raucous tale and it was literally in that very moment – just as my name was called to speak next – that I made the final decision. I drew a deep breath and began.

'My positive focus is quite a big one for me,' I began, my nerves beginning to take hold. 'I've met somebody!'

I paused and there were cheers from the room.

These were a group of people I considered to be friends as well as colleagues, some of whom I really liked and admired and, knowing I'd separated from my ex-wife the previous year, they were all genuinely pleased to hear I'd found somebody. I interrupted the babble of voices to continue my revelation.

'We're getting on really well and it's all looking good so, at the weekend I visited my mom and I came out.'

There was silence; a true tumbleweed moment.

In reality it lasted for just a couple of seconds, but it felt like an eternity. Having spoken with a number of them since, apparently nobody had even the faintest idea I might be gay, so it took a few seconds to sink in.

'Have you just come out to us too then?' one of the team asked, looking somewhat bewildered.

'Yeah, I think I have,' came my reply.

It was done!

Several people passed their congratulations and then the positive-focus carousel resumed. I looked across the room and received a few acknowledgements of my actions with a simple wink of the eye. As the meeting continued it began to dawn upon me what had just happened and the reality that, from this point onwards, I was officially a gay man.

The meeting ended, people shuffled out of the room back to their desks, and the day continued like any other. I was working in the building a few doors away with some clients so didn't see most of the team until the following day, but I was happy they knew. I was also happy that, although a big deal to me, everything had continued as normal; exactly how I wanted it to be.

There was just one more thing to do!

It was hugely important to me to have control over how I broke the news to the children. We were very close and, whilst I felt totally confident they would have no issues in understanding, there were certain things I wanted to say to them. After all, they are the two most important people in my life and I wanted them to know as soon as possible.

We saw each other on Tuesday and Thursday evenings every week, then every other Sunday we would spend the day together. My biggest concern was that they would overhear me on the phone to Johnny or, worse still, see a photograph or message on my phone and think I had deliberately kept it from them, or never intended to tell them at all.

As parents we have always impressed upon them both the importance of honesty and I would have hated for them to believe I had been anything other than open with them.

Naturally, before I could tell them I needed to inform my ex-wife, since it would be she who would be around them the most after I had shared my news, and I wanted to ensure they had somebody to talk to about it if they did have any questions or concerns. Whilst the girls and I enjoyed a close relationship, I acknowledged they were just 13 and 11 at the time and would therefore most likely find it awkward to speak directly to me if they did have any worries.

My ideal scenario was to tell them in familiar

surroundings while doing normal stuff, as I really didn't want to make it seem a bigger deal than it was by creating an unnatural situation. My ex had other ideas though and regretfully, we did clash on this.

She told me that she wanted to be there when I told them, since it would be her who would have to deal with the fallout.

'I really don't think there will be a problem,' I protested, 'they're both very mature for their ages and I will be careful with the words I choose.'

She wasn't having any of it!

Her suggestion was that I went over to their house so that we could sit them down and tell them together because she wanted to see their *genuine* reactions.

I was flabbergasted!

I had never been to their new home and I tried to explain that I wanted to keep things as *normal* as possible when I told them.

Had I arrived and sat with them in their lounge they would have instantly become worried that something major had happened. After all, they hadn't seen us together since we separated and I believed they would assume we were about to break some terrible news relating to a family member if we created a scenario like the one she was suggesting. The whole episode would have escalated into something much more dramatic than it was and besides, I didn't want to have this conversation in front of my ex-wife.

She eventually conceded and we agreed a date on which I would tell them. I promised to send her a text once I'd done it, confirming what had been said, so that she was aware of how they had reacted and could talk with them upon their return.

My plan was to grab a bag of chips and take them to the local park, as we often did during the summer evenings, and while I had their attention explain to them and give them the chance to ask me anything. The time had arrived and, although a little nervous, I was ready.

'Girls, there's something I want to tell you,' I began tentatively. 'You know mommy has met somebody…'

That's as far as I got before my youngest interrupted.

'Let me guess,' she chirped up, 'you've met somebody too?'

At this point they hadn't been aware I knew about my ex's new partner, and I could see that my eldest was uncomfortable, unsure what to say because I had taken her by surprise in mentioning his name.

'Don't worry,' I added looking at her, 'I'm happy she's found somebody.'

She looked relieved and, because I hadn't been informed he was now part of their lives – let alone living with them – I believe she had felt compromised for some time and had tried to keep it from me in case I was upset. Then, just as I finished my sentence, her sister floored me:-

'When do we get to meet her…or him?'

My head spun so fast I'm surprised it didn't detach, like Worzel Gummidge switching his regular head for a startled one (for those born after 1984 look it up on Google). I can only assume that their mom had brought same-sex relationships into conversation over the preceding weeks, in order to help prepare them for my bombshell.

'Well, it *is* a man actually!' I said, kind of amused that she had just stolen my thunder with all the nonchalance of a typical teenager, from which she was still two years away.

I went on to explain that we got on really well and that I liked him a lot.

It was important for them to know that me being with another man didn't change anything with our relationship and crucially, I wanted them to know that he lived locally, as I didn't want them to worry I might move away anywhere and upset the balance of our time together. Although they had both adjusted incredibly well to all of the recent changes in their lives and shown no signs of any problems, I was very conscious that this may have been a concern and I wanted it addressed right from the off.

The other thing I really wanted to tell them was that, although I was perfectly happy for them to tell anybody they wanted to, for their benefit I wouldn't be posting anything on Facebook that their friends could potentially see. I wanted them to think carefully about who they told because children can be vile to each other in school, and it was important they didn't expose themselves to any unnecessary hassle. *Life will deliver its own problems – you don't need to create your own.*

'Your best friends today could be your worst enemies tomorrow,' I warned them, 'so I'm just saying choose carefully who you tell, if anybody.'

I went on to let them know that, although I'd like them to meet him sometime soon, there was no rush and we would do that whenever they felt happy to.

That was pretty much it.

They both gave me a hug and, for the rest of our time together that evening we messed around on the park as we would normally have done, seeing who could complete the assault-course in the quickest time before racing each other for the last swing.

I guess I'm extremely lucky.

Perhaps it was my age that made everything seem so easy. Maybe it was because I was so comfortable with my choices or possibly, I was just fortunate that by the time I had to face up to 'coming out' it really wasn't a big deal anymore.

Whatever the reason, I actually enjoyed the whole experience. I felt excited about telling friends as I eventually caught up with them over the coming weeks and, without exception, every single person I shared my news with was encouraging and most of all, happy for me.

I believe it was probably a combination of all three things.

In my heart I knew nobody within my family would have a problem, and absolutely believed that anybody who considered themselves a true friend would be the same.

At 40 years of age I was very independent and had stopped caring about what other people thought of me a long time before, so if there were any issues they would be other people's to deal with and not mine.

Unfortunately it's not that simple for a lot of people.

I tried to imagine how difficult it would be if I had known from a young age that I was gay. I knew one guy who still lived at home with his parents and desperately wanted to tell them he was 'different'.

He suffered with anxiety and often felt really low because, although he believed they would probably be okay with him if he told them the truth, he struggled to say the words and felt he was destined to live a lie. We often talked about my experiences of coming out and I tried to reassure him on a number of occasions that, on the whole, people just don't really care anymore.

A teacher I know had told me there were several teenage kids who were openly gay or lesbian at their school. They occasionally encountered comments from the other kids, but on the whole people just accepted it and there wasn't a problem. I recall being astounded when I heard this.

How different it would have been just 25 years ago when I was that age? I wasn't aware of anybody in school who was gay and, although I found out years later that two of my friends were, they had never given any hint before we'd left school and gone our separate ways. Perhaps, like me, they'd had no idea themselves back then?

As a child I have no recollection of knowing any gay men at all. In reality there must have been someone, either within my parent's circle of friends or in the community in which I grew up, but I certainly didn't know about it.

Even as I edged into my late-teens, although there were more celebrities prepared to wave their metaphorical rainbow-coloured flag, they were still hugely in the minority and most preferred to keep their private affairs private. I can barely think of any television personalities who were open about their homosexuality in the '70s and early '80s, yet today we have the likes of Graham Norton and Alan Carr presenting hugely popular chat-shows, fully embracing who they are.

I recall vividly the now infamous circumstances in which the singer George Michael's sexuality became public knowledge. Here was a man who had more female admirers than most and who had led the popular music scene since Wham first hit the UK charts in the early '80s, with massive hits including *Club Tropicana* and *Wake Me Up*.

Despite a life in the spotlight, he had managed to keep his identity as a gay man a secret from the public for over 15 years. In an interview years later, discussing his arrest for soliciting sex in a public-toilet in Los Angeles in 1998, he told of the deep psychological toll carrying this secret had upon him and revealed that one of the reasons he had kept it private for so long was to protect his own mother from the worry surrounding HIV and AIDS.

At the time of his arrest there was still a level of stigma associated with being gay. In many ways I believe that the outing of George Michael, a public figure who sold in excess of 100m records and is the most-played artist on British radio, was a turning point for gay musicians.

In less than 10 years the number of openly gay singers has increased massively and now, in 2016, artists can finally be open about their sexuality without fear of prejudice from the music bosses. Of course, those who kept their own secret for many years had done so because attitudes to homosexuality were, until fairly recently, still in the dark ages and it was generally assumed very limiting for an artist's commercial success – especially for a member of a boy-band.

The fight for gay-rights has been a long one.

It's easy to forget that until 1967, when the *Sexual Offences Act* came into force, sex between two men was illegal. Same-sex sexual activity had been outlawed during the reign of Henry VIII, with the introduction of the *Buggery Act* in 1533, whereby anyone convicted would be sentenced to death by hanging.

The law was repealed briefly, following the accession of Queen Mary I, but later reintroduced by Elizabeth I; the last two men to be executed for sodomy in England were James Pratt and John Smith in 1835. Although the death-penalty for homosexuality was removed in 1861, male homosexual acts remained illegal and punishable by imprisonment.

It was to get worse before it got better!

The introduction of Section 11 of the *Criminal Law Amendment Act* of 1885 extended the laws regarding homosexuality to include *any* kind of sexual activity between two men. Oscar Wilde, the famous Irish playwright, novelist and poet, was prosecuted under this law and sentenced to two years' penal-labour.

By the end of 1954 there were 1,069 gay men imprisoned in England, serving time simply for being gay. Conversely, lesbians have never even been acknowledged – let alone targeted – by the penal-system, but of course have suffered similar struggles to their homosexual counterparts in other areas of life.

The term 'gay' is still regularly used in a derogatory sense, implying that a man is less 'manly' or not as 'strong' as his heterosexual counterpart. During the times of the Roman Republic it was socially acceptable, even expected, for any freeborn Roman male to indulge in sexual relations with both female and male partners, provided it was he who dominated the coupling.

Sexual liaisons with male slaves or prostitutes was considered acceptable, but to allow another man to penetrate him would threaten a man's liberty as a free-citizen and throw question upon his integrity. It was all about domination; much in the same way experts agree that rape – whether straight or gay – is less about sex and more about the offender achieving power over another human.

I am thankful to this day that, as a result of the campaigning by others and the passage of time, I felt able to make my choice to have a relationship with another man without fear of consequence or retribution.

Sure, I was conscious there are still bigots and homophobes out there and that the persecution of homosexuals still takes place in many subtle forms, but on the whole I was able to be who I wanted to be and enjoy a perfectly normal relationship with another person, regardless of their sex. I was head over heels in love and very happy, which was all I cared about.

Unfortunately happiness was to be short lived, as the otherwise okay relationship with my ex-wife was about to turn sour.

TWENTY TWO

......Sometimes I just want someone to hug me and say "I know it's hard. You're going to be okay. Here's a coffee. And 5 million Dollars" – 8 Sept 2015

Although it had come as a massive shock at the time, the separation from my ex-wife had been just about as amicable as the ending of any 24-year relationship can be, especially where there are children involved. Naturally with a house to sell, finances to sort, maintenance payments and a whole host of other things on which to agree – not least my access arrangements to the children – there were moments when things were tense, but generally we kept everything civil and cordial.

The children were at the forefront of my mind from day one and I've been conscious never to put them in an awkward position, or say anything negative or derogatory about their mom to them. Whatever my feelings toward her she is their mother – the person who has been there for them every day of their lives.

I cannot and would *never* fault her as a parent, and although I wish I could take more credit, the children's good manners, zest for life and just-do-it attitude are most certainly attributes for which they can thank their mom. It's not that they wouldn't have picked these things up from me, it's just that I wasn't around enough to instil many of my own traits upon them in their formative years.

The transition from being part of a family to living alone was tough!

Arrangements were made and access to the children was not an issue, but there was no getting away from the fact that, however often I saw them, I was no longer a part of their day-to-day life; those moments around the house when you just grab one of them and give them a hug, or sit down by their side and share in whatever they are doing to occupy their time were gone forever.

For weeks after they left the family home – before we sold the house – I would go into their bedrooms in the evenings to sit on their beds, scoop up some of the cuddly-toys which were still there, and cry.

The silence of the evenings was deafening; no shouting, no thundering footsteps above and – without question the worst thing by far – no laughter. Every evening as I returned from work I was reminded of the seismic changes that had taken place.

The British are renowned for their 'stiff upper lip' approach to life and each morning I would get up, ready myself for the day ahead and put on a brave face. For those first couple of months it was only close friends who were aware of the separation and I had wanted to keep it that way so, despite how I was feeling and the fears which were gaining momentum for my own future, I got on with it in the best way I could. Of course that also included time spent with the kids, because they had their own upheaval to work through and I absolutely could not allow them to see that I was hurting.

It amazes me even to this day how well they adjusted to everything and how they just got on with things. They had gone through some pretty dramatic changes themselves and it is to their credit that they showed no signs of this affecting them whatsoever.

Their ability to carry-on regardless often made me look at my own self-pity and wonder why I was struggling so much. After all, I wasn't sad about the marriage ending because there had been nothing there for a number of years. However, I missed the children badly and was now terrified for my own future. Both selfish emotions, but ones I couldn't control.

It was only a matter of months before my ex was back on-track. By June of 2015 she was back on the property-ladder and had met her new man.

While I hate to admit I felt a pang of jealousy that her life was already back in order, while mine felt like a train wreck, I would be lying if I said otherwise.

The financial aftermath of the separation had taken its toll and by this time my situation was pretty poor. The new job was just about covering the bills and maintenance payments and for want of a better phrase, I was struggling. I'd got some money in the bank from the sale of the house but I had to be strong and make sure I didn't start using this as a means to live, as without it I would never manage to build up a deposit to purchase another home for myself. I had to live on what I could earn and it wasn't proving easy.

Johnny's situation was completely different. Having always worked hard and taken good care of his finances, he was in an enviable position for somebody of his age.

Here I was just seven months his junior – having earned a similar salary for a number of years – struggling financially as a result of the separation, and barely able to get a mortgage big enough to purchase the one-bedroom flat I was renting. It was starting to get me down and the inequality of our positions began to play on my mind.

I really started to resent my situation.

To make matters worse, it was around this time things began to become unpleasant between my ex-wife and me.

The routine of Tuesday and Thursday evenings and alternate Sundays had always worked well and, with the exception of one or two instances where I had to work weekends to attend conferences, I stuck rigidly to this.

I felt it was important for the children to have some routine to their time with me and, since this meant we never went more than five days without seeing each other, it ensured we were always in touch. Naturally there were one or two times where evenings changed in order to accommodate things they were doing with school, or to fit around birthdays, but on the whole it worked and the time we spent together was great.

Then things began to change.

I began to receive text messages and e-mails stating she felt I should start having the children overnight at weekends, or on some of the evenings on which they came over for tea.

For as much as I loved seeing the children and missed being part of their day-to-day lives, I was now living in a one-bedroom apartment and it just wasn't viable. The tone of the messages felt more and more unpleasant and accusatory, insisting I should 'make it work' and even questioning the importance of the girls to me.

Until this point she had seemed perfectly happy with the arrangements, but I began to wonder if she had realised it would be increasingly difficult for her to juggle the children *and* work, now that she was moving out of her parents' house and into her new home.

Although I didn't know at the time, I later discovered later that these messages coincided with the time she was dating, and I therefore wonder if her suggestion had *anything* to do with the children's welfare and our relationship, or whether it was simply that she wanted some freedom for herself.

I'll never know!

I'm not the vindictive type, but I feel sure she believed my reticence was based on a desire to make *her* life difficult. To be honest I was past caring about her and that was far from my agenda, I was too focused on making the best of a bad situation with my own life to worry about upsetting somebody else's.

The messages continued!

That July, just as the school break commenced, the children were due to go away on holiday with their grandparents (her mom and dad). It had been booked prior to the separation and when everything happened I had agreed to pay half of the cost.

By the time the balance was due I was struggling financially, surviving on around £15 per week for food, which included feeding the children on two nights each week. However, I'd made the commitment and agreed to pay, so I transferred the money across from my savings.

A recent increase in the agreed maintenance figure I was paying had made things even tighter, and as a result I was no longer able to give the children pocket money on a regular basis. That hurt greatly because I knew they would not understand the financial difficulty I was under. All they would see is that I was no longer giving them the pocket money they had been receiving since we split up.

I couldn't allow them to see I was struggling! Maybe it was pride. Maybe I was protecting them. I can't be sure!

However, all of these confrontations, criticisms and feelings began to form together – compounding like a snowball gathering size.

I began to feel less and less capable!

I have never tried to shirk my financial responsibilities as a parent and understand every situation is different, but the system for calculating child-maintenance seems intrinsically flawed.

The Child Support Agency, or Child Maintenance Service as it is now known, is there to ensure regular payments are made to support the upkeep of children from broken relationships, where the parents are no longer living together as a family unit.

The system calculates the gross income of the paying parent and, depending upon the number of children and the amount of time they sleep at the paying parent's home, a figure is calculated. This is calculated as a percentage of the *gross* salary.

What the system doesn't take into account in any way is outgoings. So, with a lower-than-average annual salary and surviving on just the most basic outgoings I could – there was left very little to spare.

The rental price for an apartment is not significantly less than that of a 3-bedroom house in some towns. In addition, many of the standing charges for utilities are very similar and so the base-costs – even for a one-bedroom apartment – are still relatively high.

Living alone is not cheap!

If you've got a light on in the lounge it doesn't cost any more for three people to benefit from it than it does for one. Likewise, to heat a room is no more costly for three bodies than for one.

Take into account that the parent with whom the children live is also likely to be in receipt of a number of additional incomes, such as tax-credits and child-benefits, and you'll begin to see that the system can be quite unfair in these situations.

In essence I was left with very little each month, from which I still needed to insure, tax, MOT and service the car, purchase any clothing I needed *and* have some sort of social-life (on which I spent very little at all).

In addition, I needed to ensure I had something left so that I could do things with the girls on the Sundays and save for birthday and Christmas presents too. Seeing them receive expensive gifts from others, ones I could never match myself, was painful to say the least.

I'm a failure!

When I pointed the figures out to the Child

Maintenance Service their response was simple; we don't take outgoings into account and therefore you'll have to pay it, regardless of whether the other parent is better off than you or not.

The messages and e-mails had gone back and forth for some time and throughout I had tried my hardest not to retaliate. Despite their tone and the effect the comments had on me, I had maintained a dignified position throughout, determined that if it ever came to a legal battle of any kind I could prove I'd done everything I could along the way to remain civil.

However, the night before the children were due to fly to Crete with their grandparents, I received an e-mail to which I couldn't hold back.

She stated that she was disappointed I hadn't given the children any spending money for their holiday and that – although we had paid for half of the holiday each – *she* would also have to find extra money for clothes and food.

I was absolutely furious!

I was doing everything I could and it seemed it still wasn't enough.

Whether it was her intention or not, I felt that every opportunity to criticize me as a parent was seized with glee and it reached the point where, whenever I saw her name appear in my texts or on e-mail, I would feel physically sick – wondering what was to come next?

I wanted to scream at her to leave me alone but couldn't. I felt completely paralyzed; frightened of the possible recriminations if I aired my true thoughts – afraid that she might turn the children against me.

Why do the children need new clothes for one week away, when they already have summer stuff?

You get Child Benefit payments to help cover food – they eat like sparrows and won't be eating at home that week!

I raised both points in my response.

Her parents are very generous people and I felt it

highly unlikely they had accepted her half of the balance for the holiday, especially when she had just moved into a new home.

Of course this was conjecture so I kept it out of the response, as I could offer no proof to support my argument. I'd finally had enough though and ended my reply with the simple message that she should 'never question my finances again'.

I had no response to my e-mail!

That seemed to be her style; it felt like she would criticise me, condemn my actions and question my motives, but when I responded with answers – or asked questions pertinent to her comments – she would fall silent.

I felt angry, but mostly I felt let down.

We had spent 24 years of our lives together and the reasons for our break-up were simply that we had drifted apart; neither of us had made the effort to rescue it before it was too late. A marriage is a joint responsibility which requires regular nourishment, so when it simply withers on the vine, *both* parties must take responsibility.

Like so many couples do we had just grown apart, and that was that. So, having managed to get through the separation, sell the family home, divide the assets and even get the impending divorce underway without malice, I couldn't understand why it had come to this.

Either way, the combination of my situation and the constant unease, waiting for the next drama to unfold, began to have a serious effect upon me.

Since the day we broke-up my greatest fear had been how I would recoup my financial position after losing half of everything we'd built and, despite now being in a relationship with Johnny, I worried constantly about my own security.

I became concerned his friends may think I had an ulterior motive for being with him, I stressed about how I was going to ensure my own financial freedom for my old-age if I were to end up single again, and most of all I worried that if I didn't act fast I would end up – potentially alone – with no money to support myself through my retirement.

These thoughts weighed heavily on me and with the criticism being levelled against me about my commitment to the children, I began to feel more and more of a failure.

You need to man-up!

In truth I don't think I ever really recovered from the circumstances leading to my departure from Haunted Happenings. To have your abilities and intentions questioned can have a truly damaging impact on a person's confidence and now – less than two years since that episode had come to a close – it was happening again; but this time it felt worse.

The primary difference with the business was that I had always believed in myself and in what I was doing, and despite the situation becoming untenable I believed in my heart that I had done a good job.

I was now fighting in a completely different arena, and although I was trying to deal with it the best way I could in order to survive, I couldn't say with certainty that I was always right. After all there's no rule-book for parenting, especially for post-separation situations, and I was finding it tough.

I'd like to believe the points she was making were coming from a good place – the intention being to encourage more contact between the kids and myself in order to ensure our relationship continued to flourish – but the tone of the e-mails and texts didn't appear to support this hope. I honestly felt that she was deliberately trying to make me unhappy.

To an extent we're all responsible for our own decisions and ultimately we have to stand or fall based on the choices we make.

Whatever mistakes a person makes in their life and

whatever failings in their character, there is no excuse for anyone to take advantage. The sheer vindictiveness of someone who increases their feeling of self-worth at the expense of another is abhorrent to me and always has been.

I believe I was witness to this during a rare night out in Birmingham one evening in the summer of 2015.

A friend had arranged a night with some of her lesbian mates and we were planning to hit the bars on Hurst Street, the gay-quarter of Birmingham's bar-scene. I was well up for a night out, wishing to put some of the stresses behind me and I also arranged for another friend to join us with whom I had shared a couple of dates earlier in the year; we weren't right for each other but we had remained friends and stayed in touch. The plan was set and we arrived early to make the most of this rare night out.

The weather was unusually hot for a British summer, so we made our way to the courtyard area at the rear of The Village and enjoyed a few drinks, the evening sun still beating down upon us.

I'd never met the group before so had no expectations of what they might be like, although I had been pre-warned that two of them were a couple and had been bickering for most of the day on the trip south from where they lived.

I'm a sociable type, so meeting a new group of people held no concerns for me and I've always lived by the rule that you take people on face-value and make your own perceptions of their character. So, with my usual charm, I got on with it and was determined to have a good night.

In spite of the glorious sunshine the atmosphere was decidedly chilly between the two of them. Tina was the more outgoing one of the two; her line of work demanded a strength of character and quick-witted banter which seemed to come naturally to her.

I've never been one for stereotypes, but in this case she definitely had the more masculine look of the couple; with cropped blonde-hair, slim build and harsh but not unattractive features, she had a look not dissimilar to that of actress Linda Henry, who played Shirley Carter in *Eastenders*. Our sense of humour was similar and we got on instantly; I was drawn to her outgoing character and her direct nature. I really liked her.

In contrast her partner Karen was very quiet. With long brown-hair and softer features, her initial appearance suggested a warm, friendly type, although for some reason this wasn't coming across. She sat among a group of people looking lost and out of place, and it wasn't long before I noticed there were several unkind comments being passed in her direction, from Tina.

This was one of those awkward situations where, in a social group, the lesser confident can become isolated and shrink away, leaving the more outgoing ones to gain further ground and attention. The less one person interacts the more the situation is exacerbated, and the rest of the group begin to draw naturally to the louder one, further limiting the quieter person's ability to re-enter the conversations.

I have to admit that I was just as guilty as the rest of the group at the start of the night. After all, I wasn't there to babysit somebody who, on the surface, couldn't be bothered to interact with the group; I was there for a good night. However, as the night progressed I realised I had made an error of judgement.

I'm not sure whether it was the many triple-distilled Vodkas which helped to provide some clarity on the situation, or that the behaviour became more overt. Either way, it was sometime around midnight when I noticed something was really amiss.

We had made our way to Eden, another bar just a short walk away, and had been enjoying the music down there for just over an hour. Unbeknown to me, for most of this time the girls had been arguing outside in the smoking-area, and when I returned from the gents, everyone apart from Karen was gathered in a group ready to head back up to The Village. They asked me if I was joining them.

'Where's Karen?' I asked.

'She's outside,' one of them replied, pointing in the direction of the smoking shelter. 'She says she's going home.'

'How's she going to do that?' I replied, fully aware she was in a strange city and would have absolutely no idea how to get back, assuming the trains were even running a service at that time of night, which was highly unlikely. 'You carry on. I'm going to have a word and I'll catch up with you in a bit.'

I couldn't believe what was happening!

Here were a group of girls, wholly prepared to allow one of their friends to disappear into the night – in the centre of Birmingham – more than 100 miles from home and with no knowledge of whether she had even the means to get herself safely back.

Somebody once said to me the reason men 'rule the world' is that fraternity is stronger than sorority; in essence, the guy-code is stronger than the girl-code.

His theory was that, because guys are less complicated with their emotions and tend to say what they think, arguments are generally over with quickly and everyone can move on. With women, it is arguable there is a greater level of complexity (and bitchiness) which will always prevent the creation of a strong and unifying bond in a group.

It seemed I was bearing witness to this right now.

It hadn't been my plan to have to look after somebody else, but I feared that unless somebody threw Karen a life-line and tried to talk some sense into her, something terrible could have happened that night and so, I headed outside and found her seated on a bench, with sufficient make-up running down her face you could have mistaken her for a mascara-inspired Jackson Pollock.

'What are you doing out here on your own dickhead?' I asked, trying to raise a smile.

'I'm finishing this fag then going home,' she replied, tears still streaming down her face.

'How do you plan to do that?' I shot back, feeling that a direct tough-love approach was the only way I would get through to her. 'The last train will have left already. Do you have enough money to get home and even if there was a train, do you know where the train-station is?'

The faint hint of a smile appeared on her face. I was getting through:-

'Listen, I don't know what's going on between you both but you can't go off on your own, it's just not safe.'

'Well, the rest of them aren't talking to me now, so what else can I do?' she retorted.

'Here's what you're going to do,' I began. 'You and I are going up to The Village and we are going to have a bloody good dance, have a few drinks and sod the others. You can sort everything else out tomorrow, but tonight we're going to dance. Deal?'

The change in her was astounding and, hand-on-heart, she turned out to be a great girl. All she had needed was somebody to make the first move and give her the green-light. She just wasn't a naturally overt person and, having been overshadowed by Tina's more dominant personality, had faded into the background. It wasn't that she was being rude or didn't want to be part of the group, she just didn't know how to secure her place, especially as Tina had created further obstacles because they were having a tiff.

It occurred to me that night that, in some ways, a similar thing could be happening to me. At 40 years old I believe I was *allowing* myself to be bullied!

The more criticism I received from my ex the less

confident I was becoming, and the cracks were beginning to show. It didn't help that, just as I felt things were starting to settle down and I could begin to rebuild myself, I discovered the role I had begun just three months before was to be made redundant, with immediate effect.

Without analysing and understanding the basis of an irrational fear it is almost impossible to eliminate the hold it can have on a person, or to put into place the plans and actions required to counteract it.

It had taken me a number of months to realise the true basis of my own fears, but after some soul-searching I had come to the conclusion I wasn't afraid of being alone, I was afraid of being lonely. I didn't have a fear of getting old, but I was terrified of being old *and* alone.

Having spent the whole of my adult life in a relationship with the same person, I had never experienced loneliness.

Those first months following the separation had been a huge transition, but one I had conquered and overcome. I had genuinely begun to enjoy my newly-single status and had started to tackle the issues I now faced. I had taken control of my own finances for the first time, dealt with the sale of the house, organised a new place to live and acknowledged what I needed to do in order to move forward.

The change in career from estate agency to copywriting had been the first step toward putting my life back on track and it offered me some much needed stability. Not only the financial element of having a fixed salary, and therefore the ability to budget with absolute clarity, but also the bigger picture of taking a step towards owning my own property again, one of the key things I had acknowledged I needed to do to secure some equity for my old age.

I had returned from my trip to Portugal just days before it happened.

Feeling fresh and invigorated, I'd thrown myself back into work immediately upon my return. I genuinely enjoyed my new job. The team were great, it offered me the freedom to be creative and work under my own steam, gave me the variety I craved in my work-life and, I was learning.

The bigger picture had always been to get into copywriting, learn from Nick (whose background was in this field) and eventually take my newly-honed skills to a higher-paid role, or even try my hand at freelance work which could potentially be very lucrative. I had a two-year plan and was taking action towards my future.

However, with age and experience comes a certain level of wisdom and insight and I could see there were problems on the horizon. The format I had been employed to provide services for didn't seem viable to me in the long-term.

It came with some limitations, specifically the number of clients we could service at any one time. I couldn't see how it was scalable, and with talk of making changes to fix the problem I also couldn't see where the copywriting element had a place. So, it wasn't a huge surprise when I was called into the meeting-room and given the news nobody wants to hear.

Ad, my immediate line manager at the time, is a stellar bloke.

In all of the jobs I've had I have never had the pleasure of working with such a genuine guy. The business was very casual and Americanised in its approach, with the team's development and personal goals very much at the forefront of their mind. Ad lived and breathed the values of the business but it went deeper than that; he genuinely cared about the guys he worked with, especially those in his own team.

Unfortunately I never quite felt the same way about the guy who owned the business. He stood by the ethos of 'looking after your people' but I always felt somehow uncomfortable around him.

I'm the type of person who can make small-talk with anybody, whether it be somebody picking up their groceries in Tesco or the director of a blue-chip company, but I couldn't gel with him because I always felt there was some sort of agenda.

On the few occasions we spoke one-to-one, I had the impression that if he asked me something there was a purpose behind it. It felt like he'd already considered what he would like the outcome to be from that conversation, and his questions seemed carefully crafted in order to achieve that goal. For this reason I never felt at ease with him, and although I openly admit I may have been completely wrong, I have learned over the years to trust my instincts and they were telling me something wasn't right.

I sat with Ad and the head of HR as they broke the news to me that the role I was doing was no longer required in the business. They'd been quick to follow with the information that they didn't want to lose me, and therefore wanted to know if I'd be interested in continuing to work there in the capacity of Business Coach.

The role would involve weekly coaching calls with our clients, to assist them in the development and implementation of the strategies already outlined for their businesses. There was no talk of further remuneration and I immediately pointed out I had no background or experience in this particular area, but faced with the alternative of losing my job, I agreed to give it a go.

I knew almost instantly it wasn't for me!

I'm a face-to-face kind of person and one of the most enjoyable parts of the copywriting role for me was the interaction with different people every day. To be sat on the other end of a telephone discussing business strategies wasn't what I'd signed up for and, to make matters worse, just a few weeks later it was announced that Nick – the guy whose knowledge would help me continue toward my two-year plan – was leaving.

He would be setting up his own business and I felt sure then that the writing was on the wall. The two reasons for me joining the business, to be a copywriter and to have access to Nick, were both gone.

I stuck it out and gave it my best shot because it would have been a travesty to walk away without trying, although the cards were stacked against me from the very beginning.

How can I coach somebody who'd built a business with a six-figure turnover in ways to grow this further when I'd never done it myself?

I had real issues with my credibility and, although they seemed more than happy with what I was doing, it was making me truly miserable.

The thing I had needed most in order to get my life back on track was some continuity and I knew in my heart that everything was about to go up in the air once again.

For most people work is a necessary evil; a means by which to earn the money we need to get by. Very few people are fortunate enough to truly love their jobs and I accepted that. I'd never been in that position, but had always enjoyed my roles sufficiently that the good outweighed the bad.

I hated this!

To wake up in the morning and dread going into work is the worst feeling in the world, but to feel trapped within that role because you have lost confidence in your own abilities is truly debilitating, and that's where I was. I would turn up, go through the motions and go home.

To make matters worse all the fears and uncertainty came flooding back.

I began to see a change in myself and I was aware that valuable time spent with Johnny was being wasted because I was feeling so low. In fact, there were several occasions where things just got too much and I broke down in front of him. He always said the right things and tried to help me put some perspective onto the situation, but I was losing my ability to be rational about anything.

I began to experience panic attacks and eventually realised I needed help.

Acknowledging that you need help is always a massive step and the first in a very long journey for anyone suffering from anxiety or depression. Having always been very logical in my approach to making decisions, it was unsettling for me that I couldn't seem to gain clarity. Even the smallest problems escalated in my mind and became seemingly insurmountable tasks.

I remember taking my car for its annual MOT one day and, since it would be several hours before it would be ready, I decided it would be best to leave it there and catch the bus home while I waited for the verdict.

I had no reason to be overly concerned about the outcome of the test itself, but I began to overthink the worst-case scenarios. What if it was going to cost me a lot of money to sort? If I had to resort to using my savings, that would put me even further back in my goal of getting back onto the property-ladder.

My mind began to race and my heart began thumping in my chest.

As planned, I left the car and headed for the bus station.

It had been over 20 years since I'd used a bus, but I hadn't expected it to be so difficult to ascertain which one I needed just to get me home. I looked at the charts and tried to work out the correct stand and bus number to get me to my destination. Although I knew there was a bus-stop almost directly opposite the entrance to the apartments, I could not find a route which took me there.

So, I worked out which one I *thought* would get me the closest and asked the driver; little did I know how difficult it would be!

......Just asked a bus driver in Redditch whether he goes along Birchfield Road and he had no idea. Looked blankly at me, then mumbled something in a foreign language. Clearly had no idea what I was asking (or where he was about to drive his bus) so I assumed the answer was no. Thank God I don't use buses very often! – 25 Jul 2015

I made light of the situation in my post on Facebook, but inside I was getting more and more anxious. At 40 years of age I couldn't even manage to get a bus from the town-centre to my home, just three miles away. So, rather than continue with what seemed like an impossible task, I decided to walk.

I knew the route but it was a scorching day, and after around ¼ mile I stopped. In my head I was trying to work out what best to do. If I carried on walking it would take me at least an hour – by which time the car may well be ready – and I'd then have to walk all the way back into town. So I turned back in the direction from which I'd just travelled and began to walk, but after about twenty paces I stopped again.

Quite simply, I just couldn't make a decision. It seems ridiculous but that was how I felt at the time. Even the most basic and simple things were evading me.

What is wrong with me?

That afternoon I booked an appointment at my doctor's surgery. I wasn't seeking pills and I certainly didn't want pity. What I felt I needed was somebody to talk to, with whom I had no personal connection. Somebody who I could try to explain my fears to and would hopefully help me to rationalise my situation.

In fairness to him, the doctor didn't question me and agreed immediately to add me to the waiting list to speak with a counsellor. I also left with a prescription for the anti-depressant Citalopram, which he assured me would help to calm my anxiety, but I really didn't want to take them.

I knew a couple of people who had been long-term users of anti-depressants, for quite different reasons, and I'd never really agreed with their use.

To my mind, taking a pill to mask the feelings was akin to using a sticking-plaster to fix an arterial bleed; it was never going to work. I needed to address the issue causing the anxiety rather than pretend it didn't exist and to do that, I needed to talk.

Of course, the waiting list for a counsellor was long and I accepted I wouldn't be seen anytime soon, but what I didn't expect was that it would be six months before I'd be sat in that chair and, by that time, worrying about preparing for my old age would be the very least of my problems.

TWENTY THREE

......*"The worst type of crying isn't the kind everyone can see - the wailing on street corners, the tearing at clothes. No, the worst kind happens when your soul weeps and no matter what you do, there is no way to comfort it."* - Katie McGarry – 13 Nov 2015

I had a lot in my life to be grateful for, and as 2015 progressed there were plenty of good things going on to distract me from my mounting worries.

Not only had I experienced an amazing adventure in Transylvania and enjoyed a week in the sun in Portugal, but now Johnny and I had a trip planned to Majorca and we were set to take the children camping for a couple of days over the bank-holiday weekend, leading into August. Holidays it seems were now like the proverbial buses; all coming at once!

I had been to Majorca once before, when I was just 12 years old. It was a place I remembered fondly and, although this would only be a mini-break of just four days – to fit around Johnny's commitments and our planned break with the children – I was counting down the days until our departure.

The island is famous for its beach resorts, sheltered

coves, limestone-mountains and Roman remains and Porto Colom, situated on the south-eastern side of the island, was no different.

Centred on a natural harbour this traditional fishing-village is a haven of relaxation, where the crystal-clear waters of the warm Mediterranean-Sea dance gracefully against craggy rock-faces. With less commercialisation than towns such as Magaluf and Palma Nova, Porto Colom has resisted full-scale tourism and become a favourite spot for those seeking a quiet break; exactly what I needed – a few days of sun, lying around a pool at the all-inclusive apartment complex, and just a stone's throw from a beautifully sandy beach.

I've never been one for long holidays.

One week is never quite enough, but after ten days I'm usually sick of sun-cream, sand and living out of a suitcase. Boredom sets in relatively quickly and I'm too fidgety to sit on the beach all day. Disappearing off for long walks has always been a favourite pastime for me when abroad. During family holidays I would often walk the length of the beaches, sometimes for miles, simply enjoying my own thoughts while the sea crept around my toes at the water's edge.

During our family holidays in Mastihari, a small village on the Greek island of Kos, I would rise at around 6am most mornings, slip on my trainers and head off for a 5k run along the coastal-path before walking back along the empty beach without another soul in sight. I'd strip off and have a swim in the cool waters, then head back, quietly make myself a strong black-coffee and sit on the balcony reading for at least an hour before anybody else woke. Those were treasured moments and ones in which I truly felt I was recharging my batteries from the long hours at work back at home.

This trip was no different.

On the final day I decided to venture off for a walk on my own, intent on exploring the small dirt-track we had spotted the day before which disappeared into the countryside.

I walked for miles in the heat of the midday sun, marvelling at the stunning buildings along the way, paying particular interest to the gates on many of the properties – all identical – made from rustic lengths of crooked wood that wouldn't look out of place at the entrance to the home of a gnarly old witch. I concluded there must be some historic influence to this style, although Google failed to back-up my theory.

The walk was amazing!

I enjoyed the solitude, absorbed myself in the beautiful surroundings and cleared my mind of the events of the past few months. The hot, smooth tarmac surfaces of the road felt wonderful on my bare feet and, but for the occasional car or bleating goat, the gentle rustling of the trees in the warm breeze provided the only soundtrack to my journey.

This was mine and Johnny's first time away together and it had crossed my mind that, if there is ever a way of testing the strength of a new relationship it is most definitely to spend a few days in each other's company, 24/7. I had absolutely no reason to think there would be any issues so it came as little surprise that, after three full days there hadn't been a single cross-word between us.

I had felt he was a little distant at times but attributed this to the fact he had been working hard recently, and needed time to recharge his batteries just as much as I did. The sign of a strong relationship is when a partner doesn't need to fill silences and, since I have always been happy in my own company, this didn't faze me at all.

However, there was something which was beginning to play on my mind around this time.

Despite being close to his family, Johnny still hadn't introduced me to them. This began to raise some questions in my mind and grate on me a little, but I reminded myself that we were only three months into our relationship tried not to worry about it too much. I have never been one to invite myself or force something where there was reticence, and just reconciled that it would happen sooner or later.

Stop stressing about everything.

No sooner had we landed back in the UK than it was time to head off with the children to Devon for a weekend of camping at the idyllic Stowford Farm Meadows near Coombe Martin, just a few miles from the beautiful seaside town of Ilfracombe on the north-Devonshire coast.

The children had met Johnny on a couple of occasions by this time and had really taken to him. He had a natural charm and an understanding of how to handle kids so this, combined with their laid-back demeanour, made for a truly relaxed and fun weekend.

As you'd expect, the British weather at the end of July was changeable to say the least. In a climate where you can experience all four seasons in one day, you can never quite plan for every eventuality, so the fact we went from wearing shorts and t-shirts the day we arrived, to waterproof jackets and umbrellas the next, will come as no surprise to anyone who has ever spent a Bank Holiday in England.

Nevertheless we made the most of our time. From crabbing amongst the rocky coves of Coombe Martin beach, to games of Crazy Golf and drawing shapes in the sand with the tip of an umbrella, we enjoyed what many would call a 'traditional' family holiday. Seaside chips, plenty of ice-cream and hours spent in the amusement arcade; a staple diet for a British holiday, and we did it all.

It felt amazing and, as I watched the girls compete fiercely with Johnny for victory on the air-hockey table, I was filled with a warmth I hadn't felt in a very long time. Everything felt right and in that moment we were a family.

Sadly, it wouldn't last!

I had begun to notice something different in the way Johnny was acting. For some weeks he had seemed less keen. I couldn't put my finger on it, but it always appeared to fall upon me to make arrangements to see each other and even the time we did spent together felt somewhat distant.

As anybody who has suffered from anxiety will testify, most will do everything possible to keep things to themselves, only revealing their true fears to those closest to them (if anyone at all). In my case the only outlet I gave myself to share my feelings with was Johnny.

Only he had been privy to the content of the many text messages and e-mails from my ex-wife and therefore, he was the only person to whom I could truly speak about how things were developing. Of course, I was conscious that our relationship was still relatively new, and on several occasions apologised that he was having to hear all of this. After all, he hadn't signed up to get involved in my problems and by this point I most certainly wasn't the fun-loving person he'd first encountered that night in May.

I tried my hardest to put on a brave face and even kept a lot of things to myself – for fear of damaging what we had – but there were some pretty dark days where I needed somebody to listen, and that person was him.

Work was okay.

I continued to bed-in to the coaching role I had been assigned and, although I knew deep down this wasn't where my future lay, I tried my best to make it work; unfortunately the cracks were beginning to show there too.

I recall a conversation with my boss when, during a review meeting to discuss my performance, he noted a change in my mood. We had a system where both the employee and their line-manager would score themselves each month across a number of things, including 'attitude' and 'interaction with the team'. Having scored me a 10 the previous month, he revealed he had reduced this score to an eight, where I had given myself a nine. He went on to explain his reasons:-

'I've scored you a bit lower this time because you've not been yourself for a while,' he began. 'I know we've talked about the stuff that has been going on with your ex and I understand it's got you down, but the rest of the team here look up to you and when they see you come into work not smiling and being your normal happy-self, it affects their mood too.'

I was gobsmacked!

Don't get me wrong, Ad is a great guy and I love him to bits, but I was astounded that I had been marked-down in my review on the basis that, on some of the days when things had been really shit, I hadn't been my 'normal happy-self'.

It wasn't as though I'd gone in there and done anything wrong; I was still doing my job well and nobody I spoke with on the telephone would ever have known there was a problem, but the fact I wasn't chatty and keeping everyone else's mood elevated was now being held against me. I didn't have the fight in me to argue and switched off at that point, resolving to get to the end of the meeting and crack-on.

Everybody wants a piece of me.

It was just a couple of weeks after the camping trip that I first addressed my concerns with Johnny while at his house one evening.

'Are we okay?' I asked him.

He looked shocked at the directness of my question and quickly reassured me that everything was fine, asking me why I would think otherwise.

'I've noticed recently that you don't seem as interested' I replied. 'In fact, you haven't seemed bothered for the past six weeks and I'm a bit concerned something is wrong.'

The conversation was difficult and I'm certainly no expert in this kind of situation, but he reassured me he'd been very busy with work and that he was just tired. He was adamant nothing was wrong and, although I gave him every opportunity to be honest – without fear of any dramatics – he put my concerns to bed and apologised for making me feel that way.

At this point I also mentioned he'd yet to introduce me to his family, but he assured me there was no deliberate intention to keep that from happening, just that he hadn't arranged it yet.

Why do you keep looking for problems?

With my concerns put aside I set about organising my forthcoming birthday celebrations.

With the marriage breakdown occurring just five weeks prior to my 40th the year before, I had allowed that birthday to pass me by. I certainly wasn't in the mood for celebration at the time and, other than a birthday meal with mom, her partner and the children, it had slipped away quietly. So, now I was in a relationship and life was generally back on track, I was determined to make up for it and make my 41st birthday *everything* my 40th failed to be.

The big day fell on a Sunday, so plans were laid to hit the bars in Birmingham's gay-quarter on Saturday night, then join together with all of the family – nieces, aunts, uncles and cousins included – for a meal in a local pub on the Sunday afternoon.

We have never been overly close as an extended-family since growing-up, and it was rare to get everyone together but – to my surprise – one by one they all confirmed and the resulting meal was wonderful; 21 people seated around the table in a cornered-off area of the restaurant, reminiscing about our childhood holidays and catching up with people's lives.

The meal was everything I had hoped for and, with the children chatting away to Johnny once again, it reaffirmed everything I had felt back in Devon.

The previous night had been small-scale but pretty full-on. Two of my closest friends at the time had decided to come along with us and, following a few drinks and nibbles at my place, we headed into Birmingham.

I was still very new to the 'gay-scene', although I had felt instantly at ease on the first couple of occasions I had been out there. Compared to many 'straight' bars the atmosphere in the majority of these places is considerably different. The people are far chattier and much friendlier and there's a tangible buzz which you can't quite put your finger on.

The number of straight women who frequent gay bars was a surprise to me. It's easy to understand why a group of girls wishing for a night of drinking and dancing would choose a gay-bar, since the boys would – more often than not – be looking at the other boys and therefore leave them alone to enjoy their night.

What I found harder to grasp was the number of straight guys who came to bars like this. On one of the nights I found myself chatting to a guy who turned out to be straight, and I posed the question to him.

'So, what's a handsome bugger like you doing in a place like this?'

The flirty sarcasm in my voice wasn't lost on him and a wry smile crept across his perfectly-formed lips.

'Well here's the thing,' he began. 'loads of fit women come here with their mates, so not only is their guard down because they assume I'm gay, but there's also less competition for me down here than up the road.'

His reasoning was well thought-out and made complete sense. After all, this was a gay bar and he was drop-dead gorgeous; don't the ladies always say 'the best looking men are gay'? Why wouldn't they assume he preferred guys?

However, he was very much straight and he was incredibly hot.

WHAT'S ON YOUR MIND?

Standing around 6ft in height, with shoulders broad enough to warrant the widening of a doorframe to accommodate them, his physique would not have looked out of place on the cover of *Men's Health* magazine.

Groomed tufts of dark chest-hair peaked teasingly from the V-neck of his crisp white shirt, and a pair of fitted Chinos hugged his muscular legs and tight bum. To top it off he had been blessed with the most piercing blue-eyes which met your gaze whenever he spoke, and teeth so perfect Colgate toothpaste would probably pay thousands to have him advertise their product.

In short, he was ridiculously handsome but, despite the stereotype, he was also a really nice bloke.

I'm not shallow and I'm fully aware that beauty is, more often than not, only skin deep. It's a sad fact that with some people you can scratch the veneer and uncover nothing more than additional layers of veneer. I recall thinking how fortunate he was to have been graced with both looks and personality and, if I'm honest, I kind of felt honoured that he was even talking to me.

It's ridiculous and probably an indication of my insecurities, but in that moment I remember feeling flattered and just a little bit smug; clearly nothing was going to happen between us other than conversation, but the rest of the club – who would undoubtedly have been admiring him – didn't know that at the time, and must have been wondering how the hell it was me he was talking to.

I have no idea whether he managed to bag himself a single lady that night, but I had to admire his creative thinking.

Following a few drinks in Missing we headed down to The Village once more and spent the night dancing, drinking and generally having a great night.

One of my good mates from work had come along later to join us for a few bevvies following a dinner-date he'd just been on somewhere nearby. He is totally straight but, once again, his 6'3" muscular-frame attracted much attention from the guys in the bar. I lost count of the number of men who, after seeing us talking, prodded me in the back or tapped me on the shoulder to ask about him.

'Who's your mate?' they would ask. 'Please tell me he's gay.'

'Sorry, he's about as straight as they come,' came my stock response.

It was funny to see the disappointment on their faces and yet, even though I was happily committed to my relationship, I couldn't help but think to myself 'don't you want to know whether I'm single?'

The whole night had been exactly what I'd wanted it to be, providing some much-needed respite from the problems I'd been having with work and the concerns I'd raised with Johnny a few weeks before.

Although we saw each other most nights, we still lived separately and socialised with our own friends and colleagues individually at times.

That said, I was a little surprised and disappointed when he shot-off relatively early on the Sunday morning – my actual birthday – to keep his regular fitness-training session and visit his family, before returning later that afternoon to join me for the family meal.

I began to question myself again.

You're being too sensitive. Your birthday isn't important.

Was is too much to ask for him to spend my birthday with me as a couple and change his routine just this once?

I felt like a bit of a spare part for most of the day.

I'd be seeing the kids and mom later, so I ended up spending the majority of it slumped in front of the TV, waiting until it was time to head off for the meal. This was to be the only dampener across the whole weekend but it was Johnny – who professed I was the 'most important person' to him – who caused this relatively small hiccup in an otherwise perfect weekend, and that began to raise alarm bells.

As it turned out, I didn't have to wait long before my fears were confirmed, and on the evening of 8th November I received a WhatsApp message asking if I was free for a video Skype-call.

During the conversation he seemed somewhat distracted and a little manic, a trait I'd never seen in him before. The conversation was nothing out of the ordinary and after about 10 minutes we said our goodbyes and agreed to meet-up the following evening. Then just as I was thinking about going to bed there came a knock at my door. I peered through the spy-hole and was surprised to see it was him.

As I opened the door, thrilled and confused in equal measure at the prospect of a surprise visit, I immediately realised something was wrong.

Tears were streaming down his face as he brushed past me and walked straight into the lounge. A thousand thoughts ran through my head in less than a few seconds, but I concluded something must have happened to someone in his family in order to elicit such an emotional state, as he was normally such a controlled character. Of all the scenarios to run through my mind, what he was about to say didn't even feature.

'Johnny,' I began, my hands now on his shoulders to offer some comfort, 'what's wrong?' He didn't make eye contact, his eyes fixed downwards and his head bowed.

He proceeded to tell me that he had chatted to another guy online and they had met up for a drink…and kissed.

My head began to spin. I couldn't believe what I'd just heard and my mind clouded over.

He insisted Tony (the other guy) meant nothing to him, and went on to explain that he believed the attention this young, handsome man had shown him had massaged his ego sufficiently to make him act out of character. He assured me his 'error of judgement' had made him realise how much *I* meant to him and told me he hadn't been able to live with the guilt; he wanted to be honest with me, even if it jeopardised our relationship.

Naturally I was devastated but, after a lengthy conversation I pointed out he hadn't killed anybody and that we're all capable of making mistakes.

It would be difficult for me to deal with, knowing he had deliberately entered into conversation with this guy and met up with him behind my back, but providing he meant what he was saying and it would never happen again I preferred to put it behind us, rather than let it destroy what we had.

It's your fault Wayne – you're too needy!

He stayed over that night, having made swift work of a large Brandy to help calm him down, and we talked until the early hours before eventually falling asleep. During the night I woke to find him, seated on the bed in tears again, lambasting himself for his actions. I held and comforted him as he cried, reassuring him it would be okay and that we could get past this.

We moved on and, as far as I was concerned it was all behind us. I had plenty of other problems occupying my headspace and in spite of his indiscretion I still loved the man.

Little did I know that in just 25 days I would discover he had been somewhat creative and selective with the truth regarding Tony.

There were far worse revelations still to come!

TWENTY FOUR

...... "When you get into bed and your brain decides to run through every possible result of every possible scenario in every parallel Universe". Insomnia sucks balls – 19 Nov 2015

Making life-changing decisions is never easy!

A clear head, well thought-out plan and considerable strength of character are absolute necessities when it comes to making a significant change in your life; whether that be your career, issues with a relationship or anything that will cause a chain-reaction of events and alter the course on which you are currently travelling. I had none of these at the time, yet I needed to make some decisions and fast.

By the beginning of October I had reached breaking point with my job. The overwhelming anxiety I was feeling as a result of the situation I had found myself in at work was consuming me, and the bad days were far outnumbering the good ones. I had become a master of disguise; my colleagues at work were aware I was unhappy but – thanks to my well-rehearsed poker-face – none of them truly knew the daily struggle I faced just to turn up and get through the day.

There were numerous occasions when I would disappear from the office for a while, into the empty building next-door, simply because I was unable to control my emotions or even my breathing, and panic had overcome me.

When the human mind becomes overly anxious about a situation, whether real or perceived, the body's natural response is to release a rush of adrenaline; a natural, physiological response to the primitive 'fight or flight' syndrome where – when faced with potential danger – a person will instinctively stand strong and face up to the challenge, or do a runner to protect themselves from harm. Whichever is the chosen path, the brain understands that the body will require additional adrenaline, either to generate the energy required to survive the battle, or to facilitate the extra pace required to flee the scene. The needs may be different, but the body's response is the same.

However, where no actual danger exists and no physical response is required, this adrenaline becomes surplus to requirement and can have a significant impact on the person's physical state; the heart-rate increases to pump blood to the area most needed and breathing becomes faster to supply oxygen to the muscles, which are now tense in readiness to respond. Everyone's body is different and some parts are more sensitive to adrenaline than others, hence the symptoms of anxiety may not necessarily manifest themselves in the same way for each individual.

By far the most frightening experience for me, and I suspect for most sufferers of anxiety, were the episodes of hyperventilation.

When we become panicked about a situation it is not uncommon to over-breathe, and as a result we take far too much oxygen into the bloodstream. When the oxygen and carbon-dioxide balance is disturbed this also leads to an increased heart-rate and a release of further adrenaline into the system, resulting in tingling sensations and a light-headed, spacey feeling, which may then cause further anxiety and exacerbate the situation.

Simple breathing techniques can help to bring this under control and even prevent further episodes, but when your mind is overloaded with worry and anxiety, the effects are often already underway before you even realise. This was happening to me more and more, but neither my stubborn nature nor my pride would allow me to reveal the problem to anyone, not even Johnny.

I was unravelling fast and there was no sign of the counselling appointment coming any time soon.

Something had to give!

I had to take back some control and remove some of the things from my life which were feeding these irrational feelings. So, at the beginning of October I handed in my notice at work.

I had nothing to go to, but quite simply I couldn't continue. I was making myself physically ill, and although Johnny was there for me to talk to – bearing witness to several inconsolable tears along the way – I kept much of it from him for fear of damaging the solid relationship I thought we had.

The obvious thing to have done would be to go back to the doctor and request to be signed-off from work. After all, there was no question I wasn't physically or emotionally capable at the time, but I'd convinced myself that once you have depression or anxiety on your records, any future prospects for gaining employment were going to be even more difficult than they already would be.

I had no intention of remaining in my current job for the long-term, as I knew in my heart it would never get any better and it was a million miles from what I wanted to do, or felt comfortable doing; so I just left.

My plan wasn't very well thought through.

I'd got some money in the bank and I hoped I could still earn some money from the ghost hunting events, but since I had already planned one day to set up a freelance copywriting-service, I decided to go for it now.

I had also toyed with the idea of studying for my licence to become a qualified driving-instructor. This was a role I believed would suit my natural personality and also provide me the freedom to work for myself while delivering a relatively stable income.

As it turned out things got in the way, and it would be eight months before I made the commitment to this study, but from 6th November 2015 I was officially unemployed and began building a website to advertise my services as a freelance copywriter.

Anybody who has ever attempted to set up a business or work for themselves will know just how hard it can be.

The uncertainty of knowing where the next (or even the first) customer will come from, combined with the pressure of paying bills is difficult under the best of circumstances, but when you factor in the emotional turmoil I was feeling at the time, you'll quickly understand why this was doomed to failure from the very beginning.

However, fate was about to deal me another crushing blow; one that I just didn't see coming.

Just three days after leaving my job, and one day after Johnny's revelation about his dalliance with Tony, I received a text message from my ex-wife.

The ink was barely dry on the decree-absolute (the legal paperwork to confirm the marriage was now officially dissolved) and she had requested that I meet her and her partner at a local pub, to discuss something related to the children.

My mind went into overdrive.

It must have been something important for her to request a meeting. Was there a major problem at school? Was one of them ill? Was she about to hit me with something financial?

I had absolutely no idea.

By the time I approached the doorway to the pub on the Monday evening I had convinced myself that – since we were now legally divorced – she was going to announce they were set to marry and wanted to change the children's surname; something I would not have agreed to.

It was a very awkward few moments as we waited to be served a drink at the bar, but no sooner had we seated ourselves at a table in the corner than the mystery was revealed. Her partner had been offered a work-opportunity and they were moving away as a family; to Manchester.

My heart stopped!

I hadn't seen it coming and I was speechless.

Apparently it was too good a deal to pass up. They'd already spoken to the children about moving and they were happy and excited to go. She went on to say that the business had wanted them to move further north, towards Carlisle, but they had refused to go any farther than Manchester.

If the psychology of telling me it could have been worse was somehow designed to soften the blow; it didn't.

'You're talking as though it's already been decided,' I said, trying to control the complex mixture of anger and devastation I felt.

They went on to explain the decision had been taken, the job had been accepted and that, subject to a few arrangements which needed to be made -- not least the sale of the house – they expected to be moving sometime around the end of January, just 11 weeks away.

As the conversation continued she reassured me I would still be able to see the children regularly – perhaps every *other* weekend – and made a statement that the time we spent together on Tuesdays and Thursdays couldn't possibly be quality time anyway, as it was only for a couple of hours each night, during part of which I would be cooking their tea.

I couldn't believe what I was hearing.

How could a mother of two seriously pitch the idea to me that seeing my kids every other weekend was as good as what we had at the moment; twice a week and every other Sunday?

Those moments in the evenings were precious. It was then – after eating dinner together – that I would get to keep in touch with the day-to-day activities they were getting up to. It was those times when we would talk, about nothing in particular, and enjoy hugs and laughs.

With the best will in the world Skype conversations would *never* be a replacement for actual time together. If you've ever tried holding a conversation over the phone with a teenager you'll understand.

Chats by telephone and Skype would be more like a question and answer session – inevitably led by me – with lots of 'it was okay' and 'nothing much' responses when asked about school and what they had been up to.

I had already lost the closeness of being able to pop up to their rooms and give them a hug for no reason and now they would be moving 100 miles to the north, along one of the most notoriously congested sections of motorway in England, the M6.

There was nothing I could do!

This will change everything!

Sure, I could have caused havoc and demanded it didn't happen, or even consult a solicitor in an attempt to throw a legal spanner in the works, but it would have been futile.

We had joint legal-custody of the kids but she has always has been their primary-carer, and I wouldn't have a leg to stand on. Besides, with no spare funds available with which to even send a solicitor's letter, it was checkmate. They were going to leave and there was nothing I could do to stop it.

A few weeks down the line it was announced they

had set a date and would actually be leaving sooner than originally planned; the week between Christmas and New Year. For many reasons, not least that the children would be able to start their new school at the very beginning of term – which I totally understood – the move had been brought forward by four weeks.

It's impossible to convey how I truly felt, but what I recall vividly is the effect this had on my time with them going forward. For months I had been doing everything possible to hide from them the way I had been feeling, and it had just got a whole lot harder.

As a parent, no matter the heartache it causes you personally, the last thing you ever want to do it to hurt your children and I feared that, although they seemed perfectly happy and excited about their new life, if they saw me getting upset it would potentially cause them distress or make them feel guilty.

That was the last thing I wanted.

From the time I found out until the day they left, every moment with them hurt. Every meal I cooked, every time we went somewhere and every hug we shared served to remind me this was all about to change.

With the best intentions in the world, long distance relationships of any kind are hard to maintain, and the closeness achieved by regular contact is certain to wane over time. They would have a whole new life up there which I would not be part of and, even as they grew, their adult lives would surely be built in Manchester or the surrounding areas; when grandchildren came along the distance alone would dictate that I would be just a small part of their lives too.

My fears about getting older and being lonely, with no family nearby to visit, had just taken a turn for the worse.

I held things together in front of them, and to my knowledge they never knew how bad things were before they left, but this would only serve to cause problems further down the line and bite me firmly in the ass.

Sleepless nights came one after another and, with no job to drag myself out of bed for each morning, I began to decline fast.

There were many days where I simply didn't set foot out of the apartment. I completed a couple of small pieces of work for some clients who I had been in touch with via my previous job, but was completely unable to focus on getting the freelance copywriting underway and, despite assurances to the outside world and ex-colleagues that all was going well, it most certainly wasn't.

The greatest difficulty for anybody suffering with low-moods and issues of self-esteem is to pick yourself up and keep going.

For me, the desire to hide from the world was growing and, even though I knew the worst possible thing I could do was hide, there were days I just couldn't face seeing people. The effort it took to put a brave face on became greater and greater and on many occasions, while en route to host an event, I would pull over to the side of the road and break-down.

The one thing I always felt absolute confidence in doing was hosting the events, and now even this was starting to evade me. The worst episode occurred while travelling to Warwick, to work an event at a masonic lodge called Guy's Cliffe House.

Time behind the wheel allowed time for thinking.

As I drove my head became flooded with a thousand thoughts and I began to panic. Tears streamed down my face as I navigated the country-roads between Redditch and Warwick and, as I neared the location, my hands began to shake and I lost control of my breathing.

After pulling over into a cul-de-sac, I reached for my phone and called Johnny. I needed to hear a friendly voice and for somebody to talk me down from the stupor I had worked myself into. It was one of the most demeaning moments of my life; not only did I feel I had failed at everything I'd ever done, but now I couldn't even control my emotions without help.

Less than 15 minutes later I arrived at the location to set up for the impending ghost hunt and that night, stood before 30 guests who never suspected anything was wrong. Somehow I'd managed to put the poker-face back on and get through those six hours, but to this day I really don't know how.

It was a successful night in the sense that all the guests had a great experience and in a way it helped me, for I realised – despite falling apart earlier that evening – there was still something I could do. It gave me a glimmer of hope that I hadn't completely lost the plot.

That would come later!

……So far today I have burnt my toast, boiled the kettle dry, closed my laptop and lost some work and put the washing machine on without any detergent in it. Maybe it's time for me to dye my hair blonde – 23 Dec 2015

For a while, Johnny and I seemed okay.

Obviously it was tough and there had been further conversations about what had happened, but on the whole we seemed to have got past it and things had returned to normal.

A theatre-trip to see the Welsh National Opera's production of Sondheim's *Sweeney Todd* provided a much-needed night out and, with Christmas approaching, we had taken the children ice-skating at a local garden-centre where an outdoor-rink had been installed. The kids had a great afternoon, and despite the events of the previous fortnight things were good. The following week Johnny and I had tickets to see a band at the Academy in Birmingham; a birthday gift for me.

The gig was amazing!

Only a few weeks had passed since the atrocities of the shootings at the Bataclan Theatre in Paris, in which 89 innocent concert-goers had lost their lives, and I couldn't help but look around the venue, wondering of the chaos which must have ensued during the attacks.

I remember a moment of reflection while standing in the crowd and waiting for the band to come on stage – a moment of perspective; a realisation that no matter the problems I *felt* I was facing in life, they were nothing when compared with the horrors those people had endured and the torment their families would face in the aftermath of their loss. I reminded myself that however bad life felt at the moment, there are always people who are far worse off and with far greater problems than the insignificant ones I faced.

Basically I told myself I needed to man-up!

Following the gig I would be staying the night at Johnny's house, and as we climbed into bed I felt genuine happiness for the first time in weeks.

There are moments in your life you will always remember. For those alive at the time the day JFK was assassinated in Dallas is no doubt one of them. For today's generation, the tragic events of 11th September 2001 in New York is surely another.

For me, the morning of 3rd December 2015 has been added to the list and, although the world continued around me, mine came crashing down once again.

As was often the case at the time, Johnny had left for work fairly early that morning, leaving me in bed. I had a Skype call planned for 9.30am back at home, so dragged myself out of bed and headed downstairs for a coffee.

I'd recently finished the website for my copywriting services and, having had a few issues with the layout – website design is most definitely not on my CV – I took the opportunity to check it on his iPad, which was on charge on the kitchen worktop. Although password protected, he had opened it on several occasions while sitting next to me and, since he had made no effort to hide the pattern to open the device, I didn't think he would mind me using it briefly to confirm the website looked okay on Apple devices.

It was in that moment, standing in his kitchen, that I discovered everything I believed our relationship to be was a lie.

My uncertainty about his feelings had not been unfounded and I discovered several messages which convinced me that – in addition to Tony – there had been other men since we had been together.

I felt sick to my stomach!

How could this man have looked me in the eye and lied to me so blatantly, still maintaining that he loved me? It was too much to take in and I left the house.

I had to take that Skype call!

The phone call and messages which followed are etched on my mind forever. I told him what I had seen and, to my amazement, he turned it around on me.

His reply was so indignant that I began to doubt myself.

Had I misread what I had seen? Were those conversations actually from long ago and I'd got the dates wrong? I didn't understand how he could be so emphatic about his innocence when I'd seen the evidence with my own eyes.

His response led me to question my own sanity and almost convinced me I'd made a mistake so – since he was stuck in a conference until lunchtime – I drove back to his house and took another look.

I wasn't wrong!

Worse still, I now *believed* the reason for his tears the night he had arrived unannounced at the apartment – for which I had put aside my own heartache to comfort him – were actually the result of an argument with Tony and not remorse for his actions as he portrayed.

You deserve this – it's your fault!

I'd taken several photographs of the messages on his iPad before he had the opportunity to delete them and, although I removed them from my phone some weeks later, I retained them on my laptop to serve as a reminder of my foolishness.

He eventually opened up to me, but to this day I have never received an explanation for his actions.

In many ways, not knowing the reason for something is often worse than the thing itself. Without being furnished with an honest reason for someone's actions, it can leave you feeling insecure; it's not uncommon for people to blame themselves for the other person's actions.

This, of course, is what I began to do!

I convinced myself that it was my fault; somehow the problems I'd been having in other areas of my life had pushed him away.

Then I recalled his reaction to something he'd seen during my birthday celebrations in Birmingham; his friend's partner kissing and dancing with another guy in one of the clubs. At the time he was unaware they had already split-up and was appalled that this bloke was cheating on his boyfriend.

The hypocrisy astounded me! It seemed that despite his outward appearance, this man had no moral compass at all.

Under normal circumstances I would have walked away and that would have been the end, but I was vulnerable. I loved this man and, despite what I'd seen, I couldn't imagine my life without him.

I've seen many documentaries on television in the past where people come to rely upon their partner for strength; abusive relationships where the stronger of the two controls the other and seeks to reduce their self-worth, so that they become dependent upon them in *every* way.

Johnny was far from controlling and had never done anything like that, but I began to realise I had relied too much on him for support throughout my troubles and had come to need him far more than he had ever needed me.

Hindsight leads me to believe that with so many elements of my life in turmoil, I was once again clinging onto some normality and something familiar – even if I knew deep down that it wasn't right. Feeling as low as I did, being out of work and with the children preparing to leave, I needed a constant. If I lost him too I felt there would be nothing left to live for and I had nobody to turn to about it.

Even more oddly, having witnessed this strong and positive character break down in tears after being confronted, I couldn't find it in me to let anybody else know what had happened – even my closest friends. I had always admired and respected him and – although he'd hurt me greatly – I didn't want a living soul to know he was anything less than that which everybody believed him to be; I felt like I needed to protect him.

Despite everything I continued to try, but from that day we were broken. Nine months on, I see there was really no way back from this and, less than three weeks later, the relationship was over.

We had engaged in many, many conversations before the end finally came. Long walks along the canal where some of our first days together had taken place, many evenings on the sofa, and several conversations on WhatsApp; it was all futile.

I finally realised there was no going back during a trip to the cinema, where we felt a thousand miles apart. I don't really remember much of the movie because my head was so full of everything that was happening between us.

Two days later I arrived unannounced at his home to return some books which belonged to him. He finally admitted that he didn't want to continue and, in what was one of the worst hours of my life, the relationship ended.

I'm ashamed to say that I broke down and cried –

part sadness and mostly relief – but I was also determined I would *never* try to win him back. I simply didn't have the strength in me to be the one to finish it, but I knew when I knocked on that door I'd gone there to force the issue and bring it to a close; I just needed him to be the one to say it.

It probably seems ridiculous to anybody reading this but, in an attempt to retain some continuity in my life, I agreed to remain friends; we met for coffee several times over the coming weeks.

Once again I was lying to everyone around me and telling the world everything was fine, when all I wanted to do was scream out loud for help.

We chatted on many occasions about all manner of things and I genuinely believed that, whatever happened along the way, one thing I would always be able to rely on was his honesty.

He had nothing to lose!

I had *nothing* to offer this man other than love, and so I couldn't understand why he hadn't just called it off as soon as he realised he wanted something different.

For weeks I sat and thought about it, trying my hardest to empathise with his position in an attempt to better understand his actions. I know my mental-state must have weighed heavily on him at times, and perhaps it was because he cared for my feelings that he felt he couldn't just bring things to a close. I wanted so badly to find a way of redeeming his actions and continued to blame myself.

It wasn't until around two months later, while re-reading some of the messages I'd photographed that morning, that I understood I hadn't driven him away – he was never mine!

This was a pivotal realisation for me and gave me the strength to finally release myself from the blame I'd laid upon my own door.

The timing couldn't have been worse!

The previous Christmas had been difficult – the first since the break-up – but now I was truly dreading this one and desperate for it to pass-by as soon as possible. My relationship had broken down just three days before Christmas day and, only three days afterwards, I would have to say my final goodbyes to the children who were moving north on the morning of 29th December.

To have so many of the things that matter to you taken away in such a short space of time is unbearable.

I had the support of Hazel and Jayne, two of my closest friends and of course my mother and Paul – who were there for me every step of the way – but despite their unwavering help I felt so alone and vulnerable at the worst possible time of the year.

I spent Christmas Eve and Christmas afternoon with the children and, although we had a lovely time, my thoughts were absorbed by the reality that in just four days they would be living 100 miles away.

There were a number of occasions where I slipped away unnoticed, struggling to hold back my emotions but desperate for the children not to see my heartbreak. They were excited to begin their new lives and although utterly broken inside, I wanted them to believe everything was okay so they wouldn't be thinking about me after they had left.

Saying goodbye was the hardest thing I've ever done. I'd spent one last hour with them and driven down to my mom's so that she could say her farewells, before driving them back into town where my ex's fella would be meeting us.

I stopped the car and we stood on the pavement.

I believe he is a very good man and I am truly thankful they think so highly of him. It must be unbearable for a father to see his children living with somebody they don't like, or worse, somebody they fear. In his case, I am absolutely confident he treats them as his own and, although it hurts knowing another man has taken my place, I'm grateful it's him.

The children threw their arms around me as we stood in the crisp fresh-air. I told them how much I loved them both and, trying hard to keep my emotions in check just for a few moments longer, I held them tight. The overriding memory, and one which I'm sure will remain with me forever, was the scent of their hair as I held them close. My mind raced back to the morning after the separation where I had watched them walk out of the family home, and now I was doing it all over again.

Tears began to well-up in my eyes.

'Have a fab time in Manchester,' I said, my voice beginning to crack with emotion, 'and promise me you'll look after each other.'

As they walked towards him, standing a short distance away to allow us the space and privacy for this difficult moment, the tears began to roll down my face. They climbed into the car and, as they pulled away waving, I blew them both a kiss.

They were gone!

It took me around ten minutes before I was able to drive away and get myself home. Anybody who has ever suffered a bereavement will know exactly the feelings that consumed me. I longed to hold them again in an instant. I could still smell the sweet scent of perfume on my clothes and yet they were no longer there.

That evening I sat and cried almost constantly. I felt that I'd lost everything in life that made me happy and I just wanted an end to the pain I was feeling.

TWENTY FIVE

......I guess tomorrow is a fresh start. The world goes back to normal even though 'normal' is gonna be very different from now on. Need an über productive day and to put some things in place to make this year one to remember for the all right reasons – 3 Jan 2016

Life is a gift!

No matter how dark things become – and it can happen to even the strongest of people – it is important to remember there is always something worth living for. In my case the love and support of my mom and my closest friends kept me going over the coming weeks. There were good days and bad days and I will never forget something my friend Jayne said to me during that first week of the new-year.

'Some days will be good and some will be rubbish; just keep turning up.'

She was right, as she always is!

Jayne is an amazing person. One of those on whom you can always rely and, without question, has the biggest heart of anybody I've ever met. We had become close friends following the trip to Transylvania in April of the previous year, and since then we'd shared many fun evenings at my place, drinking, enjoying food and sometimes just chatting.

Jayne doesn't have things easy herself. She works long hours managing a residential care-home for people with dual-sensory impairment, while also caring for her parents, both with health difficulties of their own. Never once have I heard her complain about her situation. Sure, it gets her down sometimes and she has faced some incredible challenges herself along the way, but despite her ridiculously busy schedule she will always find the time to help a friend. I am thankful to this day that I was fortunate to become one of those friends and, I hope, will remain so for the rest of my days.

However, despite the support I received from those around me, my decline continued and the bad days began to outweigh the good.

Thankfully those counselling sessions I'd requested some six months before finally came through and I had my first appointment booked. The timing couldn't have been better. When I first asked to see somebody I was feeling very low and beginning to let my fears for the future control my ability to deal with the present, but now I really was in the darkest place of my life and there were so many things I needed to talk about, I wasn't quite sure where to begin.

My expectations regarding what they would be able to do for me were not high. I had a vague understanding of how counselling worked and knew this lady would not be able to offer any answers to my problems. What I needed right from the very beginning was somebody impartial to talk to. Somebody to whom I could express the feelings I had, talk through my fears and, most importantly, who would listen without judgement or emotional involvement.

A common misconception about counselling is that they are there to give advice. In truth, all a counsellor can offer is a safe environment in which to discuss and explore the difficulties and feelings of the client and assist them in seeing things more clearly. By the time I sat in that chair I realised my situation had escalated and I was suffering from severe depression. The physical issues I had encountered as a result of the anxiety had passed many weeks earlier - I was now far beyond that point.

The anxiety which had consumed me for several months had its foundation in the desire to fix elements of my life, so that I could rebuild my confidence and secure a better future; now – I realise with hindsight – I had given up on my future and stopped caring about finding ways to resolve those issues. As a result, the physical state of anxiety had passed. All I wanted now was for the pain to stop and would do whatever it took to make that so.

The sessions were difficult.

As I mentioned I had always been very black & white in my approach to life, and never been one to reveal my emotions or fears. If you asked my ex-wife to list the number of occasions on which she had seen me cry in the 24 years we were together, she would struggle to use the fingers on one hand to count them. I just wasn't programmed that way and, although the last few months had driven me to a point where this was no longer the case, I still had my pride. So, to sit in front of a complete stranger and tell them of your innermost fears was extremely hard.

'Tell me a little bit about what it is that's brought you here Wayne,' she had begun.

I explained there were a number of things which had happened that had crushed my confidence and my belief that it would ever get better. I detailed the individual events to her in the hope she would lead the way on where to start.

'Well,' I began, 'I took a chance on a career which went badly wrong and left me feeling a bit useless. Just as I got back on my feet and got a new job my wife left me and took the kids, leaving me in an uncertain financial position. Since then I've changed jobs again, come out as gay, been made redundant, discovered my partner has cheated on me and now – over Christmas – the children have moved away to live in Manchester. Where would you like to start?'

She looked shocked.

'Good grief,' she said, 'we've only got an hour.'

She was exactly what I needed; a motherly gentle-soul with compassion, life-experience and most importantly, a good pair of listening-ears.

The process of talking about these individual things was amazing!

To hear yourself vocalise the feelings in which you have been immersed for so long is truly cathartic and, with her help I began to understand and believe that the sequence of events had been mostly out of my control and therefore, I should not blame myself for them. In some cases they were decisions I had made and therefore had to take accountability for, but on the whole things had been taken out of my hands and therefore it was understandable to feel insecure.

I never revealed to her that just a few days prior to our first session I had given up altogether, and come within minutes of dying on my bed, with a plastic bag over my head.

I felt ashamed and embarrassed.

One of the first elements we focused on was Johnny, simply for the reason that without getting past this I would struggle to move forward with anything else. It wasn't that the children moving away was less significant or causing any less pain, but even in my current state I could reconcile I had no control over this and therefore, could find no resolution.

As far as Johnny was concerned I explained that I didn't want him back. The biggest emotion I felt when we finally broke up was relief.

Had the situation happened at any other point of my life I would have walked out of the door the moment I found out and never spoken to him again, but I had been clinging onto the threads of what we had, purely to provide some continuity; it was that simple. However, by forcing the conversation that day it had brought things to a close, and by removing hope from the equation he could no longer disappoint me further, which would in turn allow me to move forward.

Hate is an all-consuming and completely destructive emotion. I have never been a vengeful person, preferring to walk away and let Karma do its work in the long-run, but in the days leading to the first counselling session I had been completely engulfed with these feelings. I wasn't sure whether I hated Johnny, or just the fact I had allowed another person to treat me in this way, but I lost count of the number of nights leading up to these sessions where I lay awake, plotting his downfall.

The reason he had to be dealt with first was that, unlike the situation with the children, I had some control over how this chapter ended, and therefore I had a decision to make. The photographs I'd taken of the messages on his iPad would almost certainly destroy the budding romance which I believed was still developing with Tony, who was blissfully unaware of my existence.

Johnny wasn't on Facebook but Tony was and – although we were obviously not friends – it would have been possible for me to use the messenger-app to send him photographs of Johnny with the girls and me just prior to Christmas, thereby revealing *our* relationship to his new man.

My mind swayed one way and another.

The desire to destroy the thing that had been part of our downfall was overwhelming, but my conscience kept telling me no. None of this was Tony's fault, and from the messages between them I believe he had been hurt in relationships before. If I did this *I* would potentially be the cause of great pain for him and I didn't want that. I would then have to live with the guilt of this and I couldn't bring myself to do it.

When I expressed this to the counsellor she simply told me to do whatever I *needed* to do. She wasn't advocating the action and pointed out there would be consequences, but equally she didn't tell me not to do it. The process of hearing my own voice expressing this desire to exact revenge, along with my own moral understanding of how wrong this would be, was enough to make me realise it was not the right thing to do.

That was the turning point!

I had needed to hate him in order to move on, and now I had reached this point I could begin to piece my life back together.

Until then I'd remained in touch with him and had even met for a coffee on a few occasions. Now I knew I needed to remove him from my life in order to move forward and, despite telling me he truly wanted to remain friends, I'm sure he was relieved when I revealed I couldn't see him any longer. Let's face it, with his relationship seeming to develop with Tony, it would have been awkward to have me still around.

But, there was one thing left to do!

Even though we'd broken up days before, Johnny bought me a Christmas present; tickets for he and I to see Mariah Carey in March at Birmingham's Barclaycard Arena. Having seen her once before I was thrilled to receive this gift but, as he had ordered them, I didn't have the physical ticket and therefore some cunning was required.

I told Johnny I needed some time without speaking to him in order to move on as I was really struggling. This obviously wasn't all a lie, but the truth was that now I had reached a point of feeling nothing for him, I could have ended it there and never had to speak with him or see him again. That would have been my preference, but I wanted to see that concert and I felt he owed me.

So, after six weeks of complete radio-silence I sent him a message to say hi. Some idle chit-chat was exchanged; he asked if the children had settled in Manchester, I asked how he was and then – following a few messages back and forth – I broached the all-important question:-

'You still okay for the Mariah gig?'

'I am if you are,' came the reply.

Gotcha!

Everything was in place and just a week later it was time to face him. Mom expressed concerns, worried that seeing him again may set me back, but I was determined.

I felt nothing for him now!

My only anger toward him was because he had allowed the children to get close to him, while knowing all along that we could never last. They really liked him – as did everyone I introduced him to – and for those actions I will never forgive him. Apart from that there was nothing left, and it was important for me that he saw I was absolutely fine without him before we parted company for good.

In the words of Rachel from the American TV sitcom *Friends*, 'I am over you – and that, my friend, is what they call closure.'

But it wasn't quite over yet and it seemed fate was on my side!

Following some polite conversation we headed into the arena to find out seats. Despite being purchased as one booking, we discovered our allocated seats were actually two rows apart, so not only did I get to see Mariah that night, but I didn't even have to sit next to him for the privilege. Somebody was watching over me and as I drove home I allowed myself a wry smile.

Days later I blocked his number on WhatsApp and deleted it from my phone.

Johnny was finally just a lesson from my past and

although I didn't know it at the time, my future was already sitting on my sofa at home, waiting for me to return.

......*Going to bed with a huge smile on my face. That's all –* 26 Jan 2016

I was absolutely determined to remain single for at least two years!

My faith in relationships had been tested to within an inch of its tolerance and I needed to 'fix' myself properly before allowing anybody else back into my life. I was vulnerable, there were things about myself I needed to focus on to get back on-track and another relationship simply did not feature in my plans. I'd been happy on my own before and that was my goal for the immediate future.

So, when I met a guy called Chris on a ghost hunt at The Station Hotel in Dudley, it was the very last thing on my mind.

The evening had begun as usual. I'd arrived at the venue, the very same one at which I had experienced my first ghost hunt, and prepared the base-room for the night ahead. The guests were directed to the hotel-bar to grab a soft-drink, while the team set-up the refreshments and chairs in the room we would be using.

I've since learned that when I entered the bar to begin checking-off the names from the guest list, a young man called Chris – who had begrudgingly joined some of his work-colleagues for the night – had spotted me and passed comment to his friend:-

'Ooh look - a tall, dark and handsome man just for me!'

In the hectic approach to the beginning of the event I didn't even register him (rather embarrassingly), but it seems his proverbial 'gaydar' was on form that night, and he maintains he was pretty certain from the beginning that I was 'on his team'.

Fate is an interesting concept to me and one in which I hold some belief. I say that because I did something on this night I'd never done before, and it's because of this one action that he and I became a couple.

After many years as a guest, my good friend Jayne had just joined the Haunted Happenings team and was providing an extra pair of hands that night. I had been conducting Ouija Board experiments in the notorious 'haunted' bedrooms on the second floor, and Jayne had joined me for the vigils. Under normal circumstances I would have walked the guests back downstairs, ready to collect my next group as they switched vigil areas, but because Jayne was there she offered to do this and I had a couple of moments alone, waiting for them to return.

It was then that I briefly disabled flight-mode on my phone and quickly checked the dating-app I had reinstalled following the break-up. When you spend time outside your home-town, your profile appears on different people's pages – due to the change in location – and therefore it wasn't uncommon to receive lots of messages in a short space of time. There were five waiting for me and the familiar sound of the app's notification filled the corridor. Then, just as I was about to switch it off, the door swung open and in walked the next group, with Chris leading the way.

I had no idea at the time, but he had recognised the colours of the app on my phone as I returned it to flight-mode and, as luck would have it, he had a profile on there too. So when I switched my phone on during the break, I was welcomed by a strange message from a faceless man.

'I'm in your group lol.'

That was all it said.

I was intrigued and couldn't resist a response. I hadn't registered him earlier and was therefore under the impression there was nobody there I'd be interested in getting to know. Besides, I was there to work and needed to remain professional.

'Really? Lol' was all I could come up with.

I figured it was just somebody having a bit of fun because they'd rumbled me, but I was determined not to ask for a photo to discover who it was. That, I thought, was what they wanted.

It was during the next break that he revealed his face to me in another message and, when I returned to the room to begin the final part of the night's ghost hunting activities, I simply gave him a wink and left it there. We didn't have the opportunity to speak once I'd found out who it was – in fact we didn't have a direct conversation the whole night – but as I pulled up at home that morning my phone sprung to life once more with another message.

We chatted for a short while and agreed to catch up later that day, after some much needed sleep. He seemed like a really nice guy and that afternoon, after exchanging numbers, we chatted via WhatsApp for over three hours.

We had a lot in common; the same sense of humour, similar tastes in lots of things and both had been hurt in the past by ex-boyfriends. I really liked our conversations and, when the proposal of meeting up for a drink was thrown into the mix, I was absolutely up for it. I was very much in a place where I needed good people around me and the idea of spending time with him – getting to know him a bit more – was instantly appealing. So no time was wasted in making arrangements for him to come over to my place the following night, for a drink.

I had no expectations and was still absolutely determined that nobody was coming into my life again anytime soon.

From the pictures he'd sent me during our chat (nothing rude I hasten to add) I could see he was a handsome guy. With dark-blonde hair, blue eyes and a cheeky smile, there was something very appealing about him. However, at 27 years of age he fell way short of my age criteria of +/- 5 years, so no matter how well we got along, there was absolutely no way anything would develop between us; at most, he would hopefully become a good friend.

How wrong can one person be?

That night we spent hours talking. I discovered all about his past in the pub-trade, shared stories about ghost hunts and generally had a brilliant time. It was late by the time he left but, living some 35 miles away in Cannock, he had a long journey home and needed to be up early for work in the morning. I lay in bed and couldn't stop smiling. I'd not felt like this for a long time (since the night I met Johnny) and I knew straight away that I really liked him.

During the following days and weeks we spent as much time together as possible. Every evening we would speak, either on the phone or by Skype, and at weekends he would travel down and stay over at mine – not returning home until Sunday night, ready for another week at work.

Hazel very kindly allowed him to join me on some of the events, seeing how happy I was for the first time in ages and understanding that weekends were the only opportunity we had to properly spend time together. At the time he shared his rented home with a housemate and therefore it was only really viable to spend quality time together at mine.

Things moved forward at an incredible pace, but not without some concern on both parts. During that first week Chris had expressed concerns that, with the distance between us and his plans to move north in the future to open a hotel, perhaps we should nip things in the bud before either of us became too attached.

Likewise, I reminded him I'd been adamant I wouldn't get into a relationship, for fear of discovering I was simply rebounding after the Johnny fiasco, and the last thing I wanted to do was hurt him if that turned out to be the case. However, it seemed we both felt too strongly about each other to allow these things to get in the way, and after just three weeks I introduced him to 'the parents'.

It's not quite as heavy as it sounds!

Mom and Paul regularly went for a Friday night drink at their local and I had often joined them during my single days. Both Jayne and Michele, another close friend, had agreed to join us down there for a casual drink and, after cooking up a storm for Jayne – who was having an incredibly tough time herself – we descended upon The Shakespeare in Studley, for a few drinks and plenty of giggles.

It was one of the best nights I'd had in a very long time. There's nothing better than an impromptu evening and this is most definitely one I'll not forget in a hurry. Most importantly, Chris and mom got on like a house-on-fire, and the following day he received the official stamp of approval.

I've only had three proper relationships in my life, so I would say I'm far from an expert, but something occurred to me shortly after meeting Chris.

My criteria for another relationship had been pretty clear in my mind; somebody close in age so that we had similar reference points from our youth and would grow old together, nobody who lived any further away than around 10 miles and – ideally – somebody of similar height, with that all-important bald/shaved-head and stubble. Had I stuck fast to these ideals I would absolutely have missed out on getting to know the person I now truly believe is my soul-mate.

In Johnny I'd found everything I *believed* I wanted in a man, but he turned out to have nothing I needed. Chris didn't fit any of the things I believed I wanted and yet, turned out to be *everything* I needed, and more.

I realised very quickly into the relationship that I had fallen in love with this guy and, despite the potential difficulties the distance would pose, I wanted more than anything to make it work.

The apartment had been my only constant through the recent turmoil and was very important to me. When I first moved it had become clear this was by far the best in my price range and I truly loved the place. Situated on the corner of the building I could look from my lounge and bedroom windows straight onto the lawns outside; it was peaceful, private and most importantly, it was my constant. Chris was in a similar position, except he had his job to consider too, so it wasn't even a consideration that – should it ever get that far – he would be moving to Redditch.

Then, fate took another turn.

Chris' housemate had begun to notice how close we had become and had asked him how long it would be before I'd be moving in.

We had talked about it eventually happening, although we hadn't gone any further than that. After Chris explained this he'd begun to look at an apartment for himself and – within a day or so – had found the perfect place. So, in an unexpected twist, he would be getting the keys to his new place in just a few days and that left Chris without a housemate to help pay the rent and, more importantly, it gave us the opportunity to take that step.

Of course, there were financial benefits on both our parts, but that wasn't the deciding factor. I had nothing to really keep me in Redditch – other than mom – but I was frightened. What if I moved, gave up the apartment and then discovered this wasn't going to work? I'd be living miles away from my family and would be completely alone should it all go horribly wrong. Then, during a conversation with Hazel, it hit me. I was focusing purely on the negative outcomes and not the positives.

'What's the worst that can happen?' Hazel had asked me. 'You move, it doesn't work and you have to find somewhere else to live. But, what are the possibilities?'

She was absolutely right.

I loved Chris deeply and truly felt, from the very first weeks, he was absolutely the right person for me. I don't believe there is just one person for everyone on this planet, otherwise the odds of somebody ever meeting their perfect match would be infinite and it would simply never happen.

However, I do believe that when you meet a person with whom you feel a close bond and who you would do anything for, you stop looking.

There will always be people you meet in life who turn your head from an attraction point of view, and you will doubtless meet others with whom you would forge an equally strong bond – given the right circumstances. But, when you find a partner with whom you can imagine yourself for the rest of your life, grab the opportunity with both hands and never let it go.

So my mind was made up, and just 11 weeks after we first began talking I packed my things into the back of a van and moved to Cannock.

It was that simple!

Esther Rantzen, star of '80s television show *That's Life* and founder of the Childline charity, recently made an appearance on *Celebrity First Dates* and – in her subsequent interview – made a statement which completely resonated with my position at this time.

'I have lots of people to do something with, but nobody to do nothing with.'

She could not have summed up my thoughts any more succinctly if she tried. I had so many great friends around me that I was never short of somebody to invite for dinner or go out for drinks with, but there was something I truly missed about being in a relationship.

I didn't miss Johnny at all – not once since I reached

that point of anger — but I sorely missed having somebody by my side to chat with while making dinner, to sit with while watching nothing special on TV and to wander around town with for no particular reason.

Maybe *The Law of Attraction* was on my side once more and the universe answered my prayers by delivering Chris to me; who knows?

......WARNING: Apologies in advance for the soppy, gushy nature of this post.....

I'm sat here today reflecting on stuff and it has kinda hit me how much things have turned around in just 3 months. I feel really lucky to have met someone who gets my odd sense of humour, laughs at my ridiculous jokes & nonsense comments and most of all, who loves me just for who I am. Nobody has ever treated me the way that he does and been so good to me (and good for me).

He has restored my faith in relationships and that there are decent people out there! Thank you for stumbling across me Chris - you're the best and I can't wait to make lots of great memories for us to look back on when we're sat on a Pier in our old age, gumming an Ice Cream and being generally cantankerous — feeling blessed —
15 Apr 2016

Whatever it was that conspired to bring us together, I was having the time of my life and had never been happier. But - there were still things I needed to resolve.

I needed to find work and continue to put my own life back in order, but the move to Cannock would allow me to finally put into action those plans I had conceived several months before and begin my ADI qualification to become a driving instructor; a significant step towards putting things right and achieving the security I longed for.

It was finally my time!

TWENTY SIX

......When the past calls, let it go to voicemail. It has nothing new to say. Dear Past, thanks for all the lessons. Dear future, I'm ready – 10 Mar 2016

Nobody knows what challenges life will throw at them! From the day we are born until the moment we take our last breath, our journey is ever changing.

Every decision we make, every opportunity which is presented to us, every test we overcome and every person who influences us – both positively and negatively – changes the course of our existence and leads us toward our final destination.

Everyone's journey is different, but for each and every person one common goal is shared; we all seek happiness. Whether achieved through the accumulation of personal wealth, the satisfaction of helping others, or simply the joy of a loving family, we are all responsible for our own time on this Earth and how we choose to live our lives.

Scrolling through my Facebook page recently, I came across a meme which sums it up perfectly.

'Always live for today, because you never know what tomorrow may bring, or what it may take away.'

Although statistically only half-complete, my journey has certainly been an interesting one so far, and one from which I have learned many valuable lessons.

Of course I have regrets – we all do – but as Sinatra once sang, 'too few to mention'. I for one never appreciated how fortunate I was to have a well-paid job, a home and two amazing children, until they were gone.

The personal struggles I faced during those three tumultuous years is barely a drop in the ocean when compared with the struggles some have to face through their whole lives. I have my health, have always had a roof over my head and – most importantly – I have people around me who care. It took some time for me to realise just how many friends I have, but I will never take them for granted.

Mistakes are inevitable; we all make them!

Whether that be misjudging another person, unintentionally causing hurt and upset to somebody, or simply making the wrong choice when selecting from a menu in a restaurant and wanting what somebody else ordered (we've all been there). It's what we do with those mistakes which defines who we are and reveals our true character. Every hurdle we jump, every obstruction we swerve and every wall we knock down in order to achieve happiness serves to make us stronger, whether we realise it at the time or not. Mistakes are nothing more than teachings; the decision is yours whether you learn from that particular lesson or set it aside.

I have wasted a number of precious years focusing on the wrong things and those years can never be recovered. As my children grew I worked far too many hours, intent upon providing the security of a home and giving them the material things they wanted. The one thing I failed to provide them with was my time.

It's an age-old story, often recounted in the medium of a sappy Christmas-movie, but one which thousands of people – both men and women – fall foul of.

Those years are gone! I cannot turn back the clock and for that I am truly sorry.

I lost my way on so many levels during my darkest moments and, when I should have turned to those closest to me for support, I slammed the doors shut and tried to hide what was happening; not only to friends and colleagues but to my own children.

The intention was good. I simply wanted to protect them from seeing my hurt but I misjudged the situation, and as a result my eldest felt I didn't care about her. I am now paying the price for this and, whilst I hope each and every day that we will recover our relationship, I must accept responsibility for making her feel that way.

One hundred years from now will you have made any lasting impact? Will those figures you must get done before leaving work for the day have made a difference? Could they have waited, in favour of returning home in time to kiss your children goodnight before they fell asleep? The only impact most of us will ever truly have in this world is upon others.

Life is good now!

At 41 years of age I understand what is important. I have unburdened myself from the chains which prevented me finding happiness and have embraced who I am. I will soon be qualified to begin my career as a driving instructor which, I feel sure, will provide me with plenty of great anecdotes for another book sometime in the future.

I now see that, whatever else life throws at me during the remainder of my years, nothing is insurmountable. As 2015 drew to a close I made the decision to post something on my Facebook page in the hope that, one year down the line, it would re-appear as 'memory' and serve as a positive reminder.

......MESSAGE TO MYSELF

Remember how 2015 started? You were settled in your own life, time spent with the kids was fun and kept you close to them and you were happy living alone.

Remember how you met someone and fell in love, how this changed your whole world and how you couldn't see any outcome other than spending the whole of your lives together?

Remember how by the end of 2015 you felt you'd lost everything in the world that meant something to your future and how you couldn't see any happiness ahead without them?

Well, you're reading this one year on and you're still around! You survived what was the worst time of your life and now you're stronger for it. Whatever 2016 has brought you, good or bad, whether you are sharing your life with someone and showing them this post or not, you survived.

Keep going - you're doing fine! – 30 Dec 2015

AUTHOR'S NOTE

The events are portrayed here are to the best of my memory. While the stories and conversations in this book are based on actual events, some names and identifying details have been changed or omitted to protect the privacy and anonymity of the people involved. The situations and characters described are written from my perspective and therefore, not necessarily fact.

The process of writing What's On Your Mind? was a cathartic one and, although painful to revisit some of the experiences described, it has helped me to put the past into a box – where it belongs!

One of the things I wanted to achieve, by sharing so candidly my experience of depression, was to highlight the fact that – in many cases – even those closest to somebody suffering this awful illness may not be aware of their suffering. I now have a far greater understanding of anxiety and depression, a silent-killer, and feel I am a better, more caring person for it.

If by writing this book I have made even one person think differently about mental illness, depression or anxiety then it would all have been worthwhile. And, if you have read about my experiences and recognise *any* of the same symptoms or feelings within yourself, I would urge you to talk to somebody without hesitation – I left it far too late and almost paid the ultimate price!

Printed in Great Britain
by Amazon